Praise for the twenti
Judaism and Global Survival

"For many years now, Richard Schwartz has been a clear, unwavering voice for a more compassionate, more humane and holier Judaism. *Judaism and Global Survival* offers Jews and non-Jews alike an authentic and inspirational view of what traditional Judaism is and should be."—**Professor Alon Tal**, former MK, former department chair at Ben Gurion University of the Negev; chairman of "The Green Movement" (Israel's Green Party); author of *Pollution in the Promised Land* and many other books and articles on environmental issues in Israel

"This is an inspirational and prophetic book that explores the deep issues that are facing us today, not only for the purpose of healing the ecological world, but more importantly for saving the soul of Judaism. The essential message Richard Schwartz, a modern Orthodox Jew, is promoting highlights that it is time to apply the deep God-centered and, consequently, moral and ethical way of living in which humanistic ideals and actions are essential outflowing of a God-centered way of life."—**Rabbi Gabriel Cousens**, MD, MD(H), DD, director of the Tree of Life Foundation; author of *Torah as a Guide to Enlightenment*, *Spiritual Nutrition*, *Conscious Eating*, and *Creating Peace by Being Peace*

"I consider it an honor and a mitzvah to commend Professor Richard Schwartz's work and all his endeavors to bring Jewish teachings on diet, health, the environment, and related issues to public attention, especially to those of us who seek to lead a religiously observant lifestyle, in keeping with the precepts and goals of the Torah. May his efforts merit Divine blessing and success."—**Rabbi David Rosen**, former chief rabbi of Ireland; president for Israel of the International Jewish Vegetarian Society

"I applaud Richard Schwartz's valiant efforts to raise the issue of a plant-based diet within the Jewish community. He taps into a millennia-old Jewish tradition supporting compassion toward animals, and does so at a time when all life on Earth depends on wise human action. He thoughtfully examines what type of food consumption fits with the ethics of kosher, which means appropriate. May God bless his holy efforts!"—**Rabbi Yonatan Neril**, founder and executive director of the Interfaith Center for Sustainable Development and of Jewish Eco Seminars

"This book is so crucial and urgently necessary! We once again owe deep gratitude to Professor Richard Schwartz for opening our minds and hearts to the essence of Jewish ethics!"—**Rabbi Dr. Shmuly Yanklowitz**, founder and CEO of Shamayim v'Aretz: Jewish Animal Advocacy; author and editor of over a dozen books of Judaica, including three on Jewish dietary teachings

"No one has been more creative, committed, and consistent than Richard Schwartz in arguing for a Judaism that can address in all its depth the world crisis that all humanity and all the life forms of our planet face today."—**Rabbi Arthur Waskow,** director of The Shalom Center; author of *Down-to-Earth Judaism, Seasons of Our Joy,* and many other works on Jewish thought and action

"The challenging title of this welcome new edition by Professor Richard Schwartz, one of the most insightful commentators on Jewish scriptural interpretation, says a great deal about his struggle to reclaim Judaism in the 21st century from those who would narrow its scope to ethnocentrism and self-interest. Schwartz is a major protagonist in the battle to present the humanitarian insights and universal truths that have been part of the Jewish tradition, from its earliest holy texts to the present day."—**Rabbi Gerald Serotta**, founder of Rabbis for Human Rights, North America; executive director of Clergy Beyond Borders

"I commend Dr. Schwartz for his courage and integrity in reminding the Jewish community of its historic mission to serve as a light unto the nations. While it is always safer to tell people what they want to hear, I am thrilled that at least one person has the guts to challenge our people to live up to the highest ideals of the prophets by acting as responsible stewards of our planet, fighting to protect those who need our help, and practicing kindness to animals. His new edition of *Judaism and Global Survival* will serve as a lightning rod to stimulate critically needed discussion about what it means to be Jewish and how we can live an ethically Jewish life."—**Rabbi Barry Silver**, rabbi of Congregation L'Dor Va-Dor in Lake Worth, Florida; former Florida State Representative; founder and co-chairman of the Palm Beach County Environmental Coalition

"Once again Richard Schwartz has produced a thought-provoking book. This new edition of *Judaism and Global Survival* will be a very positive addition to our libraries. His writing is powerful and thought-provoking. As always, Richard is not afraid to challenge us."—**Rabbi Michael M. Cohen**, Director of Development at Friends of the Arava Institute for Environmental Studies

"*Tekiah!* The venerable Richard Schwartz once again sounds a shofar blast of warning to wake up the Jewish community and the world. No one has done more than him to advance the understanding of the relationship between Judaism, the environment, and respect for nonhuman animals. Like a modern-day prophet, Schwartz sees Jews straying from biblical edicts for Earth stewardship and prods us to embrace divinely ordained and inspired environmental action. As unabated greed and climate change threaten life and religion as we know them, Schwartz urges actions rooted in the very heart of Judaism. We all would be wise to heed his call." **David Krantz**, president and chairperson of Aytzim: Ecological Judaism

"There are woefully few examples in history of lone individuals who bravely rose up to identify the underlying causes of problems that have plagued nations, societies, and indeed the world at large. All too often those voices were rapidly silenced, either through political subjugation, ignorance, or indifference. Fortunately, despite overwhelming odds, there are those who have made a profound difference to the reigning status quo. Richard Schwartz is one such person. His new book identifies much of what we as Jews have failed to recognize as our planet heads inexorably towards an ecological meltdown. Politically, ethically, morally, economically, and scientifically, we are guilty of wearing blinkers when we look around and perceive what is happening to our world, especially in the face of climate change and also in our inability to obtain a just and peaceful settlement to the Israeli–Palestinian conflict

"Soundly basing his views on the profound teachings of the Torah and the inherent wisdom and compassion of our ancient faith, he provides an alarming analysis of how we are failing not only ourselves, but also our duty to be a 'light unto the nations.' This book should be essential reading for everyone. I applaud Richard as a maverick and as a *tzaddik,* a truly righteous man in every sense of the word. He is one of the few individuals who gives me a sense that there is still hope if we act now to reverse the trends that are pushing us towards disaster."—**Lionel Friedberg**, Emmy Award-winning producer, director, writer, and documentarian; producer of *A Sacred Duty: Applying Jewish Values to Help Heal the World*

"If you think Judaism consists of occasional visits to a synagogue or temple where congregants perform rituals and recite prayers without feeling and attend mainly to socialize, then this book is a must-read. Schwartz reminds us that the very essence of Judaism is to struggle to find what is right and to have the courage to do right, including speaking out against evil. Worship accompanied by indifference to evil, the prophets said, is an abomination to God. Schwartz fulfills the best of Judaism by urging us to cry out against immorality, injustice, deceit, cruelty, and violence toward all living beings, rather than condone it with our silence, for in condoning empty rituals and standing silent in the face of immoral deeds, we make a mockery of Judaism itself."—**Nina Natelson**, director of Concern for Helping Animals in Israel (CHAI)

"Richard Schwartz has been a consistent, clear, compassionate voice for the planet. This book once again illustrates his wisdom, insight, and willingness to speak up. If the Jewish community takes this book to heart and makes the necessary changes, the world can follow. We can co-create a world that respects all life."—**Rae Sikora**, co-founder of Plant Peace Daily, Institute for Humane Education, and Vegfund

"This book by Professor Richard Schwartz not only offers the reader a comprehensive research of Jewish teachings and their relevance to contemporary science and world affairs, but also challenges the reader with an urgent cry for action. For about forty years, Schwartz has been a world authority on the deep linkage between Judaism and vegetarianism. Now he shows that a vegan revolution has started—in Israel and worldwide. But is it fast enough to save us from ecological catastrophe? And is the Jewish establishment assuming the role it should play within it? These are questions Schwartz addresses."—**Yossi Wolfson**, vegan and animal rights activist in Israel; coordinator of the Israeli Jewish Vegetarian Society in Jerusalem

"When I consider Judaism and its highest ideals, I realize how consistent it is with veganism: being respectful and compassionate, protecting life and resources, guarding and increasing health, pursuing peace and justice, living by one's values. I have worked with Richard Schwartz for a long time and know him to be extraordinarily sincere, diligent, conscientious, respectful, caring, compassionate, intelligent, and deeply dedicated to Judaism—so much so that he is deserving of the Nobel Peace Prize. As with his previous books that have illuminated so many lives with their insight and wisdom, I likewise heartily recommend this book. Well-researched, well-written, well-thought-out, and absolutely vital for the continuation of life on our planet. Especially in this era of population explosion, overconsumption, globalization, and our climate crisis, this book needs to be read and shared."—**Dan Brook, PhD**, professor of sociology at San Jose State University; board member of San Francisco Veg Society

"Richard Schwartz's new book is a clarion call, a shofar blast, to disturb the slumber of indifference and to align Judaism with its noblest values."—**Jeffrey Spitz Cohan**, executive director of Jewish Veg, formerly Jewish Vegetarians of North America

"This pioneering book by Richard Schwartz, the world's greatest living authority on the teachings of Judaism on protecting animals and nature, provides nothing short of the revolution in our way of thinking and acting that is now required in efforts to avert a climate catastrophe and other environmental disasters. This compelling, magisterial book is a must-read. Its message must be heeded. Our future depends on it."—**Lewis Regenstein**, author of "Commandments of Compassion: Jewish Teachings on Protecting the Planet and Its Creatures," *Replenish the Earth*, and other writings on Judaism and animals

Praise for the first edition of
Judaism and Global Survival

"This masterful volume provides a treasure of insights into the perspective of Judaism on many urgent social problems. People committed to the vital force of the Jewish heritage will discover in this work both richness of expression and creative application of old texts to new situations. This volume can make a significant contribution to the shaping of the social consciousness of our community."—**Rabbi Saul J. Berman**, professor of Jewish studies at Stern College of Yeshiva University; founder and executive director of Edah (modern Orthodox community organization)

"Everyone who believes in Tikkun Olam will be strengthened by this rich compendium of Jewish sources and ethical insights, which should stimulate many dialogues in the Jewish community about critical issues. Everyone who wants to apply Jewish values to the great concerns of our time will be nourished when they eat of this feast of Jewish values and treasures that is spread before us."—**Rabbi Irving Greenberg**, president of Jewish Life Network; founder of CLAL, National Jewish Center for Learning and Leadership

"A superb task of research, compilation, and writing. This book brings to bear scholarly insight in a way that is accessible to the interested layperson. The insights and the values of the Jewish tradition regarding crucial social issues of our time come alive in this presentation. Whether used as a textbook or as a personal guide for Jews who care about making Jewish values live in our world, this book makes a significant contribution to the modern understanding of Jewish social justice."—**Rabbi David Saperstein**, director of Religious Action Center of Reform Judaism

"Dr. Schwartz's erudition and moral passion are admirable, as well as his ability to deal with so many subjects so readably and succinctly."—**Dr. Andre Ungar**, rabbi at Temple Emanuel, Woodcliff Lake, New Jersey; former chairperson of the Hebraic studies department at Rutgers University

"[Richard Schwartz] shows with eloquence and intelligence that Jewish tradition has much to teach us all about how to protect the earth and the human race from destruction—and how to nurture a decent world."—**Rabbi Arthur Waskow,** director of the Shalom Center; author of *Godwrestling: Round 2* and many other books

"My undergraduate years at Brandeis University were just beginning when the first edition of this book came out—and this one-stop collection of Judaic textual sources on issues of the day had a profound influence on me. It served me well through years of learning and activism, and was one of the few to accompany me on a cross-country walk for the environment ten years ago. In seminary at the Reconstructionist Rabbinical College, hardly a month went by without occasion to consult this important work. As a pulpit rabbi and Jewish-environmental educator, I still keep it handy. Not only is it time for me to replace my own dog-eared copy, but it's time for the newly updated edition of this work to find a position of prominence on every Jewish bookshelf."—**Rabbi Fred Scherlinder Dobb**, Adat Shalom Reconstructionist Congregation, Bethesda, MD; member of board of trustees at Coalition on the Environment and Jewish Life

"I urge every rabbi, Jewish teacher, and concerned Jew to read *Judaism and Global Survival*. We face the future with a great need for ancient wisdom from our tradition dealing with justice and how to sustain our life on Earth. Schwartz's visionary and wise book provides us with the spiritual tools to guide our way."—**Rabbi Warren Stone,** environmental chair of CCAR (Central Conference of American Rabbis)

"An excellent sourcebook. Many of its ideas have found their way into my sermons."—**Rabbi Gerald Serotta**, Campus Hillel rabbi at the George Washington University; associate rabbi at Temple Shalom of Chevy Chase, MD

"Among Judaism's most basic principles are God's affirmation of both the world and the moral potential of humankind. Therefore, to the Jewish mind, the proper concerns of religion are not only of a private, subjective nature, but necessarily extend to the spiritual and physical improvement of the world. Dr. Schwartz echoes the impassioned protest of the ancient prophets of Israel in his pointed consideration of contemporary social issues. In doing so, he also demonstrates that Judaism cannot be pigeonholed into the convenient ideological categories of 'conservative,' 'liberal,' and so on, but must be encountered on its own terms." **Rabbi Dovid Sears**, author of *Compassion for Humanity in the Jewish Tradition*

"Richard Schwartz has written a profound and inspiring call to Jews to involve themselves in saving our planet from disaster. His book makes us proud of our Jewish heritage and eager to engage in environmental activism."—**Susannah Heschel**, Eli Black professor of Jewish studies at Dartmouth College

"This extremely eloquent, important, and timely book addresses a subject of the utmost importance, one of vital concern to everyone—how we can save the earth and prevent the destruction of its life-supporting systems and of humanity itself."—**Lewis G. Regenstein**, president of the Interfaith Council for the Protection of Animals and Nature; author of *Replenish the Earth: The Teachings of the World's Religions on Protecting Animals and Nature*

"Richard Schwartz has crafted a magnificent contribution to Jewish ethical writing. He has insightfully raised important questions for concerned Jews and courageously taught a simple, yet profound Jewish message."—**Rabbi Hillel Norry**, Shaare Tzedeck Synagogue, New York City; member of the Law and Standards Committee of the Rabbinical Assembly

Judaism and Global Survival

20th anniversary edition

Richard H. Schwartz, Ph.D.

Lantern Publishing & Media ● Woodstock & Brooklyn, NY

2023
Lantern Publishing & Media
PO Box 1350
Woodstock, NY 12498
www.lanternpm.org

Printed in the United States of America

Library of Congress Cataloging-in-Publication Data

Names: Schwartz, Richard H, author.
Title: Judaism and global survival / Richard H. Schwartz, PhD.
Description: Woodstock, NY : Lantern Publishing & Media,
    [2023] | 20th anniversary edition. | Includes bibliographical
    references.
Identifiers: LCCN 2023001806 (print) | LCCN 2023001807
    (ebook) | ISBN 9781590567067 (paperback) | ISBN
    9781590567074 (epub)
Subjects: LCSH: Judaism and social problems.
Classification: LCC HN40.J5 S38 2023 (print) | LCC HN40.J5
    (ebook) | DDC 296.3/8—dc23/eng/20230612
LC record available at https://lccn.loc.gov/2023001806
LC ebook record available at https://lccn.loc.gov/2023001807

Contents

To my wife Loretta and our children, Susan Esther (and David Meir) Kleid, David Schwartz, and Devorah Chana (and Ariel) Gluch, and our grandchildren, Shalom Eliyahu (and Temima) Kleid, Ayelet Breindel (and Yehezkel) Stepner, Avital (and Elad) Nissenboim, Michal Naama Kleid, Eliyahu Gluch, Yosef Gluch, Yael Shachar Gluch, Talya Nitzan Gluch, and Ayala Neta Gluch, for their love, encouragement, and support, and with my hope that this book will help produce a healthy, environmentally sustainable world for them and for all future generations.

Foreword

Rabbi David Rosen

The Talmud declares that a one who is not compassionate cannot truly be of the seed of Abraham our father (Betzah 32b). In other words, to be authentically Jewish means to emulate Abraham's compassionate conduct towards others. Underlying this statement is the view of Abraham in our Tradition as the pioneer of ethical monotheism. He not only recognized that there is one Creative Source of the one Creation, but that this very unity conveys a moral imperative concerning ethical behavior and conduct (Genesis 18:19). Accordingly, based on the above statement, our sages declare: the more we are compassionate and engaged in relation to the world around us, the truer we are to the moral essence of the Abrahamic faith affirmation.

Of course, there is also a very pragmatic dimension of enlightened self-interest that demands such conduct of us. This is expressed in the Talmud in the words of our sages, that Heaven grants compassion to those who have compassion for others, but withdraws it from those who do not (Shabbat 151b). In other words, compassion is the means by which we secure our own future! Indeed, Judaism teaches that it is our responsibility as human beings to be constructive co-workers in the Creation, ensuring its sustainable development (Genesis 2:15; Shabbat 10a; Ecclesiastes Rabbah 7:28).

For thousands of years we have recited daily, evening and morning, the *"kriyat shema,"* the second paragraph of which (Deuteronomy 11:13–21) deals with the direct link between the observance of the Biblical commandments and the condition of our ecosystem. Today, this connection between our ethical behavior or misbehavior and our environment is evident to us as it has never been before.

In this excellent book, Professor Richard Schwartz clarifies this connection most vividly, together with the dangers and injustices with which our planet has to contend. However, also in keeping with Biblical teaching, he makes it powerfully clear that we have the means to significantly address these challenges. Indeed, the degree to which we take up his call is the degree to which we demonstrate whether or not we are worthy and authentic children of Abraham, our father.

Rabbi David Rosen, former Chief Rabbi of Ireland; President for Israel of the International Jewish Vegetarian Society; International Director of Interreligious Affairs of the American Jewish Committee; President of the International Council of Christians and Jews; International President of the World Conference of Religions for Peace

PREFACE

In this hour we, the living [post-Holocaust Jews], are "the people of Israel." The tasks begun by the patriarchs and prophets and continued by their descendants are now entrusted to us. We are either the last Jews or those who will hand over the entire past to generations to come. We will either forfeit or enrich the legacy of ages.
—Rabbi Abraham Joshua Heschel[1]

On some positions, Cowardice asks the question, "Is it safe?" Expediency asks the question, "Is it politic?" And Vanity comes along and asks the question, "Is it popular?" But Conscience asks the question, "Is it right?" And there comes a time when one must take a position that is neither safe, nor politic, nor popular, but he must do it because Conscience tells him it is right.—Dr. Martin Luther King, Jr.[2]

Rabbi Tarfon said: "The day is short, the work is urgent, the workers are lazy but the reward is great and the Owner is insistent. . . . It is not for you to complete the task [of perfecting the world], but neither are you free to desist [from doing all you can]."—Pirkei Avot 2:17–18

Here is my long-held vision for Judaism in this time of multiple crises:

To be a Jew is to see the world through the eyes of God, to be unreconciled to the world as it is, to be discontented with the status quo and unafraid to challenge it.

To be a Jew is to be a co-worker with God in the task of perfecting the world, to know that the world remains unredeemed and that we must work with God to redeem it.

To be a Jew is to feel deeply the harms done to others, to speak out in the face of wrongdoing, and to prod the conscience of those who passively accept the status quo.

To be a Jew is to stand apart from the world, to be a nonconformist, to shout "NO" when others murmur "yes" to injustice, to actively help uplift those in need and try to correct injustices, even if others stand idly by.

To be a Jew is to be intoxicated with a dream of social justice, to have an abiding concern for others, to have compassion without condescension for people who are poor, weak, and suffering.

To be a Jew means to know that God's name can be sanctified by our actions, and to try to live a life compatible with being created in God's image by doing justly, acting kindly, and in all ways imitating God's attributes.

To be a Jew means to believe in the unlimited potential of people in spite of the evil and injustice around us, recognizing that we have been chosen to serve as an example, to strive to be "a light unto the nations."

To be a Jew means of course many specific practices concerning Shabbat, kashrut, and much more. It means study and worship, and most of all action and observance. It means all these things and far, far more. It is not always easy to be a Jew, but it is a very significant and worthy lifelong endeavor.

* * * * *

Why a twentieth anniversary edition of *Judaism and Global Survival*? The answer is really captured in the title of this book. It has become abundantly clear in the past twenty years that global survival is increasingly threatened and that it is urgent that Jewish values be applied to avert a climate catastrophe and other environmental disasters.

As discussed in much more detail later, the scientific consensus about climate threats has become far stronger. Facts on the ground reinforce that very strong consensus. Temperatures have increased significantly; glaciers worldwide, Arctic ice, and permafrost have been melting rapidly; and there has been an increase in the frequency and severity of heatwaves, droughts, wildfires, storms, floods, and other climate events. Climate experts are predicting that the world could soon reach an irreversible tipping point when climate will spin out of control, with cataclysmic consequences. Human survival is increasingly at risk. UN Secretary General Antonio Guterres has claimed that the situation is a "Code Red for humanity" and that "delay means death."[3]

This book is intended as a wake-up call, the most urgent that I can make, to Jews and all of humanity that we must do everything we can to apply Jewish and other religions' values to help shift our imperiled planet onto a sustainable path.

A primary aim is to show that the world is heading toward a "perfect storm" of existential crises: sudden, catastrophic climate change; severe environmental degradation; devastating scarcities of food, water, and energy; widening terrorism; and other critical threats to life as we know and value it. It is meant to represent a cause and a crusade, to increase awareness that the application of Jewish values can make a major difference in shifting our imperiled world away from its present perilous path.

Please consider the following brief discussions of some issues, in addition to the climate threats discussed above, that are also addressed thoroughly later in this book:

* **World hunger.** There is a potential for major food shortages due to growing demand caused by 1) increasing population (projected to increase by about 40 percent by 2100);[4] 2) increasing affluence, leading to a rise in grain-intensive meat consumption and a surge in the purchase of material items;[5] 3) continued production of corn-based ethanol, and 4) decreased production of food due to the conversion of cropland into land used for houses, roads, parking lots, factories, and other needs of the growing population, as well as the negative effects of heat waves, droughts, floods, and other consequences of climate change.

* **Water scarcity.** The world is also experiencing increasing water shortages. Climate change is causing severe droughts in many parts of the world, even as it is causing flooding in other areas. Trying to grow adequate food for the world's increasing population (and the growing appetite for water-intensive meat production in the developing world) through irrigation of feed crops is causing aquifers to shrink in many countries, and some may soon be completely depleted. In addition, because of global warming, glaciers that provide replenishing water to rivers and streams in the spring are rapidly receding. There is an increasing likelihood that nations may go to war over water and other natural resources.

* **Meeting energy needs.** Because the burning of coal and oil contributes to climate change and other environmental problems and there are dangers related to nuclear energy, it is essential that renewable sources of energy—solar, wind, and hydroelectric—be rapidly developed.

* **Climate wars.** Many military leaders and security experts are increasingly concerned about the national security implications of climate change. Military and security experts are increasingly concerned that millions of hungry, thirsty, desperate refugees fleeing from droughts, floods, heat waves, storms, wildfires, and other effects of climate change will amplify the likelihood of instability, violence, terrorism, and war.

* **Threats of increased violence, terrorism, and war.** As I write this in June 2022, the Russian invasion of Ukraine is having devastating consequences. In addition to the deaths of people and destruction of property in Ukraine, the war is causing major increases in the costs of food and energy, threatening widespread famine recessions. It is also distracting from the urgency of responding to climate threats, forcing countries to use more fossil fuels in the immediate term and dedicate increasing energy to producing weapons of war. It will require far more energy to rebuild the destroyed homes, vehicles, and infrastructure, making a future climate catastrophe more likely. At the same time, Israel was experiencing a terror wave, with increasing risks of renewed warfare.

* **Other threats.** Unfortunately, there are many other threats to humanity's future. These include deforestation, desertification, rapid species extinction, pollution, increasing poverty, soaring financial deficits in some countries, and the inability of many countries to meet the needs of their people.

Everything possible must be done to avert the potential catastrophes indicated above, since they threaten humanity and all life on the planet. This book argues that the application of Jewish values, such as pursuing justice and peace and working as partners with God in protecting the environment, can contribute greatly to solving these problems. Fortunately, other religions have similar values, so hopefully others will increase efforts to encourage their co-religionists to apply their religions' values to today's crises.

A main focus of this book is that, in the face of today's urgent problems, Jews must return to our universal Jewish values and to our missions: to be "a light unto the nations," a kingdom of priests and a holy people, descendants of prophets, champions of social justice, eternal protestants against a corrupt, unjust world, and dissenters against destructive and unjust systems. Jews must become actively involved in the missions of global survival and Jewish renewal, working for major changes that will lead to a society where there is far less oppression, injustice, violence, hunger, poverty, and alienation.

I hope that this book will contribute to and help expand open dialogues about Jewish teachings concerning these critically important issues, playing a part in moving our precious planet away from its present perilous path onto one that is more compassionate, just, humane, peaceful, and environmentally sustainable.

Unfortunately, as with other religions, with important exceptions, there has been too little effort by Jews to apply our Jewish values to the many critical problems that threaten the world today. In fact, as discussed in Chapter 1, along with the many positive developments in Jewish life today, sadly there has been a shift by many Jews away from these basic Jewish values just when the world needs them more than ever before.

I hope that this book will contribute to and help expand widespread open dialogues about Jewish teachings concerning these critically important issues, playing a part in helping to move our precious planet away from its present perilous path and onto one that is more compassionate, just, humane, peaceful, and environmentally sustainable.

For Whom Is This Book Intended?

For Jews who look to Judaism for moral and spiritual guidance, but who find that contemporary interpretations of our faith's traditions do not address the pressing issues of today. For Jews who are seeking a Judaism that will make a difference in responding to the crises of today and will help guide humanity in directions that can bring a more just, compassionate, peaceful, environmentally sustainable future for generations to come. For Jews who recognize that the Jewish calling to be a light unto the nations gives them a special responsibility to live in ways that benefit all of God's creation. And, since other religions have similar problems and concerns, I believe that non-Jews will also find this book interesting, challenging, informative, relevant, and valuable.

* * * * *

More information about the issues in this book can be found in the books mentioned in the bibliography, including my books *Vegan Revolution: Saving Our World, Revitalizing Judaism*; *Who Stole My Religion: Revitalizing Judaism and Applying Jewish Values to Help Heal Our Imperiled Planet*; and *Judaism and Vegetarianism*, as well as the website www. JewishVeg.org/schwartz, where over 250 of my related articles are archived. These issues are also presented in a documentary called *A Sacred Duty: Applying Jewish Values to Help Heal the World* that I helped produce, along with multiple-award-winning producer, director, writer, and cinematographer Lionel Friedberg. It can be viewed for free on YouTube.

If you have specific questions, points of disagreement (or of agreement that you would like to share), suggestions about promoting the ideas in this book, or just points you would like to discuss, please contact me at veggierich@gmail.com. I welcome your comments and suggestions, especially about how to get dialogues started within your community and social and religious groups about the application of Jewish values to current critical issues.

Many thanks!

Acknowledgements

First, I want to express my thanks to God by reciting the traditional Jewish blessing pronounced when a person reaches a milestone in life: "Blessed are you, Lord our God, King of the universe, Who has kept us alive and sustained us and brought us to this season."

While it is essential that the issues discussed in this book be put on the Jewish agenda and beyond, I recognize my limitations in presenting this information. I have been very fortunate, however, to have input and suggestions from a wide variety of dedicated, extremely knowledgeable individuals.

The following (in alphabetical order) reviewed all or a major part of a previous edition of the manuscript and made valuable suggestions, many of which are reflected in this twentieth anniversary edition:

1. Rabbi Yonasson Gershom: Breslov Chassid; author of *Kapporos Then and Now: Toward a More Compassionate Tradition.*
2. Ari Knoll: attorney; a longtime friend and advisor.
3. Mark Nagurka, Ph.D. (MIT): former associate professor of mechanical and biomedical engineering at Marquette University in Milwaukee, Wisconsin.
4. Charles Patterson, Ph.D.: author of *Anti-Semitism: The Road to the Holocaust and Beyond, From Buchenwald to*

Carnegie Hall, and *Eternal Treblinka: Our Treatment of Animals and the Holocaust.*

5. Lewis Regenstein: author of *Replenish the Earth: The Teachings of the World's Religions on Protecting Animals and Nature, America the Poisoned,* and *The Politics of Extinction;* president of the Interfaith Council for the Protection of Animals and Nature in Atlanta; an affiliate of the Humane Society of the United States.

6. Rabbi Dovid Sears: Breslov Chassid; author of many books, including *Compassion for Humanity in the Jewish Tradition: A Source Book, The Path of the Bal Shem Tov: Early Chassidic Teachings and Customs,* and *The Vision of Eden: Animal Welfare and Vegetarianism in Jewish Law and Mysticism.*

7. Jonathan Wolf: longtime vegetarian and vegan; environmental and social justice activist.

People who made major contributions to specific parts of previous editions of the book include Arnold Aronowitz, Yosef Ben Shlomo Hakohen, Aaron Gross, and Asher Waldman.

Two people who read the entire manuscript for this edition and made very valuable suggestions are Irene Landcaster and Jayn Meinhardt. Others who contributed very useful suggestions for one or more chapters include Rina Deych, Joanne Kong, and Lewis Regenstein.

I apologize to any contributors whom I have inadvertently omitted.

I also want to express deep appreciation to Brian Normoyle, Emily Lavieri-Scull, Liza Barkova, and others at Lantern Publishing & Media for their consistent encouragement and valuable suggestions.

I wish to express deep appreciation to my wife, Loretta, our children, Susan (and David) Kleid, David Schwartz, and Deborah (and Ariel) Gluch, and our grandchildren, Shalom Eliahu, Ayelet Breindel, Avital P'nina, and Michal Na'ama Kleid, and Eliyahu, Ilan Avraham, Yosef, Yael Shachar, Talya Nitzan, and Ayala Netta Gluch, for their patience, understanding, and encouragement as I took time away from other responsibilities to gather and write this material.

Although all of these people have been very helpful, I take full responsibility for the final selection of material and interpretations. The reviewers mentioned above do not necessarily agree with everything in this book.

Finally, I wish to thank in advance all who read this volume and send me ideas and suggestions for improvements so this book can more effectively show how the application of Jewish values can help shift our imperiled planet onto a sustainable path. My e-mail address is veggierich@gmail.com.

1

INVOLVEMENT AND PROTEST

If a person of learning participates in public affairs and
serves as judge or arbiter, he gives stability to the land.
But if he sits in his home and says to himself, "What have
the affairs of society to do with me? . . . Why should I
trouble myself with the people's voices of protest? Let my
soul dwell in peace!"—if he does this, he overthrows the
world. (*Tanchuma to Mishpatim*)

Judaism urges active involvement in issues facing society.
A Jew must not be concerned only about his or her own
personal affairs when the community is in trouble:

Whoever is able to protest against the transgressions of
his own family and does not do so is punished [liable, held
responsible] for the transgressions of his family. Whoever
is able to protest against the transgressions of the people
of his community and does not do so is punished for the
transgressions of his community. Whoever is able to
protest against the transgressions of the entire world and
does not do so is punished for the transgressions of the
entire world. (*Shabbat* 54b)

Judaism teaches that people must struggle to create a better
society. The Torah frequently admonishes: "And you shall
eradicate evil from your midst" (Deuteronomy 13:6, 17:7,
21:21, 24:7). Injustice cannot be passively accepted; it must be

actively resisted and, ultimately, eliminated. The Talmudic sages teach that one reason Jerusalem was destroyed was because its citizens failed in their responsibility to constructively criticize one another's improper behavior (*Shabbat* 99b). They indicate that, "Love which does not contain the element of criticism is not really love" (*Genesis Rabbah* 54:3).

The essential elements of Jewish practice include devotion to Torah, study, prayer, performing good deeds and other *mitzvot* (Commandments), and cultivating a life of piety. But, as indicated in the following Midrash (a rabbinic story or teaching based on Biblical events or concepts), in order to be considered pious, a person must protest against injustice. Even God is challenged to apply this standard in judging people:

> R. Acha ben R. Chanina said: Never did a favorable decree go forth from the mouth of the Holy One which He withdrew and changed into an unfavorable judgment, except the following,
>
> "And the Lord said to His angel: 'Go through the city, through Jerusalem, and put a mark upon the foreheads of the men who sigh and groan over all the abominations that are committed there'" (Ezekiel 9:4). [Thus, they will be protected from the angels who are slaying the wicked.]
>
> At that moment, the indignant prosecutor came forward in the Heavenly Court.
>
> Prosecutor: Lord, wherein are these (marked ones) different from those (the rest)?
>
> God: These are wholly righteous men, while those are wholly wicked.
>
> Prosecutor: But Lord, they had the power to protest, but did not.

God: I knew that had they protested, they would not have been heeded.

Prosecutor: But Lord, if it was revealed to You, was it revealed to them? Accordingly, they should have protested and incurred scorn for thy holy Name, and have been ready to suffer blows . . . as the prophets of Israel suffered.

God revoked his original order, and the righteous were found guilty, because of their failure to protest. (Shabbat 55a; Tanchuma Tazria 9)

Hence, it is not sufficient merely to do *mitzvot* while acquiescing in unjust conditions. The *Maharal* of Prague, a sixteenth-century sage, states that individual piety pales in the face of the sin of not protesting against an emerging communal evil, and a person will be held accountable for not preventing wickedness when capable of doing so.[1] One of the most important dangers of silence in the face of evil is that it implies acceptance or possibly even support. According to Rabbeinu Yonah, a medieval sage, sinners may think to themselves, "Since others are neither reproving nor contending against us, our deeds are permissible."[2]

Rabbi Joachim Prinz, a refugee from pre–World War II Nazi Germany and former president of the American Jewish Congress, spoke to the 250,000 people who took part in the "March on Washington" organized by the Reverend Martin Luther King and others in 1963 on behalf of Civil Rights. He stated that under Hitler's rule, he had learned about the problem of apathy toward fellow human beings: "Bigotry and hatred are not the most urgent problem. The most urgent, the most disgraceful, the most shameful and most tragic problem is silence."[3]

Rabbi Abraham Joshua Heschel, a leading twentieth-century philosopher, believed that apathy toward injustice results in greater wickedness. He writes that, "Indifference to evil is more insidious than evil itself," and that silent acquiescence leads to evil being accepted and becoming the rule.[4]

A famous Talmudic story tells that Jerusalem was destroyed because of a failure to protest. A man in Jerusalem was a friend of Kamtza and a bitter enemy of Bar-Kamtza. When the man made a party, his servant mistakenly invited Bar-Kamtza. When Bar-Kamtza arrived, the man insisted that he leave, even after Bar-Kamtza offered to pay for the entire feast if he would be allowed to stay. Bar-Kamtza was very angry at being insulted in public and sought revenge. Because the sages who were present failed to protest, he went to the Romans and slandered the Jews. This led to a series of events which resulted in the destruction of Jerusalem. Hence, the failure of the Jewish sages to protest an injustice that they witnessed had very negative consequences for the Jews (*Gittin* 55b–66a).

Jews are required to protest against injustice and to try to agitate for change even when successful implementation appears very difficult. The Talmudic sage Rabbi Zera states, "Even though people will not accept it, you should rebuke them" (*Shabbat* 55a). We can never be sure that our words and actions will be ineffective. Thus, the only responsible approach is to try our best. In Rabbi Tarfon's famous formulation in the *Mishna*: "It is not your obligation to complete the task. But neither are you free to desist from it" (*Pirkei Avot* 2:21).

Just as many drops of water can eventually carve a hole in a rock, many small efforts can result in a major impact.

There are times when a person must continue to protest in order to avoid being corrupted:

> A man stood at the entrance of Sodom crying out against the injustice and evil in that city. Someone passed by and said to him, "For years you have been urging the people to repent, and yet no one has changed. Why do you continue?" He responded: "When I first came, I protested because I hoped to change the people of Sodom. Now I continue to cry out, because if I don't, they will have changed me."[5]

In his article "The Rabbinic Ethics of Protest," Rabbi Reuven Kimelman observes that the means of protest must be consistent with responsibility to the community. He states that protest must involve both love and truth, since love implies the willingness to suffer, and truth, the willingness to resist. Together, he concludes, they encompass an approach of nonviolent resistance, toward the ends of justice and peace.[6]

The Talmud teaches that controversy and protest must be "for the sake of Heaven" (*Pirkei Avot* 5:20). The protest of Korach against the rule of Moses in the wilderness (Numbers 16:1–35) is considered negatively by the Jewish tradition because it was based on jealousy and personal motives.

INVOLVEMENT AND PROTEST IN JEWISH HISTORY

From its beginning, Judaism has often protested against greed, injustice, and the misuse of power. Abraham, the first Jew, smashed the idols of his father although his action challenged the common belief of the time. He established the precedent that a Jew should not conform to society's values when they are evil. Later he even challenged God, exclaiming, "Shall not the Judge of all the earth do justly?" (Genesis 18:25). By contrast, Noah, though personally righteous, was later rebuked by the Talmudic sages because he failed to criticize the immorality of the society around him.

At the beginning of the book of Exodus, the Torah relates three incidents in Moses' life before God chose him to deliver the Israelites from Egypt. They teach that Jews must be involved in helping resolve disputes, whether they are between two Jews, a Jew and a non-Jew, or two non-Jews. On the first day that Moses goes out to his people from the palace of Pharaoh in which he was raised, he rushes to defend a Hebrew against an Egyptian aggressor (Exodus 2:11, 12). When Moses next goes out, he defends a Hebrew who is being beaten by another Jew (Exodus 2:13). Later, after being forced to flee from Egypt and arriving at a well in Midian, Moses comes to the aid of the shepherd daughters of Jethro who were being harassed by other shepherds (Exodus 2:15–17).

Balaam, the biblical pagan prophet, intends to curse Israel but ends up blessing them. He describes the role of the Jewish people: "Lo, it is a people dwelling alone, and not reckoning itself among the nations" (Numbers 23:9). To the Israelites, the keynote of their existence is: "I am the Lord your God, Who has separated you from the nations that you should be Mine" (Leviticus 20:26). Throughout their history, Jews have often been nonconformists who refused to acquiesce in the false values of the surrounding community.

When the Jews were in Persia, Mordechai refused to defer to an evil ruler. As the book of Esther states: "And all the king's servants . . . bowed down and prostrated themselves before Haman. . . . But Mordechai would not bow down nor pay homage before him" (Esther 3:2). Mordechai believed that bowing down to a human being is inconsistent with his obligation to worship only God. Later, Mordechai condemns inaction in urging Esther to take risks to save the Jewish people (Esther 4:13, 14).

The greatest champions of protest against unjust conditions were the Hebrew prophets. Rabbi Abraham Heschel summarizes the attributes of these spokespeople for God: they had the ability to hold God and people in one thought at the same time; they could not be tranquil in an unjust world; they were supremely impatient with evil due to their intense sensitivity to God's concern for right and wrong; they were advocates for those too weak to plead their own cause (the widow, the orphan, and the oppressed); their major activity was interference, remonstrating against wrongs inflicted on other people.[7]

In sharp contrast, although Jews are supposed to be *b'nei nevi'im* (descendants of the Biblical prophets), our communities often respond rather placidly to immoral acts and conditions. We try to maintain a balanced tone while victims of oppression are in extreme agony. But not so the prophets:

> Cry aloud, spare not, Lift up your voice like a trumpet, and declare unto My people their transgression. . . . Is this not the fast that I have chosen: To loosen the chains of wickedness, to undo the bonds of oppression, to let the crushed go free, and to break every yoke of tyranny? (Isaiah 58:1, 6)

The prophet Amos berates those content amidst destruction and injustice (6:1, 4–6):

Woe to those who are at ease in Zion,

And to those who feel secure on the mountains of
    Samaria. . . .

Woe to those who lie upon beds of ivory,

And stretch themselves upon their couches,

And eat lambs from the flock,

And calves from the midst of the stall;

Who sing idle songs to the sound of the harp. . . .

Who drink wine in bowls,

And anoint themselves in the finest oils,

But are not grieved on the ruin of Joseph!

In order to carry out their role, to be a kingdom of priests and a light unto the nations, Jews throughout history were compelled to live in the world, but apart from it—in effect, on the other side. This, the sage's comment, is implied in the very name "Hebrew" (*ivri*), from "*ever,*" the other side: "The whole world is on one side [idolaters] and he [Abraham, the Hebrew] is on the other side" (*Midrash Genesis Rabbah*). Jacques Maritain, a French Catholic philosopher, wrote in 1939 that the Jewish people were found at the very heart of the world's structure, stimulating it, exasperating it, moving it. . . . They give the world no peace, it bars slumber, it teaches the world to be discontented and restless as long as the world has not accepted God.[8]

Several distinguished Orthodox rabbis of the past two centuries, including Rabbis Samson Raphael Hirsch, Jonathan Sacks, Joseph B. Soloveitchik, and Lord Immanuel Jakobovitz, stress that Judaism has a message for their surrounding cultures and that Jews should convey it to their host societies.[9] Rabbi Soloveitchik (the Rav), one of the foremost Torah leaders of the twentieth century, believed that Jews have a responsibility to work with others to promote the welfare of civilization. He felt that Jews must aid those in need and protect human rights, because such obligations are "implicit in human existence." He states: "We stand shoulder to shoulder with the rest of civilized society against an order that defies us all."[10] Rabbi Sacks, the former Chief Rabbi of England, believed that working for *tikkun olam* (healing and improving the planet) can be a powerful counterforce to the dominance of secularism, as well as an antidote to religious isolationism. He notes:

> One of the most powerful [wrong] assumptions of the twentieth century is that faith … belongs [only] to private life. Religion and society, many believe, are two independent entities, so we can edit God out of the language and leave our social world unchanged.[11]

Based on Jewish tradition and values, Jews have been active in many protest movements. Some of these movements were on behalf of Jewish needs, such as the effort to rescue European Jews from the Holocaust, the battle to support Jewish independence and survival in Israel, and the struggles for Soviet Jewry and later for Syrian and Ethiopian Jewry. But Jews also have been actively involved in struggles for a more peaceful world, human rights, and a cleaner environment. A group of rabbis, acting in accordance with the Jewish ethic of protest, explain why they came to St. Augustine, Florida, in 1964 to demonstrate against segregation in that community:

> We came because we could not stand silently by our brother's blood. We had done that too many times before. We have been vocal in our exhortation of others, but the idleness of our hands too often revealed an inner silence. . . . We came as Jews who remember the millions

of faceless people who stood quietly, watching the smoke rise from Hitler's crematoria. We came because we know that second only to silence, the greatest danger to man is loss of faith in man's capacity to act.[12]

THE CURRENT LACK OF INVOLVEMENT AND PROTEST[13]

Religious practitioners frequently mischaracterize God's demands. Instead of crying out against immorality, injustice, deceit, cruelty, and violence, they too often condone these evils, while emphasizing mostly ceremonies and ritual. To many Jews today, Judaism involves occasional visits to the Synagogue or Temple, prayers recited with little feeling, rituals performed with little meaning, and socializing. But, to the prophets, worship accompanied by indifference to evil is an absurdity, an abomination to God.[14] Judaism is mocked when Jews indulge in or condone empty rituals side-by-side with immoral deeds.

While ritual is extremely important, God's great concern for justice is powerfully expressed by the prophet Amos:

> Even though you offer Me your burnt offerings and cereal offerings, I will not accept them, And the peace offerings of your fatted beasts I will not look upon. Take away from Me the noise of your songs; to the melody of your harps I will not listen. But let justice well up as waters, and righteousness as a mighty stream. (5:22–24)

The prophet Hosea similarly states God's preference for moral and spiritual dedication, rather than mere outward ritual: "For I desire kindness and not sacrifice, attachment to God rather than burnt offerings." (6:6)

Yet all too often, Jews today have failed to speak out against an unjust, immoral society. While claiming to follow the ethical teachings of the prophets, many Jews have equivocated and rationalized inaction. Rabbi Heschel blames religion's failure to speak out and be involved in critical current issues for its losses:

> Religion declined not because it was refuted but because it became irrelevant, dull, oppressive, insipid. When faith is completely replaced by habit, when the crisis of today is ignored because of the splendor of the past, when faith becomes an heirloom rather than a living fountain, when religion speaks only in the name of authority rather than with the voice of compassion, its message becomes meaningless.[15]

Many Jews are turned off to Judaism by the lack of moral commitment and involvement in struggles for a better world within some Jewish religious institutions. Rabbi Abraham Karp, who taught at Dartmouth College, felt that students would only be attracted to a "church or synagogue which dares, which challenges, which disturbs, which acts as a critic, which leads in causes which are moral."[16] Reinhold Niebuhr, the prominent Christian theologian, attributes religion's failure to attract idealistic people to its failure to protest injustice. He states that the chief reason that many people turn from religion is that the "social impotence of religion outrages their conscience."[17]

Many Jews today justify their lack of involvement with the world's problems by stating that Jews have enough troubles of their own and that we can leave it to others to involve themselves in "non-Jewish" issues. Certainly, Jews must be actively involved in battling antisemitism, working for a secure and just Israel, and interact with many other Jewish issues. But can we divorce ourselves from active involvement with more general problems? Are they really "non-Jewish" issues? Don't Jews also suffer from polluted air and water, resource shortages, the effects of climate change, and other societal threats? Can we ignore issues critical to our nation's future?

Perhaps the situation is, in mathematical terms, one of conditional probability. If conditions in the world are good, it is still possible that Jews will suffer. But if these conditions are bad, it is almost certain that Jews will be negatively affected. Hence, even considering self-interest alone, Jews must be involved in working for a just and harmonious world.

It is essential that Jews (and others) actively apply Jewish values to current critical problems. We must be God's loyal opposition to injustice, greed, and immorality, rousing the conscience of humanity. We must shout "NO" when others are whispering "yes" to injustice. We must restore Judaism to the task of "comforting the afflicted and afflicting the comfortable." We must act as befits "descendants of the prophets" (*Pesachim* 66b), reminding the world that there exists a God of justice, compassion, and kindness. Nothing less than global survival is at stake.

As later chapters will show, the world is moving on a very perilous path due to its failure to take seriously religious values that have a direct impact on society at large, such as justice, kindness, compassion, peaceful relations, and concern for the environment. We must act to inform and influence Jews (and others) to become involved and to protest to help move the world to a more sustainable path before it is too late.

2

HUMAN RIGHTS AND OBLIGATIONS

One person (Adam) was created as the common ancestor of all people, for the sake of the peace of the human race, so that one should not be able to say to a neighbor, "My ancestor was better than yours."

One person was created to teach us the sanctity and importance of every life, for one who destroys a single life is considered by scripture to have destroyed an entire world, and one who saves a single life is considered by scripture to have saved an entire world.

One person was created to teach us the importance of the actions of every individual, for we should treat the world as half good and half bad, so that if we do one good deed, it will tip the whole world to the side of good. (*Mishna Sanhedrin* 4:5)

A fundamental Jewish principle is the equality and unity of humanity. We all have one Creator; God is the Divine Parent of every person. Judaism is a universal religion that condemns discrimination based on race, color, or nationality. God endows each person with basic human dignity.

Ben Azzai, a disciple of Rabbi Akiva, reinforces this concept in the Talmud. He states that a fundamental teaching of the Torah is the verse: "This is the book of the generations of *humanity (Adam)* [emphasis mine]" (Genesis 5:1).[1] The statement does not talk about black or white, or

Jew or Gentile, but *humanity*. Since all human beings share a common ancestor, they must necessarily be brothers and sisters. Hence these words proclaim the essential message that there is a unity to the human race.

IMITATION OF GOD'S WAYS

One of the most important ideas about the creation of humanity is that, "God created people in God's own image; in the image of God He created him; male and female He created them" (Genesis 1:27). According to Rabbi Akiva, a Talmudic sage, "Beloved are human beings who were created in the image of God, and it is an even greater act of love [by God] that it was made known to people that they were created in the Divine image" (*Pirkei Avot* 3:18, citing Genesis 1:27).

Because human beings are created in God's image, we are to imitate God's attributes of holiness, kindness, and compassion: "And the Lord spoke unto Moses, saying: 'Speak unto all the congregation of the children of Israel, and say unto them: You shall be holy, as I, the Lord Your God, am holy'" (Leviticus 19:1, 2). The fact that the above mandate was delivered to the entire congregation means that it applies to every Jew, not just to a small elite group of spiritual or moral specialists.

In the following verses, the Torah mandates that we walk in God's ways:

> And now, Israel, what does the Lord your God ask of you, but to revere the Lord your God, to walk in all His ways and to love Him, and to serve the Lord your God with all your heart and with all your soul. (Deuteronomy 10:12)

You shall diligently keep this entire commandment which I command you to do it, to love the Lord your God, to walk in all His ways, and to cleave to Him. (Deuteronomy 11:22)

The Midrash interprets the expression "walking in God's ways" to mean "Just as God is 'merciful,' you should be merciful, just as God is 'compassionate,' you should be compassionate" (*Sifre to Deuteronomy* 11:22). The third-century sage Hama ben Hanina expands on the duty of imitating God:

What is the meaning of the verse "You shall walk after the Lord your God" (Deuteronomy 13:5)? Is it possible for a human being to walk after the *Shechinah* (God's presence), for has it not been said, "For the Lord your God is a devouring fire" (Deuteronomy 4:24)? But the verse means to walk after the *attributes* of the Holy One, Blessed is He. As God clothes the naked, for it is written, "And the Lord God made for Adam and his wife coats of skin and clothed them" (Genesis 3:21), so should you clothe the naked. The Holy One, Blessed is He, visits the sick, for it is written, "And the Lord appeared to him (Abraham), while he was recovering from circumcision), by the oaks of Mamre" (Genesis 18:1), so should you also visit the sick. The Holy One, Blessed is He, comforts mourners, for it is written, "And it came to pass after the death of Abraham, that God blessed Isaac, his son" (Genesis 25:11), so should you comfort mourners. The Holy One, Blessed is He, buries the dead, for it is written, "And He buried Moses in the valley" (Deuteronomy 34:6), so should you also bury the dead. (Sotah 14a)

Maimonides finds a powerful statement about the importance of imitating God's positive attributes in these words from the prophet Jeremiah:

Thus says the Lord:
Let not the wise person take pride in his wisdom;
Neither let the mighty person take pride in his might;
Let not the rich person take pride in his riches;
But let him that takes pride, take pride in this:
That he understands and knows Me,
That I am the Lord who exercises mercy, justice, and
    righteousness, on the earth;
For in these things I delight, says the Lord. (Jeremiah
    9:22–23)

Maimonides interprets this statement to mean that a person should find fulfillment in the imitation of God, in being "like God in one's actions."[2] According to Rabbi Abraham Joshua Heschel, Maimonides originally considered the highest human goal to be contemplation of God's essence, but later came to believe that one's ultimate purpose is to emulate God's traits of kindness, justice, and righteousness. He renounced his former practice of seclusion and ministered to the sick throughout each day (as a physician).[3]

    While Judaism has many beautiful symbols, such as the *mezuzah*, *menorah*, and *sukkah*, there is only one symbol that represents God, and that is each person. As Rabbi Heschel taught, more important than to have a symbol is to *be* a symbol. And every person can consider themselves a symbol of God. This is our challenge: to live in a way compatible with being a symbol of God, to walk in God's ways, to remember who we are and Whom we represent, and to remember our role as partners of God in working to redeem the world.

LOVE OF NEIGHBOR

A central commandment in Judaism is "You shall love your neighbor as yourself" (Leviticus 19:18). According to Rabbi Akiva, this is a (or perhaps *the*) "great principle of the Torah."[4] Rabbi Levi Yitzhak of Berditchev taught: "Whether a person really loves God can be determined by the love he or she bears toward other human beings."[5]

Many Torah authorities write that this should be applied not only to Jews but to all humanity. Rabbi J. H. Hertz, former Chief Rabbi of England, states that the translation of the Hebrew word *rea* (neighbor) does not mean "fellow Israelite." He cites several examples in the Torah where that word means "neighbor of whatever race or creed."[6] His view reflects that of Rabbi Pinchas Eliyahu of Vilna, author of the classic *Sefer HaBrit*, who states: "Love of one's neighbor means that we should love all people, no matter to which nation they belong or what language they speak. For all [people] are created in the Divine image, and all engage in improving civilization. . . ."[7] Rabbi Pinchas stated that "All of the commandments between man and man are included in this precept of loving one's neighbor,"[8] and he also provides a scriptural proof text in which a non-Jew is also called "neighbor."[9]

The commandment "Love your neighbor as yourself" logically follows from the Jewish principle that each person has been created in God's image. Hence, since my neighbor is like myself, I should love him as myself. In fact, the proper translation of the commandment may be "Love your neighbor; he is like yourself."

In the same chapter of Leviticus in which "Love your neighbor as yourself" appears, the Torah outlines some specific ways that this mandate can be put into practice:

> You shall not steal; nor shall you deal falsely nor lie to one another. . . . You shall not oppress your neighbor, nor rob him. You shall not curse the deaf, and you shall not put a stumbling block before the blind. You shall do no injustice in judgment; be not partial to the poor, and favor not the mighty; in righteousness shall you judge your neighbor. You shall not go up and down as a talebearer among your people; neither shall you stand idly by the blood of your neighbor: I am the Lord. (Leviticus 19:11, 14–16)

The Talmudic sages spell out how one should practice love for human beings:

> One should practice loving-kindness (*gemilut chasadim*), not only by giving of one's possessions, but by personal effort on behalf of one's fellowman, such as extending a free loan, visiting the sick, offering comfort to mourners and attending weddings. For alms giving (*tzedakah*) there is the minimum of the *tithe* (one-tenth) and the maximum of one-fifth of one's income. But there is no fixed measure of personal service. (*Mishnah Pe'ah* 1)

Rabbi Moshe Leib of Sassov tells how to love our neighbor as ourselves by relating an experience in his life:

> How to love people is something I learned from a peasant. He was sitting in an inn along with the other peasants, drinking . . . he asked one of the men seated beside him: "Tell me, do you love me or don't you love me?" The other replied, "I love you very much." The first peasant nodded his head, was silent for a while, then remarked: "You say that you love me, but you do not know what

I need. If you really loved me, you should know." The other had not a word to say to this, and the peasant who asked the question fell silent again. But I understood. To know the needs of men and to bear the burden of their sorrow—that is the true love of man.[10]

Aaron, the brother of Moses, also teaches how we can love our neighbors. When two people were quarreling, he would go to each separately and tell him how the other deeply regretted their argument and wished reconciliation. When the two would next meet, they would often embrace and reestablish friendly relations. Because of such acts of love and kindness by Aaron, the great Talmudic master Hillel exhorts people to "Be of the disciples of Aaron, loving peace and pursuing peace, loving humanity, and drawing them closer to the Torah." (*Pirkei Avot* 1:12)

When a pagan confronted Hillel and demanded that the sage explain all of the Torah while he, the potential convert, stood on one leg, Hillel's response was: "What is hateful to you, do not do unto others—that is the entire Torah; everything else is commentary. Go and learn." (*Shabbat* 31a)

KINDNESS TO STRANGERS

To further emphasize that "love of neighbor" applies to every human being, the Torah frequently commands that we show love and consideration for the stranger, "for you know the heart of the stranger, since you were strangers in the land of Egypt" (Exodus 23:9). The stranger was one who came from distant parts of the land of Israel or, like the immigrants of our own day, from a foreign country. The

Torah stresses the importance of treating them with respect and empathy.

The importance placed on the commandment not to mistreat the stranger in our midst is indicated by its appearance thirty-six times in the Torah—far more than any other mitzvah.[11] It is placed on the same level as the duty of kindness to and protection of the widow and the orphan.[12] According to rabbinic tradition, most of these references to the "stranger" allude to one who converts to Judaism (*ger tzedek*) or to non-Jews living in the land of Israel who accept Jewish sovereignty, observe basic laws of morality, and repudiate idolatry (*ger toshav*). But since we were neither converts nor formally accepted fellow travelers in Egypt, there must be additional meaning in our obligation to the "stranger."

The German Jewish philosopher Hermann Cohen (1842–1918) stated that true religion involves shielding the "alien" from all wrong. He commented:

> The alien was to be protected, although he was not a member of one's family, clan, religious community, or people; simply because he was a human being. In the alien, therefore, man discovered the idea of humanity.[13]

In our world, with its great clannishness and nationalism, with its often-harsh treatment of people who don't share the local religion, nationality, or culture, the Torah's teachings about the "stranger" are remarkable:

> And a stranger shall you not wrong, neither shall you oppress him; for you were strangers in the land of Egypt. (Exodus 22:20; Leviticus 19:33)

> Love you therefore the stranger; for you were strangers in
> the land of Egypt. (Deuteronomy 10:19; Leviticus 19:34)

> And you shall rejoice in all the good which the Lord,
> your God has given you . . . along with the stranger who
> is in the midst of you. (Deuteronomy 26:11)

The stranger is guaranteed the same protection in the law court and in payment of wages as the native:

> Judge righteously between a man and his brother and the
> stranger that is with him. (Deuteronomy 1:16)

> You shall not oppress a hired servant who is poor and [in
> need], whether he be of your brethren, or of the strangers
> that are in your land within your gates. In the same day
> you shall pay him. (Deuteronomy 24:14, 15)

When it comes to Divine forgiveness, the stranger stands on an equal footing with the native:

> And all the congregation of the children of Israel shall
> be forgiven, and the stranger that sojourns among them.
> (Numbers 15:26)

Like any other person in need, the "stranger" had free access to the grain that was to be left unharvested in the corners of the field and to the gleanings of the harvest, as well as to fallen grapes or odd clusters of grapes remaining on the vine after picking (Leviticus 19:9, 10; 23:22; Deuteronomy 24:21). The stranger, like the widow and the fatherless, was welcome to the forgotten sheaves in the fields (Deuteronomy 24:19) and to the olives clinging to the beaten trees (Deuteronomy 24:20). He also partook of the tithe (the

tenth part of the produce) every third year of the Sabbatical
cycle. (Deuteronomy 14:28, 29; 26:12)[14]

TREATMENT OF NON-JEWS

Since God is the Creator and Divine Parent of every person,
each human being is entitled to proper treatment. A person's
actions, and not their faith or creed, are most important, as
indicated in the following Talmudic teachings:

> I bring heaven and earth to witness that the Holy Spirit
> dwells upon a non-Jew as well as upon a Jew, upon a
> woman as well as upon a man, upon maidservant as well
> as manservant. All depends on the deeds of the particular
> individual! (*Yalkut to Judges* 4:4 from *Tannade Vei Eliyahu*)

> In all nations, there are righteous individuals who will
> have a share in the world to come. (*Tosefta Sanhedrin* 13:2)

The Talmud contains many statutes that require us to assist
and care for non-Jews along with Jews:

> We support the poor of the non-Jew along with the poor
> of Israel and visit the sick of the non-Jew along with the
> sick of Israel and bury the dead of the non-Jew along with
> the dead of Israel, for the sake of peace (*mipnei darchei
> shalom*). . . . (*Gittin* 61a)

> In a city where there are both Jews and Gentiles, the
> collectors of alms collect from both; they feed the poor
> of both, visit the sick of both, bury both, comfort the
> mourners whether they be Jews or Gentiles, and restore
> the lost goods of both, *mipnei darchei shalom*: to promote
> peace and cooperation. (*Yerushalmi Demai* 4:6 (24a))

The essential spirit of Judaism toward other people was expressed by Maimonides in his *Mishneh Torah*:

> Jew and non-Jew are to be treated alike. If a (Jewish) vendor knows that his merchandise is defective, he must inform the purchaser (whatever his or her religion). (18:1)

Influenced by this statement by Maimonides, Rabbi Menachem Meiri of Provence ruled in the fourteenth century that a Jew *should* desecrate the Sabbath if it might help to save the life of a Gentile.[15] He stated that any previous ruling to the contrary had been intended only for ancient times for those non-Jews who were pagans and morally deficient.[16] The late Israeli Chief Rabbi Chaim Unterman in a *responsum* (reply to a religiously-based question) in which he vigorously denied a charge raised by a Dr. Israel Shahak that Jewish law forbids violating the Sabbath to save a Gentile's life, quotes this decision.[17]

Rabbi Ezekiel Landau, eighteenth century author of *Noda B'Yehuda*, ruled:

> I emphatically declare that in all laws contained in the Jewish writings concerning theft, fraud, etc., no distinction is made between Jew and Gentile; that the (Talmudic) legal categories goy, *akum* (idolater), etc., in no way apply to the people among whom we live.

The following Midrash dramatically shows that Jews are to treat every person, not just fellow Jews, justly:

> Shimon ben Shetach worked hard preparing flax. His disciples said to him, "Rabbi, desist. We will buy you an ass, and you will not have to work so hard." They went and bought an ass from an Arab, and a pearl was found on it (hidden in the saddle), whereupon they came

to Rabbi Shimon and said, "From now on you need not work anymore." "Why?" he asked. They said, "We bought you an ass from an Arab, and a pearl was found on it." He said to them, "Does its owner know of that?" They answered, "No." He said to them, "Go and give the pearl back to him." To their argument that he need not return the pearl because the Arab was a heathen, he responded, "Do you think that Shimon ben Shetach is a barbarian? He would prefer to hear the Arab say, 'Blessed be the God of the Jews,' than to possess all the riches of the world. . . . It is written, 'You shall not oppress your neighbor.' Now your neighbor is as your brother, and your brother is as your neighbor. Hence you learn that to rob a Gentile is robbery." (*Deuteronomy Rabbah* 3:3)

According to the late Rabbi Ahron Soloveichik, the late rabbinic leader, scholar, and Professor of Talmud at Yeshiva University, Shimon Ben Shetach in the above story gave a remarkable definition of a barbarian: "Anyone who fails to apply a uniform standard of *mishpat* (justice) and *tzedek* (righteousness) to all human beings, regardless of origin, color, or creed, is deemed barbaric."[18]

SLAVERY IN THE BIBLICAL PERIOD

From today's perspective, the widespread and legalized practice of slavery in biblical times seems to contradict Jewish values with regard to the treatment of human beings. However, we must look at slavery as an evolving process; it was a common practice in ancient times and was thought to be an economic necessity. Therefore, the Torah does not outlaw it immediately but, through its teachings and laws, the Torah paved the way toward the eventual elimination of slavery.

Slavery in Israel's early history had many humane features in comparison with practices in other countries. Enslaved people's rights were guarded and regulated with humanitarian legislation. They were recognized as having certain inalienable rights based on their humanity. For example, enslaved people had to be allowed to rest on the Sabbath Day, just like people who had power over them.

The Talmud proclaimed legislation in order to mitigate slavery's harshness, especially with regard to an enslaved Hebrew:

> He [the enslaved person] should be with you in food and with you in drink, lest you eat clean bread and he moldy bread, or lest you drink old wine and he new wine, or lest you sleep on soft feathers and he on straw. So it was said, "Whoever buys a Hebrew slave, it is as if he purchased a master for himself." (*Kiddushin* 20a)

It is significant that, unlike the law of the U.S. before the Civil War, the Biblical fugitive law protected the runaway enslaved person:

> You shall not deliver to his master a bondsman that is escaped from his master unto you. He shall dwell with you in the midst of you, in the place which he shall choose within one of your gates, where he likes it best; you shall not wrong him. (Deuteronomy 23:16, 17)

VIOLATIONS OF HUMAN RIGHTS

One test of the decency of a community is in its attitude toward strangers. A just society teaches its members to welcome outsiders and to be kind to those who are disadvantaged.

Unfortunately, the history of the world is largely a history of exploitation and the violation of human rights. Today in many countries there is widespread discrimination against and oppression of people of different races, religions, nationalities, sexual orientations, and economic status. As will be discussed in Chapter 10, often due to injustice and repression, much of the world's people lack adequate food, shelter, employment, education, health care, clean water, and other basic human needs.

Jews have historically been among the people who have suffered the most from prejudice. The Crusades, the Inquisition, and the Holocaust are just three of the most horrible examples in Jewish and human history. Often Jews have been killed, expelled from countries where they had lived and contributed to for many generations, subjected to pogroms, or converted at sword point (or died resisting), solely because they were Jewish. Whenever conditions were bad, the economy suffered, or there was a plague, Jews provided a convenient scapegoat.

Antisemitism continues and, in many ways, has become worse today. Many organizations use social media and other means to spread their hateful messages. There are several groups that preach that the Holocaust never occurred. Jewish organizations, such as the Anti-Defamation League, are working to reduce antisemitism, but much more needs to be done to eliminate this ancient, but still ever-present and virulent disease.

It is essential to educate all people to the evils of antisemitism and other forms of discrimination. In addition to openly confronting and opposing antisemitism and racism, it is also necessary to work to reduce and eliminate injustice, poverty, slums, hunger, illiteracy, unemployment, homelessness, and other social ills. Just, democratic societies will be far safer for everyone, including Jews.

JEWISH VIEWS ON RACISM

Rabbi Ahron Soloveichik, a twentieth-century educator and author, indicates how strong Jewish views against racism are:

> From the standpoint of the Torah there can be no distinction between one human being and another on the basis of race or color. Any discrimination shown to another human being on account of his color or her skin constitutes loathsome barbarity.[19]

He points out that Judaism *does* recognize distinctions between Jews and non-Jews, but this is not based on any concept of superiority—it "is based on the unique and special burdens that are placed upon Jews."[20]

The prophet Amos challenges the state of mind that looks down on darker-skinned people in a ringing declaration on the equality of all races and nations. He compares the Jewish people to Black people and indicates that God is even concerned with Israel's enemies, such as the Philistines and Syrians:

> Are you not as the children of the Ethiopians unto me,
> 0 children of Israel? says the Lord.
> Have I not brought up Israel out of the land of Egypt?
> And the Philistines from Caphtor,
> And the Syrians from Kir? (Amos 9:7)

Judaism teaches the sacredness of every person, but this is not what has always been practiced in our society. And, as with many other moral issues, religion has too seldom spoken out in protest.

Rabbi Heschel pointed out the tremendous threat that racism poses to humanity:

> Racism is worse than idolatry; *Racism is Satanism*, unmitigated evil. Few of us seem to realize how insidious, how radical, how universal an evil racism is. Few of us realize that racism is man's gravest threat to man, the maximum of hatred for a minimum of reason, the maximum of cruelty for a minimum of thinking.[21]

He pointed out that bigotry is inconsistent with a proper relationship with God:

> Prayer and prejudice cannot dwell in the same heart. Worship without compassion is worse than self-deception; it is an abomination.[22]

Rabbi Heschel asserted that "what is lacking is a sense of the monstrosity of inequality."[23] Consistent with the Jewish view that every person is created in God's image, he boldly states: "God is every man's pedigree. He is either the Father of all men or of no men. The image of God is either in every man or in no man."[24]

It is an embarrassing fact that most of America's religious institutions did not originally take the lead in proclaiming the evil of segregation; they had to be prodded into action by the decision of the Supreme Court of the United States in the case of *Brown v. Board of Education* in 1954.

Based on Jewish values of compassion and justice, many Jews were active in the struggle for Civil Rights. Two

Jewish college students, Andrew Goodman and Michael Schwerner, along with Black student James Chaney, were brutally murdered while working for Civil Rights in Mississippi in 1964.

After the 1967 Six-Day war, the Black Power movement, and the rise of ethnic pride in the late 1960s, some fissures developed between Jewish and Black people in their decades-long alliance for progress in America. But while some on both sides would emphasize points of disharmony, Jewish and Black people have many common interests and goals and have much to gain by working together for a more just, compassionate, peaceful, and harmonious society, as is modeled by the frequent close cooperation on many issues between the congressional Black caucus and Jewish members of Congress.

Jewish identification with disadvantaged people is rooted in Jewish historical experience: we were slaves in Egypt and have often lived as oppressed second-class citizens (or worse) in ghettos, deprived of freedom and rights. Hence, we should understand the frustrations of other minorities, here and elsewhere, and their impatient yearning for equality and human dignity.

It is significant that the government of Israel has for some time had a policy of preferential treatment for immigrants who need help adjusting to their new home. Special programs have been devised for the children of Mizrachi (Middle Eastern) and Ethiopian Jews who come from homes where there is low literacy. Compensatory measures include free nurseries, longer school days and school years, special tutoring and curricula, additional funds for equipment and supplies, extra counseling services, and preferential acceptance to academic secondary schools, although there is unfortunately also some discriminatory treatment and segregation. Like every other country, Israel is not yet ideal in its treatment of some newcomers and minorities.

In summary, Jewish values stress the equality of every person, love of neighbor, proper treatment of strangers, and the imitation of God's attributes of justice, compassion, and kindness. Hence, it is essential that Jews work for the establishment of societies that will protect the rights of every person, each of whom is entitled, as a child of God, to a life of equitable opportunities for education, employment, and human dignity.

3

SOCIAL JUSTICE

Justice, justice shall you pursue. (Deuteronomy 16:20)

The pursuit of a just society is one of the most fundamental concepts of Judaism. The prevalence of injustice in today's world makes all the more urgent Judaism's emphasis on the importance of actively seeking social justice.

Note two things about the Torah verse above, which is a keynote of Jewish social values:

1. Words are seldom repeated in the Torah. When they are, it is generally to emphasize an important teaching. In this case, the repetition of the Hebrew word *tzedek* (justice) is to stress the supreme importance of applying even-handed justice to all. Rabbenu Bachya ben Asher, a thirteenth-century Torah commentator, stresses: "justice whether to your profit or loss, whether in word or action, whether to Jew or non-Jew."[1]

2. We are told to *pursue* justice. Hence, we are not to wait for the right opportunity to come along, the right time and place, but instead we are to actively seek opportunities to practice justice.

Many other statements in the Jewish sacred writings emphasize the great importance placed on working for justice. The book of Proverbs asserts: "To do righteousness and justice is preferred by God above sacrifice" (Proverbs 21:3). The psalmist exhorts: "Give justice to the weak and the fatherless; maintain the right of the afflicted and the destitute." (Psalms 82:3)

The prophets constantly stress the importance of applying justice:

> Learn to do well—seek justice, relieve the oppressed, judge the fatherless, plead for the widow. . . . Zion shall be redeemed with justice, and they who return to her with righteousness. (Isaiah 1:17, 27)

> The Lord of Hosts shall be exalted in justice, The Holy God shows Himself holy in righteousness. (Isaiah 5:16)

To practice justice is considered among the highest demands of prophetic teachings:

> It has been told you, O human being, what is good
> And what the Lord requires of you:
> Only to do justly, love *chesed* (mercy, kindness),
> And walk humbly with your God. (Micah 6:8)

The prophet Amos warns the people that without the practice of justice, God is repelled by their worship:

> Take away from Me the noise of your songs and let Me not hear the melody of your stringed instruments, but let justice well up as waters, and righteousness as a mighty stream. (Amos 5:23, 24)

The practice of justice is even part of the symbolic betrothal between the Jewish people and God:

> And I will betroth you unto Me forever; And, I will betroth you unto Me in righteousness, justice, loving

kindness, and compassion. And I will betroth you unto
Me in faithfulness. And you shall know the Lord. (Hosea
2:21–22)

The prophets of Israel were the greatest champions of social
justice in world history. Jeremiah rebukes the Jewish people
when they fail to plead the cause of the orphan or help those
in need (5:28). He castigates an entire generation, for "in
your skirts is found the blood of the souls of the innocent
poor" (2:34). Ezekiel rebukes the whole nation for "using
oppression, robbing, defrauding the poor and the needy, and
extorting from the stranger" (22:29). Isaiah (5:8) and Micah
(2:2) criticize wealthy Jews who built up large holdings of
property at the expense of their neighbors. The prophetic
books are replete with such moral reproof.

The patriarch Abraham even challenges God to
practice justice: "That be far from You to do after this
manner, to slay the righteous with the wicked . . . shall the
Judge of all the earth not do justly?" (Genesis 18:25)

Rabbi Emanuel Rackman, former President of Bar Ilan
University, points out that Judaism teaches a special kind of
justice, an "empathic justice," which seeks to make people
identify themselves with each other—with each other's
needs, with each other's hopes and aspirations, with each
other's defeats and frustrations. Because Jews have known
the distress of slavery and the loneliness of strangers, we are
to project ourselves into other souls and try to improve their
conditions.[2]

This concept is reinforced by Rabbi Levi Yitzchak
Horowitz, the former Bostoner Rebbe:

The fact that the Jewish people had to experience 400
years of Egyptian exile, including 210 years of actual

slavery, was critical in molding our national personality into one of compassion and concern for our fellow man, informed by the realization that we have a vital role to play in the world. . . . For this reason, God begins the Ten Commandments with a reminder that "I am the Lord, your God, Who took you out of Egypt" (Exodus 20:2). We must constantly remember that we were slaves, in order to always appreciate the ideal of freedom, not only for ourselves but also for others. We must do what we can to help others to live free of the bondage of the evil spirit, free of the bondage of cruelty, of abuse and lack of caring.[3]

Based on these teachings, Jews have regarded the practice of justice and the seeking of a just society as Divine imperatives. This has inspired many Jews throughout history to be leaders in struggles for better social conditions. The teachings of the Torah, prophets, and sages have been the most powerful inspiration for justice in the history of the world.

GIVING CHARITY (*TZEDAKAH*)

To help low-income and hungry people and to support communal purposes and institutions, Judaism places great stress on the giving of charity as an act of righteousness (*tzedakah*). In the Jewish tradition, *tzedakah* is not an act of condescension from one person to another who is in need. It is the fulfillment of a *mitzvah*, a commandment, to a fellow human being, who has equal status before God. Although Jewish tradition recognizes that the sharing of our resources is also an act of love (as the Torah states, "Love your neighbor as yourself" (Leviticus 19:18)), it emphasizes that this act of sharing is an act of justice. This is to teach us that Jews are obligated to provide people in need with our love and concern. They are human beings, created in the Divine image, who have a place and a purpose within God's creation.

In the Jewish tradition, failure to give charity is equivalent to idolatry (*Ketubot* 68a). Perhaps this is because a selfish person forgets God, Who created and provides for us all, and, in becoming preoccupied with personal material needs, makes materialism into an idol. The giving of charity by Jews is so widespread that Maimonides was able to say: "Never have I seen or heard of a Jewish community that did not have a charity fund."[4]

Charity even took priority over the building of the Temple. King Solomon was prohibited from using the silver and gold that King David, his father, had accumulated for the building of the Temple, because that wealth should have been used to feed the poor during the three years of famine in King David's reign. (I Kings 7:51)

Judaism mandates lending to those in need, to help them become economically self-sufficient:

> And if your brother becomes impoverished, and his means fails in your proximity; then you shall strengthen him. . . . Take no interest from him or increase. . . . You shall not give him your money upon interest. (Leviticus 25:35–37)

Every third year of the sabbatical cycle, people in need are to receive the tithe for the poor (one-tenth of one's income) (Deuteronomy 14:28, 26:12). The following Torah verse indicates the general Jewish view about helping the impoverished:

> If there shall be among you a needy person, one of your
> brethren, within any of your gates, in your land which
> the Lord your God gives you, you shall not harden your
> heart, nor shut your hand from your needy brother; but
> you shall surely open your hand unto him, and shall
> surely lend him sufficient for his need in that which he
> wants. (Deuteronomy 15:7–8)

Jewish tradition views *tzedakah* as not only an act of love,
but also as an act of justice—in fact, the word "*tzedakah*"
comes from the word "*tzedek*" (justice). According to the
Torah, the governing institutions of the Jewish community
are responsible to help people in need.

Maimonides writes in his code of Jewish law that the
highest form of *tzedakah* is to help an individual in need
through "a gift or a loan, or by forming a business partnership
with him, or by providing him with a job, until he is no
longer dependent on the generosity of others."[5] This concept
is based on the following Talmudic teaching: "It is better to
lend to a poor person than to give him alms, and best of all is
to provide him with capital for business." (*Shabbat* 63a)

Hence, Jews should provide immediate help for poor
people while also working for a just society in which there
is no poverty. In Judaism, *tzedakah* is intertwined with the
pursuit of social justice.

An entire lengthy section of the Code of Jewish Law
(*Shulhan Arukh*), *Yoreh De'ah* 247–259, is devoted to the many
aspects of giving charity. Some of the more important
concepts are given below:

247:1: It is a positive religious obligation for a person to give
as much charity as they can afford. (A tithe of ten percent of
one's income is incumbent upon every Jew.)

247:33: God has compassion on whoever has compassion on the poor. A person should think that, just as they ask of God all the time to sustain them and as they entreat God to hear their cry, so they should hear the cry of those in need.

248:1: Every person is obliged to give charity. Even a poor person who is supported by charity is obliged to give from that which they receive.

249:3: A person should give charity cheerfully and out of the goodness of their heart. They should anticipate the grief of the poor person and speak words of comfort to them. But if they give in an angry and unwilling spirit, they lose any merit there is in giving.

250:1: How much should be given to a poor person? "Sufficient for his need in that which he requires" (Deuteronomy 15:8). This means that if the person is hungry, they should be fed; if they have no clothes, they should be given clothes; if they have no furniture, furniture should be brought for them. (This is to be dispensed by the person in charge of community charity funds.)

According to the prophet Ezekiel, failure to help those in need led to the destruction of Sodom:

> Behold this was the iniquity of thy sister Sodom; pride,
> fullness of bread, and careless ease . . . neither did she
> strengthen the hand of the poor and needy . . . therefore
> I removed them when I saw it. (Ezekiel 16:49, 50)

A relationship between personal misfortune and a failure to help the poor is indicated in Proverbs 17:5, 21:13, and 28:27. For example, Proverbs 21:13 states: "The person who fails to hear the cry of the poor will later also cry, but will not be answered."

ACTS OF LOVING KINDNESS

As important as *tzedakah* is, the Jewish tradition states that even greater is *gemilut chasadim* (acts of loving kindness):

> One who gives a coin to a poor man is rewarded with six blessings, but he who encourages him with kind words is rewarded with eleven blessings. (Baba Batra 88b)

Of course, providing both charity and kind words is best of all.

The sages interpret "acts of loving kindness" to include many types of gracious action, such as hospitality to travelers, providing for poor brides, visiting the sick, welcoming guests, burying the dead, and comforting mourners.

Gemilut chasadim is deemed superior to acts of charity in several ways: no gift is needed for it but the giving of oneself; it may be provided to the rich as well as the poor; and it may be done not only to the living, but also to the dead (through burial).[6]

The purpose of the entire Torah is to teach *gemilut chasadim*. It starts and ends with an act of loving kindness. For in the third chapter of Genesis, the verse reads: "The Lord God made for Adam and his wife garments of skin and clothed them" (Genesis 3:21), and the last book of the Torah reports: "and He buried him (Moses) in the valley." (Deuteronomy 34:6; Sotah 14a)

JEWISH VIEWS ON POVERTY

Judaism places emphasis on justice and charity and kindness to the poor because of the great difficulties people in need face:

> If all afflictions in the world were assembled on one side of
> the scale and poverty on the other, poverty would outweigh
> them all. (Midrash *Exodus Rabbah*, *Mishpatim* 31:14)

Judaism believes that poverty is destructive to the human
personality and negatively shapes a person's life experiences:
"The ruin of the poor is their poverty" (Proverbs 10:15);
"Where there is no sustenance, there is no learning" (Pirkei
Avot 3:21); "The world is darkened for the person who has to
look to others for sustenance" (*Betza* 32a); "The sufferings of
poverty cause a person to disregard his own sense (of right)
and that of his Maker." (*Eruvin* 41)

Judaism does not encourage an ascetic life. Insufficiency
of basic necessities does not ease the path toward holiness,
except perhaps for very spiritual individuals. In many cases
the opposite is true; poverty can lead to the breaking of a
person's spirit. This is one reason that holiness is linked to
justice.

Many Torah laws are designed to aid the poor: the
produce of corners of the field are to be left uncut for the
poor to take (Leviticus 19:9); the gleanings of the wheat
harvest and fallen fruit are to be left for those in need
(Leviticus 19:10); during the sabbatical year, the land is to
be left fallow so the poor (as well as animals) may eat of
whatever grows freely. (Leviticus 25:2–7)

Failure to treat the poor properly is a desecration of God:
"The person who mocks the poor blasphemes his Maker"
(Proverbs 17:5). Abraham, the founder of Judaism, always
went out of his way to aid the poor. He set up inns that were
open in all four directions on the highways so that the poor
and the wayfarers would have access to food and drink when
in need. (Genesis 18:2; *Abot de Rabbi Nathan* 7:17a, b)

The Jewish tradition sees God as siding with the poor and oppressed. God intervened in Egypt on behalf of poor and oppressed enslaved people. His prophets constantly castigated those who oppressed those in need. Two proverbs reinforce this message. A negative formulation is in Proverbs 14:31: "He who oppresses a poor man insults his Maker." Proverbs 19:17 puts it more positively: "He who is kind to the poor lends to the Lord." Hence, helping a person in need is like providing a loan to the Creator of the universe.

COMPASSION

Compassion is one of Judaism's highest values. God is referred to in synagogue services as *Ha–rachaman* (the compassionate one) and as *Av harachamim* (Father of compassion). Since Judaism teaches that human beings, uniquely created in God's image (Genesis 1:27), are to emulate God's positive attributes, we should also be compassionate.

The Talmud states that Jews are to be *rachmanim b'nei rachmanim* (compassionate children of compassionate ancestors) (*Kiddushin* 4a), and that one who is not compassionate cannot truly be of the seed of Abraham, our father (*Bezah* 32b). It also states that Heaven grants compassion to those who are compassionate to others, and withholds it from those who are not. (Shabbat 151b)

The *Baruch Sheh'amar* prayer, recited daily in the morning (*Shacharit*) services, states that "Blessed is the One [God] Who has compassion on the earth; blessed is the One Who has compassion on the creatures [nonhuman and human animals]." Hence, in emulating God, we should also exhibit concern and compassion toward the earth's environment and all of God's creatures.

The rabbis considered Jews to be distinguished by three characteristics: compassion, modesty, and benevolence (*Yebamot* 79a). As indicated previously, we are instructed to feel empathy for strangers "for you were strangers in the land of Egypt" (Deuteronomy 10:19). The *birkat ha-mazon* (grace recited after meals) speaks of God compassionately feeding the whole world.

The important *ashrei* psalm, recited three times daily, states that "God is good to all, and His compassion is over all His works." According to Rabbi Dovid Sears, author of *A Vision of Eden: Animal Welfare and Vegetarianism in Jewish Law and Mysticism*, this verse is "the touchstone of the rabbinic attitude toward animal welfare."

Referring to the Talmudic teaching that we are to emulate God's ways, Rabbi Sears states: "Therefore, compassion for all creatures, including animals, is not only God's business; it is a virtue that we too must emulate. Moreover, compassion must not be viewed as an isolated phenomenon, one of a number of religious duties in the Judaic conception of the Divine service. It is central to our entire approach to life."

In the spirit of the above teachings, the Chofetz Chaim, a sage of the late nineteenth and early twentieth centuries, wrote: "The existence of the entire world depends on this virtue [our capacity to imitate God's compassion and other positive attributes]. . . . Hence, whoever follows in this path will bear the Divine image on his person; while whoever refrains from exercising this virtue and questions himself, 'why should I do good to others?' removes himself completely from God, the Blessed One."[7]

We are not only to have compassion for Jews, but for all who are in need: "Have we not one Father? Has not one God created us?" (Malachai 2:10)

Rabbi Samson Raphael Hirsch, a noted sage and biblical commentator of the nineteenth century, wrote very eloquently about the importance of compassion:

> Compassion is the feeling of empathy which the pain of one being of itself awakens in another; and the higher and more human the beings are, the more keenly attuned are they to re-echo the note of suffering which, like a voice from heaven, penetrates the heart, bringing to all creatures a proof of their kinship in the universal God. And as for the human being, whose function it is to show respect and love for God's universe and all its creatures, his heart has been created so tender that it feels with the whole organic world . . . so that if nothing else, the very nature of his heart must teach him that he is required above everything else to feel himself the brother of all beings, and to recognize the claim of all beings to his love and beneficence.[8]

He continued:

> Do not suppress this compassion, this sympathy especially with the sufferings of your fellowman. It is the warning voice of duty, which points out to you your brother in every sufferer, and your own sufferings in his, and awakens the love which tells you that you belong to him and his sufferings with all the powers that you have. Do not suppress it! . . . See in it the admonition of God that you are to have no joy so long as a brother suffers by your side.[9]

Rabbi Samuel Dresner states that "Compassion is the way God enters our life in terms of man's relation to his fellowman."[10]

Another example of the importance of compassion in the Jewish tradition is its prominent location in God's statement to Moses as God passed before him and proclaims: "*Hashem, Hashem*, God, Compassionate and Gracious, Slow to Anger, and abundant in loving-kindness and truth." (Exodus 34:6)

The Jewish emphasis on compassion finds expression in many groups and activities in Jewish communities: a *Bikur Cholim* Society to provide medical expenses for the sick, and to visit them and bring them comfort and cheer; a *Malbish Arumim* Society to provide clothing for the poor; a *Hachnasat Kalah* Society to provide for brides in need; a *Bet Yetomin* Society to aid orphans; a Talmud Torah Organization to support a free school for poor children; a *Gemilut Chesed* Society to lend money at no interest to those in need; an *Ozer Dalim* Society to dispense charity to the poor; a *Hachnasat Orchim* Society to provide shelter for homeless travelers; a *Chevrah Kaddishah* Society to attend to the proper burial of the dead; and *Essen Teg* Institutions to provide food and shelter for low-income students who attend schools in the community.

Judaism also stresses compassion for nonhuman animals. Among the many laws in the Torah which mandate kindness to animals are the following: a farmer is commanded not to muzzle his ox when he threshes corn (Deuteronomy 25:4) and not to plow with an ox and a donkey together (Deuteronomy 22:10), since the weaker animal would not be able to keep up with the stronger one; animals must be allowed to rest on the Sabbath Day (Exodus 20:10, 23; 12), a teaching so important that it is part of the Ten Commandments; one must feed their animals before sitting down to a meal. These concepts are summarized in the Hebrew phrase *tsa'ar ba'alei chayim*—the mandate not to cause "sorrow to any living creature."

The Psalmist pictures God as "satisfying the desire of every living creature (Psalm 145:16) and "providing food for the beasts and birds" (Psalm 147:9). Perhaps the Jewish attitude toward animals is epitomized by the statement in Proverbs: "The righteous person regards the life of his or her animal" (Proverb 12:10). In Judaism, one who does not treat nonhuman animals with compassion cannot be considered a righteous individual.[11]

Rabbi Moshe Cordovero (1522–1570) indicates the importance Judaism places on the proper treatment of animals, as well as people:

> [One should] respect all creatures, recognizing in them the greatness of the Creator who formed man with wisdom, and whose wisdom is contained in all creatures. He should realize that they greatly deserve to be honored, since the One Who Forms All Things, the Wise One, Who is exalted above all, cared to create them. If one despises them, God forbid, it reflects on the honor of their Creator. . . . It is evil in the sight of the Holy One, Blessed be He, if any of His creatures are despised.[12]

The Hebrew word *rachamim* (compassion) is derived from the Hebrew word *rechem*—womb. Hence, just as a mother has compassion for the life of all the children of her womb, we should have compassion for all of God's creatures.

If more Jews become aware of the many beautiful Jewish teachings on compassion and strive to put them into practice, it will have great potential to help revitalize Judaism and move our imperiled planet toward a more just, humane, and environmentally sustainable world.

Judaism and Business Ethics

The Torah provides instruction in honest business practices:

> You shall do no wrong in judgment, in measures of length, of weight, or in quantity. Just balances, just weights, a just ephah [the standard dry measure] and a just hin [a measure for liquids], shall you have. I am the Lord your God, who brought you out of the land of Egypt. (Leviticus 19:35, 36)

The rabbis of the Talmud give concrete expression to the many Torah and prophetic teachings regarding justice and righteousness. They indicate in detail what is proper when conducting business. Rabbinic literature translates prophetic ideals into the language of the marketplace in terms of duties of employers to employees and of workers to their employers, fair prices, the avoidance of false weights and measures, proper business contracts, and fair methods of competition.

Rava, a fourth-century Babylonian teacher, taught the wealthy merchants of his town the importance of scrupulous honesty in business dealings. He stated that on Judgment Day, the first question God asks a person is, "Were you reliable in your business dealings?" (*Shabbat* 31a). The rabbis stress that a person's word is a sacred bond that should not be broken. The Mishnah states that God will exact punishment for those who do not abide by their promises. (*Baba Metzia* 4:2) Cheating a Gentile is considered even worse than cheating a Jew, for "besides being a violation of the moral law, it brings Israel's religion into contempt, and desecrates the name of Israel's God." (*Baba Kamma* 113b)

The sages are very critical of attempts to take away a person's livelihood by unfair competition (*Sanhedrin* 81a). Their overall view of business ethics can be summarized by the verses: "And you shall do that which is right and good in the sight of the Lord" (Deuteronomy 6:18), and "better is a little with righteousness than great revenues with injustice." (Proverbs 16:8)

The very high ethical standards of the Talmudic sages are exemplified by the following story:

> Reb Saphra had wine to sell. A customer came in to buy wine at a time when Reb Saphra was saying the *Sh'ma* prayer (which cannot be interrupted by speaking). The customer said, "Will you sell me the wine for such an amount?" When Reb Saphra did not respond, the customer thought he was not satisfied with the price and raised his bid. When Reb Saphra had finished his prayer, he said, "I decided in my heart to sell the wine to you at the first price you mentioned; therefore, I cannot accept your higher bid." (*She'ilot, Parshat VaYehi*)

It is essential that Jews work to establish systems and conditions consistent with the basic Jewish values of justice, compassion, kindness, the sacredness of every life, the imitation of God's attributes, love of neighbors, consideration of the stranger, compassion for animals, and the highest of business ethics.

4

ENVIRONMENT

In truth, there is no one nearer to idolatry than one who can disregard the fact that all things are the creatures and property of God, and who then presumes also to have the right, because he has the might, to destroy them according to a presumptuous act of will. Yes, that one is already serving the most powerful idols—anger, pride, and above all ego, which in its passion regards itself as the master of things.[1]

JEWISH ENVIRONMENTAL TEACHINGS

Many fundamental Torah principles express and make concrete the Biblical statement: "The earth is the Lord's and the fullness thereof" (Psalms 24:1):

1. People are to be co-workers with God in helping to preserve and improve the world.

The Talmudic sages assert that the assigned role of the Jewish people is to enhance the world as "partners of God in the work of creation" (Shabbat 10a; Sanhedrin 7). The following Psalm reinforces this concept:

> When I look at Your heavens, the work of Your hands,
> The moon and work which you have established,
> What is man that You are mindful of him, and the son of
> man that You do care for him?

> Yet you have made him little less than God, and do
>   crown him with glory and honor.
> You have given him dominion over the works of Your
>   hands;
> You have put all things under his feet. . . . (Psalms 8:4–7)

The Talmudic sages express great concern about preserving the environment and preventing pollution. They state: "It is forbidden to live in a town which has no garden or greenery" (*Kiddushin* 4:12; 66d). Threshing floors must be placed far enough from a town so that it will not be dirtied by chaff carried by winds (*Baba Batra* 2:8). Tanneries must be kept at least fifty cubits (a cubit is about half a meter, or about twenty inches) from a town and may be placed only on the east side of a town, so that odors and pollution will be carried away from the town by the prevailing winds from the west. (*Baba Batra* 2:8–9)

2. Everything belongs to God. We are to be stewards of the earth, to ensure that its produce is available for all God's children.

There is an apparent contradiction between two verses in Psalms: "The earth is the Lord's" (Psalms 24:1) and "The heavens are the heavens of God, but the earth He has given to human beings" (Psalms 115:16). The apparent discrepancy is cleared up in the following way: Before a person says a *bracha* (a blessing), before he acknowledges God's ownership of the land and its products, then "the earth is the Lord's;" after a person has said a *bracha*, acknowledging God's ownership and that we are stewards to ensure that God's works are properly used and shared, then "the earth He has given to human beings." (*Berachot* 30:5)

Property is a sacred trust given by God; it must be used to fulfill God's purposes. No person has absolute or exclusive control over his or her possessions. The concept that people have custodial care of the earth, as opposed to ownership, is illustrated by this ancient Jewish story:

> Two men were fighting over a piece of land. Each claimed ownership and bolstered his claim with apparent proof. To resolve their differences, they agreed to put the case before the rabbi. The rabbi listened but could come to no decision because both seemed to be right. Finally, he said, "Since I cannot decide to whom this land belongs, let us ask the land." He put his ear to the ground and, after a moment, straightened up. "Gentlemen, the land says it belongs to neither of you but that you belong to it."[2]

The produce of the field does not belong solely to the person who farms the land. The poor are entitled to a portion:

> And when you reap the harvest of your land, you shall not wholly reap the corner of your field, neither shall you gather the gleaning of your harvest. And you shall not glean your vineyard, neither shall you gather the fallen fruit of your vineyard; you shall leave them for the poor and for the stranger; I am the Lord, your God. (Leviticus 19:9–10)

These portions set aside for the poor were not voluntary contributions based on kindness. They were, in essence, a regular Divine assessment. Because God is the real owner of the land, He claims a share of the bounty which he has provided to be given to the poor.

As a reminder that "The earth is the Lord's," the land must be permitted to rest and lie fallow every seven years (the sabbatical year):

> And six years you shall sow your land, and gather in the increase thereof, but the seventh year you shall let it rest and lay fallow, that the poor of your people may eat; and what they leave, the animals of the field shall eat. In like manner you shall deal with your vineyard, and with your olive yard. (Exodus 23:10, 11)

The sabbatical year also has environmental benefits. Every seven years, the land was given a chance to rest and renew its fertility.

Judaism asserts that there is one God Who created the entire earth as a unity, in ecological balance, and that everything is connected to everything else. This idea is perhaps best expressed by Psalm 104:

> You [God] are the One Who sends forth springs into brooks, that they may run between mountains,
> To give drink to every animal of the fields; the creatures of the forest quench their thirst.
> Beside them dwell the fowl of the heavens; . . .
> You water the mountains from Your upper chambers, . . .
> You cause the grass to spring up for the cattle, and herb, for the service of humans, to bring forth bread from the earth . . .
> How manifold are your works, O Lord! In wisdom You have made them all; the earth is full of Your property . . .

Some argue that people have been given a license to exploit the earth and its creatures, because God gave humans "dominion over the fish of the sea, and over the fowl of the air, and over every living thing that creeps upon the earth." (Genesis 1:28) However, the Talmudic sages interpret dominion as meaning responsible guardianship or stewardship, being co-workers with God in taking care of and improving the world, not as a right to conquer and exploit animals and the earth (*Shabbat* 10a; *Sanhedrin* 7). The fact that people's dominion over animals is limited is indicated by God's first (completely vegan) dietary regime. (Genesis 1:29)

Rabbi Abraham Isaac Ha-Kohen Kook, the first Chief Rabbi of pre-state Israel, states that dominion does not mean the arbitrary power of a tyrannical ruler who cruelly governs in order to satisfy personal desires.[3] He observes that such a repulsive form of servitude could not be forever sealed in the world of God whose "tender mercies are over all His works" (Psalm 145:9).[4] God indicates the intended human role when he tells Adam and Eve that they are to work the earth and protect it. (Genesis 2:15)

3. We are not to waste or unnecessarily destroy anything of value.

This prohibition, called *bal tashchit* ("you shall not destroy"), is based on the following Torah statement:

> When you shall besiege a city for a long time, in making war against it to take it, you shall not destroy (*lo tashchit*) the trees thereof by wielding an ax against them; for you may eat of them. You shall not cut them down; for is the tree of the field man, that it should be besieged by you? Only the trees of which you know that they are not trees for food, them you may destroy and cut down, that you may build bulwarks against the city that makes war with you, until it fall. (Deuteronomy 20:19, 20)

This Torah prohibition is very specific. Taken in its most literal sense, it prohibits only the destruction of fruit trees using axes during wartime. During Talmudic times, the rabbis greatly expanded the objects, methods of destruction, and situations that are covered by *bal tashchit*:

> Whoever breaks vessels, or tears garments, or destroys a building, or clogs a well, or does away with food in a destructive manner violates the prohibition of *bal tashchit*. (Kiddushin 32a)

Early Jewish sages reasoned that if the principle applied even during a wartime situation, it must apply also at all other times. Similarly, they deduced that other means of destruction besides direct destruction with an ax (such as destroying trees by diverting a source of water) were also forbidden. Finally, they ruled, by analogy, that *bal tashchit* regulated not only trees, or even all natural objects, but anything of potential use, whether created by God or altered by people (*Sefer Hachinuch*, #530). Talmudic rulings on *bal tashchit* also prohibit the unnecessary killing of animals (*Hullin* 7b) and the eating of extravagant foods when one can easily eat simpler ones (*Shabbat* 140b). In summary, *bal tashchit* prohibits the destruction, complete or incomplete, direct or indirect, of all objects of potential benefit to people.

The following Talmudic statements illustrate the seriousness with which the rabbis considered the violation of *bal tashchit*:

> The sage Rabbi Hanina attributed the early death of his son to the fact that the boy had chopped down a fig tree. (Baba Kamma 91b)

Jews should be taught when very young that it is a sin to waste even small amounts of food. (Berachot 52b)

Rav Zutra taught: "One who covers an oil lamp or uncovers a naphtha lamp transgresses the prohibition of *bal tashchit*." [Both actions mentioned would cause a faster—hence wasteful—consumption of the fuel.] (*Shabbat* 67b)

Maimonides makes explicit the Talmudic expansion:

It is forbidden to cut down fruit-bearing trees outside a besieged city, nor may a water channel be deflected from them so that they wither. . . . Not only one who cuts down trees, but also one who smashes household goods, tears clothes, demolishes a building, stops up a spring, or destroys articles of food with destructive intent transgresses the command "you must not destroy."[5]

The *Sefer Ha-Hinukh*, a thirteenth-century text that explicates the 613 mitzvot in detail, indicates that the underlying purpose of *bal tashchit* is to help one to learn to act like the righteous, who oppose all waste and destruction:

The purpose of this mitzvah [*bal tashchit*] is to teach us to love that which is good and worthwhile and to cling to it, so that good becomes a part of us and we avoid all that is evil and destructive. This is the way of the righteous and those who improve society, who love peace and rejoice in the good in people and bring them close to Torah: that nothing, not even a grain of mustard, should be lost to the world, that they should regret any loss or destruction that they see, and if possible, they will prevent any destruction that they can. Not so are the wicked, who are like demons, who rejoice in destruction of the world, and they destroy themselves.[6]

Rabbi Samson Raphael Hirsch, the leading Orthodox rabbi of nineteenth-century Germany, viewed *bal tashchit* as the most basic Jewish principle of all—acknowledging the sovereignty of God and the limitation of our own will and ego. When we preserve the world around us, we act with the understanding that God owns everything. However, when we destroy, we are, in effect, worshipping the idols of our own desires, living only for self-gratification without remembering God. By observing *bal tashchit*, we restore our harmony not only with the world around us, but also with God's Will, which we place before our own:

> "Do not destroy anything" is the first and most general call of God. . . . If you should now raise your hand to play a childish game, to indulge in senseless rage, wishing to destroy that which you should only use, wishing to exterminate that which you should only gain advantage from, if you should regard the beings beneath you as objects without rights, not perceiving God Who created them, and therefore desire that they feel the might of your presumptuous mood, instead of using them only as the means of wise human activity—then God's call proclaims to you, "Do not destroy anything! Be a *mensch* [good human being]! Only if you use the things around you for wise human purposes, sanctified by the word of My teaching, only then are you a *mensch* and have the right over them which I have given you as a human. However, if you destroy, if you ruin, at that moment you are not a human . . . and have no right to the things around you. I lent them to you for wise use only; never forget that I lent them to you. As soon as you use them unwisely, be it the greatest or the smallest, you commit treachery against My world, you commit murder and robbery against My property, you sin against Me!" This

is what God calls unto you, and with this call does God represent the greatest and the smallest against you and grants the smallest as well as the greatest a right against your presumptuousness. . . .

In truth, there is no one nearer to idolatry than one who can disregard the fact that all things are the creatures and property of God, and who then presumes also to have the right, because he has the might, to destroy them according to a presumptuous act of will. Yes, that one is already serving the most powerful idols—anger, pride, and above all ego, which in its passion regards itself as the master of things.[7]

Rabbi Hirsch also taught that "destruction" includes using more things (or things of greater value) than is necessary to obtain one's aim.[8] The following *Midrash* is related to this concept:

Two men entered a shop. One ate coarse bread and vegetables, while the other ate fine bread, fat meat, and drank old wine. The one who ate fine food suffered harm, while the one who had coarse food escaped harm. Observe how simply animals live and how healthy they are as a result. (Ecclesiastes Rabbah 1:18)

ENVIRONMENTAL TEACHINGS IN
JEWISH HISTORY AND PRAYERS

Much of early Jewish history is closely connected to the natural environment. The patriarchs and their descendants were shepherds. Since their work led them into many types of natural settings, including mountains, prairies, wilderness, and desert, they developed a love and appreciation of natural wonders and beauty. According to Charles W. Eliot, "No race has ever surpassed the Jewish descriptions of either the beauties or the terrors of the nature which environs man."[9]

Jews have often pictured God through His handiwork in nature. While marveling at the heavenly bodies, Abraham, the father of the Jewish people, intuited that there must be a Creator of these wonders. The prophet Isaiah exclaimed:

> Lift up your eyes on high,
> And see: Who has created these?
> He that brings out their host by numbers,
> He calls them all by name;
> By the greatness of His might, for He is strong in power,
> Not one fails. (Isaiah 40:26)

During the years when he was a shepherd, Moses, the greatest prophet, learned many facts about nature, which were later useful in leading the Israelites in the desert. The Torah, including the Ten Commandments, were revealed to the Jews at Mount Sinai, in a natural setting. The forty years of wandering in the wilderness trained Israel in the appreciation of natural beauty.

Many Jewish prayers extol God for His wondrous creations. Before reciting the *Sh'ma* every morning, religious Jews say the following prayer to thank God for the new day:

> Blessed are You, Oh Lord our God, King of the universe.
> Who forms light and creates darkness,
> Who makes peace and creates all things.
> Who in mercy gives light to the earth
> And to them who dwell thereon,
> And in Your goodness renews the creation
> Every day continually.
> How manifold are Your works, O Lord!
> In wisdom You have made them all;

> The earth is full of Your possessions . . .
> Be blessed, O Lord our God,
> For the excellency of Your handiwork,
> And for the bright luminaries
> Which You have made:
> They shall glorify You forever.

In the Sabbath morning service, the following prayer is recited: "The heavens declare the glory of God, and the firmament shows His handiwork" (Psalms 19:2). However, Judaism does not only consider the "heavens above." It also deals with practical, down-to-earth issues. The following law, which commands disposal of excrement, even in wartime, illustrates the sensitivity of the Torah to environmental cleanliness by mandating the burial of waste in the ground, not dumping it into rivers or by littering the countryside:

> You shall have a place outside the military camp, when you shall go forth abroad. And you shall have a spade among your weapons; and it shall be when you sit down outside, you shall dig therewith, and shall turn back and cover that which comes from you. (Deuteronomy 23:13–15)

Traditionally, the preservation of the land of Israel has been a central theme in Judaism. The three pilgrimage festivals (*Pesach*, *Shavuot*, and *Sukkot*) are agricultural as well as spiritual celebrations. Jews pray for dew and rain in their proper times so that there will be abundant harvests in Israel.

CURRENT ENVIRONMENTAL THREATS

When God created the world, He was able to say, "It is very good" (Genesis 1:31). Everything was in harmony as God had planned, the waters were clean, and the air was pure. But what must God think about the world today?

What must God think when the rain He provided to nourish our crops is often acid rain, due to the many chemicals emitted into the air by industries and automobiles; when the abundance of species of plants and animals that He created are becoming extinct at such an alarming rate in tropical rain forests and other threatened habitats, before we are even able to study and catalog many of them; when the abundant fertile soil He provided is quickly being depleted and eroded; when the climatic conditions that He designed to meet our needs are threatened?

Consider the extreme differences between conditions at the time of creation and conditions today:

* In the beginning God created the heavens and the earth. The earth was without form and void, and darkness was upon the face of the deep; and the Spirit of God hovered over the face of the waters. (Genesis 1:1–2)

   In the beginning of the technological age, man recreated the heavens and the earth. To the earth he gave new form with dynamite and bulldozer, and the void of the heavens he filled with smog.

* And God said, "Let there be a firmament in the midst of the waters. . . . Let the waters under the heavens be gathered into one place, and let the dry land appear." (Genesis 1:6)

   Then man took oil from beneath the ground and spread it over the waters, until it coated the beaches with slime. He washed the topsoil from the fertile prairies and sank it in the ocean depths. He took waste from his mines and filled in the valleys, while real estate developers leveled the hills. And man said, "Well, business is business."

* Then God said, "Let the earth put forth vegetation, plants yielding seed and fruit trees bearing fruit in which is their seed, each according to its kind, upon the earth. . . . Let the earth bring forth living creatures according to their kinds." And it was so. And God saw that it was good. (Genesis 1:11, 24)

But man was not so sure. He found that mosquitoes annoyed him, so he killed them with DDT. And the robins died, too, and man said, "What a pity." Man defoliated forests in the name of modern warfare. He filled the streams with industrial waste, and his children read about fish . . . in the history books.

* So God created humans in His own image; in the image of God He created them. And God blessed them, and God said to them, "Be fruitful and multiply, and fill the earth and subdue it, and have dominion over . . . every living thing." (Genesis 1:27–28)

So man multiplied and multiplied—and spread his works across the land until the last green blade was black with asphalt, until the skies were ashen and the waters reeked, until neither bird sang nor child ran laughing through cool grass. So man subdued the earth and made it over in his image, and in the name of progress he drained it of its life. . . . Until the earth was without form and void, and darkness was once again upon the face of the deep, and man himself was but a painful memory in the mind of God.[10]

Today's environmental threats bring to mind the Biblical ten plagues that appear in the Torah portions which are read in synagogues in the weeks before the environmental holiday of Tu Bishvat:

*   When we consider the threats to our land, waters, and air due to pesticides and other chemical pollutants, resource scarcities, acid rain, threats to our climate, etc., we can easily enumerate ten modern "plagues."
*   The Egyptians were subjected to one plague at a time, while the modern plagues threaten us simultaneously.
*   The Jews in Goshen were spared most of the Biblical plagues, while every person on earth is imperiled by the modern plagues.
*   Instead of an ancient Pharaoh's heart being hardened, our hearts today have been hardened by the greed, materialism, and waste that are at the root of current environmental threats.
*   God provided the Biblical plagues to free the Israelites, while today we must apply God's teachings in order to save ourselves and our precious but endangered planet.
*   God inflicted the plagues to free the Israelites from oppression. But today we must apply God's teachings to save ourselves.
*   Had Pharaoh heeded the warning of the first plague and simply let the Israelites go, there would have

been no need for the nine others. Unfortunately, he did not. We must learn from Pharaoh's mistake and heed the warnings that are coming almost daily.

* We must apply our traditional Judaic teachings in the light of modern science to save our earthly homes, before we are destroyed because of our own hard-heartedness.
* It is we ourselves who are the causes of these modern plagues, though it is future generations who will be most severely afflicted.
* Instead of recognizing that we are partners and co-workers with God in protecting the environment, modern commerce is driven by the unsustainable societal ideals of wealth, material gain, unrestrained economic growth, and consumerism.

As long ago as 1992, over 1,670 scientists, including 104 Nobel laureates in science, signed a "World Scientists' Warning To Humanity," which argues that human beings are inflicting "irreversible damage on the environment and on critical resources," and that "Fundamental changes are urgent" if "vast human misery is to be avoided and our global home on this planet is not to be irretrievably mutilated."[11]

In 2017, a new generation of scientists reinforced their message and issued a second warning. Reflecting on the 1992 message, 15,364 signatories from 184 countries responded as follows:

On the twenty-fifth anniversary of their call, we look back at their warning and evaluate the human response by exploring available time-series data. Since 1992, with the exception of stabilizing the stratospheric ozone layer, humanity has failed to make sufficient progress in generally solving these foreseen environmental challenges, and alarmingly, most of them are getting far worse.

Especially troubling is the current trajectory of potentially catastrophic climate change due to rising greenhouse gases from burning fossil fuels, deforestation, and agricultural production—particularly from farming ruminants for meat consumption.

Moreover, we have unleashed a mass extinction event, the sixth in world history, wherein many current life forms could be annihilated or at least committed to extinction by the end of this century. Humanity is now being given a second notice, as illustrated by these alarming trends. We are jeopardizing our future by not reining in our intense but geographically and demographically uneven material consumption and by not perceiving continued rapid population growth as a primary driver behind many ecological and even societal threats. By failing to adequately limit population growth, reassess the role of an economy rooted in growth, reduce greenhouse gases, incentivize renewable energy, protect habitat, restore ecosystems, curb pollution, halt defaunation [extinction of animal species], and constrain invasive alien species, humanity is not taking the urgent steps needed to safeguard our imperiled biosphere.[12]

The biggest environmental threat today is from climate change. It will be discussed in Chapter 5. The very serious climate and other environmental problems for Israel will be considered in Chapter 6.

Unless otherwise indicated, facts in the remainder of this section are from Earth-Org's August 21, 2021 article "11 Biggest Environmental Problems of 2021," its June 5,

2022 article "Biggest Environmental Problems Of 2022," and its October 8, 2020 analysis "Key Takeaways From David Attenborough's New Film, 'A Life on Our Planet.'" Some of the environmental problems considered in these articles will be discussed in the chapters 5 and 7 on climate change and on hunger. An entire book could be written on these issues, but this section will consider highlights on several current environmental problems.

Deforestation

The very rapid loss of forests is a major threat to humanity. Forests the size of twenty football fields are destroyed every minute. If this continues, only about 10 percent of the world's forests may remain by 2030, and they could all be gone within 100 years.

The leading cause of deforestation is animal agriculture, as over 40 percent of the world's ice-free land is used to graze animals and to grow feed crops for them. As discussed in more detail in Chapter 5 on climate change, the only way to avert a climate catastrophe is to reforest and rewild this vast area, permitting the sequestering of much of the atmospheric CO_2 and bringing its current very dangerous level to a safer one. This would require a society-wide shift to plant-based diets.

The 2021 Glasgow climate conference delegates pledged to cut deforestation by 30 percent by 2030. This would be a very positive development, but possibly far from enough and far too late.

In addition to being able to sequester atmospheric CO_2, forests help prevent soil erosion because tree roots bind the soil and prevent it from washing away.

Alarmingly, if Amazon deforestation continues, it will be degraded to such a degree that it will no longer produce enough moisture, transforming it into a dry savanna. This would decimate the rainforest's biodiversity and alter the global water cycle, which would greatly affect the world's climate.

According to the UN Food and Agricultural Organization (FAO), the world has lost about a billion acres of forest, mainly in South America and Africa, since 1990.[13]

Biodiversity Loss

Environmental experts believe that we are in the 6th mass extinction of wildlife, with over 500 species of land animals on the brink of extinction, with most of them likely to be gone within 20 years. According to the World Wildlife Fund, there has been a decline of an average of 68 percent in the population sizes of mammals, birds, fish, reptiles, and amphibians between 1970 and 2016.

Since the 1950s, animal populations have decreased by more than half, while farmed bird populations have soared. About 70 percent of the planet's bird mass are farmed birds—mostly chickens. People account for over a third of the weight of mammals on Earth. A further 60 percent of weight of animals are those that are raised for human consumption. Wild animals make up only about four percent of the planet's animal mass. As discussed later, the huge expansion in the number of farmed animals is a major cause of climate change and other environmental threats.

Fish populations are also declining rapidly. About 30 percent of aquatic life has been fished to critical levels, and freshwater fish populations have decreased by over 80 percent.

Biodiversity loss has occurred mainly due to a rapid growth of human population, consumption, global trade, and urbanization, and major land-use changes, especially the conversion of habitats, such as forests, grasslands, and mangroves, into agricultural systems. In addition, the illegal wildlife trade endangers such animals as pangolins, sharks, and seahorses.

Plastic Pollution

The world's annual production of plastics multiplied from 2 million tons in 1950 to 419 million tons in 2015, greatly increasing plastic waste in the environment. According to the science journal *Nature*, about 11 million tons of plastic enter the oceans annually, harming wildlife habitats and the animals that reside in them. The study found that if present trends continue, by 2040, the plastic crisis will grow to 29 million metric tons per year.

According to *National Geographic,* 91 percent of all plastic that has ever been made is not recycled, resulting in one of the biggest current environmental problems, a major market failure. Plastic takes 400 years to decompose. There is uncertainty about how serious the future effects of plastic pollution will be on the environment.

Air Pollution

Air pollution is caused mainly by motor vehicles and industrial sources, with additional contributions from dust storms and burning biomass.

According to World Health Organization (WHO) research, about 90 percent of people worldwide breathe polluted air, and an estimated 4.2 to 7 million people die annually worldwide from air pollution. A recent European

Union environment agency report indicated that air pollution contributed to 400,000 annual deaths in the E.U. in 2012 (the last year for which data were available). In Africa, according to UNICEF, deaths from outdoor air pollution increased from 164,000 people in 1990 to 258,000 people in 2017.

According to the 2021 "State of the Air" report by the American Lung Association (ALA), about 40 percent of US residents live in counties with unhealthy air pollution levels.[14] A UN report published on February 15, 2022 indicated that more people die annually worldwide from pollution than from COVID 19.[15]

Ocean Acidification

Global temperature rise is the main cause of ocean acidification. The world's oceans absorb about 30 percent of the carbon dioxide that is released into the earth's atmosphere. As higher concentrations of carbon emissions are released due to human activities, the amount of carbon dioxide that is absorbed back into the sea also increases.

Even a small change in the pH scale can significantly impact the ocean acidity. Ocean acidification can negatively affect marine ecosystems, species, and food webs and can reduce habitat quality. If pH levels become too low, the shells and skeleton of marine organisms, such as oysters, could start to dissolve.

One of the biggest ocean acidification effects is coral bleaching, resulting in coral reef losses. This is the result of rising ocean temperatures reducing the symbiotic relationship between the reefs and algae that live within it, driving away the algae and causing coral reefs to lose their natural vibrant colors.

Alarmingly, some scientists project that coral reefs may be completely destroyed by 2050. Higher acidity in the ocean would obstruct coral reef systems' ability to rebuild their exoskeletons and recover from these coral bleaching events. This will cause a substantial decrease in fish populations, affecting millions of people whose livelihoods depend on the ocean.

CAUSES OF CURRENT ENVIRONMENTAL PROBLEMS

The root cause of current environmental crises is that the realities of our economic and production systems are completely contrary to Torah values:

* While Judaism stresses that "the earth is the Lord's" and that we are to be partners with God in protecting the environment, many corporations consider the earth only in terms of how it can be used to maximize profits, with only minor regard for damaging environmental effects. Instead of starting with protection of the earth as a prime value and building production and economic systems consistent with this value, our production is generally based on the desire for maximum gain, regardless of the potential harmful ecological consequences. Corporations' shortsighted application of technology is a prime cause of current ecological crises.

* While Judaism mandates *bal tashchit*, most economies are based on waste, buying, using, and disposing. Advertising constantly tries to make people feel guilty if they don't have the newest

gadgets and the latest styles. Every national holiday has become a compulsive consumption with the attraction of department store sales filling mall parking lots with cars. The United States has become a throwaway society. People now use increasing numbers of plastic containers, although they harm the environment more than glass or metal containers. For convenience, we are also using greater amounts of paper products each year. Many potentially valuable products that could be used for fertilizer are instead discarded.

* While Judaism established a Sabbatical year in which the land is allowed to lie fallow and recover its fertility and farmers may rest, learn, and restore their spiritual values, today, under economic pressure to constantly produce more, farmers plant single crops (the same crops in the same land, with no crop rotation) and use excessive amounts of chemical pesticides and fertilizer, thereby reducing soil fertility and badly polluting air and water.

The effects of animal-based diets on the environment is discussed in Chapter 8 on veganism.

JEWISH VALUES CAN HELP SOLVE THE ENVIRONMENTAL CRISIS

Based on biblical values, including "The earth is the Lord's" and *bal tashchit,* Jews and others who take religious values seriously must lead efforts to preserve the environment. We must work to change a system based primarily on greed and maximization of profits that entices people to seek unnecessary material goods, thus causing great ecological damage. We must work for approaches that place primary emphasis on protection of our vital ecosystems.

To reduce potential threats to the U.S. and to the world, we must change over to simpler, saner lifestyles. Religious institutions, schools, and private and governmental organizations must all play a role. We must reapply some of our industrial capacity toward recycling, renewable forms of energy, and mass transit. We must design products for long-term durability and ease of repair. We must revise our agricultural and industrial methods so that they are less wasteful of resources and energy. Perhaps there should be a presidential commission appointed solely to consider how we can stop being such a wasteful society. Changing will not be easy, since our society and economy are based on consumption and convenience, using and discarding. But it is essential that we make supreme efforts. Nothing less than human survival is at stake.

Given the extent of the crisis, it's essential that we, in the Jewish community, apply our rich tradition of environmental responsibility and stewardship to the world's fragile environment. This means, for example, embracing an energy policy based not on destructive energy sources, but on CARE (conservation and renewable energy), consistent with Jewish teachings on environmental stewardship, creation of jobs, protection of human life, and concern for future generations.

Too often the Jewish establishment, like the rest of the world, has been silent while our climate is rapidly worsening, our air is bombarded with poisons, our rivers and streams are polluted by industrial wastes, our fertile soil is both eroded and depleted, and the ecological balance is endangered by the destruction of rainforests and other vital habitats.

The Jewish community must become more actively involved. We must proclaim that it is a *chillul Hashem* (a desecration of God's name) to pollute the air and water that God created pure; to slash and burn forests that existed before there were human beings; and to wantonly destroy the abundant resources that God has so generously provided for all of humanity to enjoy and be sustained by. We have a choice, as proclaimed in the Torah:

> This day, I call upon the heaven and the earth as witnesses; I have set before you life and death, the blessing and the curse. You shall choose life, so that you and your offspring will live. (Deuteronomy 30:19)

The proper application of Sabbath values would help reduce environmental pollution. The Sabbath teaches that we should not be constantly involved in exploiting the world's resources and amassing more and more possessions. On that day each week we are to contemplate our dependence on God and our responsibility to treat the earth with care and respect. Rabbi Samson Raphael Hirsch powerfully expresses this:

> To really observe the Sabbath in our day and age! To cease for a whole day from all business, from all work, amidst the frenzied hurry-scurry of our age! [And Rabbi Hirsch was writing well over 100 years ago, when commerce and production were far less frenzied.] To close the stock exchanges, the stores, the factories—how would it be possible? The pulse of life would stop beating and the world perish! The world perish? On the contrary; it would be saved.[16]

The philosophy of the Sabbatical year provides yet another approach to environmental problems. There could be great benefits if land, on a rotating basis, could be left fallow, free from the tremendous amounts of chemicals and fertilizer that pollute air and water and reduce soil fertility. If people could spend a (Sabbatical) year from their usually hurried lives, away from the numbing bustle of the marketplace, and from the constant pressure to produce and buy goods, they would have the opportunity to use their time for mental and spiritual development. Perhaps they might even have time to study methods of reducing pollution and other current problems.

As co-workers with God, charged with the task of being a light unto the nations and accomplishing *tikkun olam* (restoring and healing the earth), it is essential that we Jews take an active role in struggles to end pollution and waste of natural resources. Based on the central Jewish mandate to work with God in preserving the earth, we Jews must work with others in applying Jewish values toward significant changes in our economic and production systems and our lifestyles, in order to help shift our imperiled planet onto a sustainable path.

5

CLIMATE CHANGE

In the hour when the Blessed Holy One created the first human being, God took him and let him pass before all the trees of the Garden of Eden and said to him: "See my works, how fine and excellent they are! All that I have created, for you have I created them. Think upon this and do not despoil and destroy My world. For if you destroy it, there is no one to set it right after you."
—Ecclesiastes Rabbah 7:28

In ancient times, Jews may have wondered about the significance of this *Midrash* (rabbinic teaching). How could it be possible to destroy the world that God had created? Did humans have such power? Today, we know that it is not only possible, but probable.[1]

HOW SERIOUS ARE CLIMATE THREATS?

The greatest threat to humanity today is climate change. Our human civilization is set on a path that could lead to a possibly uninhabitable planet by the end of the century— or one so torn asunder by climate disaster and its social, political, economic, and health consequences that few of us would want to inhabit it.[2] And the catastrophe could occur much sooner because, as explained below, self-reinforcing positive feedback loops (vicious cycles) could result in an irreversible tipping point, when climate spins out of control, with disastrous consequences.[3]

Is this an outrageous exaggeration, considering how many previous predictions there have been about an end to the world? Not according to some 97 percent of climate scientists, every major science academy, and virtually all peer-reviewed papers (thousands of them) on this issue in respected scientific journals. These scientists convincingly argue that global warming and the resulting climate change we see today are the product of our own activities and pose an existential threat to humanity.[4]

The leaders of the almost 200 nations that attended both the December 2015 Paris and the December 2021 Glasgow Climate Change conferences, including Israel and the United States, agreed that immediate steps must be taken to avert a climate catastrophe, and almost all the nations pledged to reduce their greenhouse gas emissions.[5] Although this was an important step forward, climate experts believe that even if all these pledges are kept (they are not binding), the measures would still be insufficient to prevent severe climate disruption later in this century.

Indeed, in October 2018, when the UN's Intergovernmental Panel on Climate Change (IPCC) released its much-anticipated update on the science (the work of ninety-one climate experts from forty countries reviewing thousands of the latest climate-related studies and reports), the authors warned that the world has until 2030 to make "rapid, far-reaching and unprecedented changes in all aspects of society" if we're to have a reasonable chance of limiting global warming to 1.5°C above pre-industrial levels and averting the climate disasters that would likely follow if we don't.[6]

A year later, the urgency of the IPCC's report was echoed when over eleven thousand scientists signed on to a paper in the journal *BioScience*, declaring that "the climate crisis has arrived and is accelerating faster than most scientists expected."[7] They warned: "It is more severe than anticipated, threatening natural ecosystems and the fate of humanity."[8]

"We declare, with more than 11,000 scientist signatories from around the world, clearly and unequivocally, that planet Earth is facing a climate emergency," the paper began. "To secure a sustainable future," it continued, "we must change how we live. [This] entails major transformations in the ways our global society functions and interacts with natural ecosystems."[9] The scientists' prescription for humanity included leaving fossil fuels in the ground, ending population growth, and halting forest destruction—and massively reducing the amount of meat produced and eaten.[10]

A UN report of November 26, 2019, was also extremely alarming.[11] It pointed out that, despite many nations' pledges to reduce them, greenhouse gases are still rising perilously, growing an average of 1.5 percent annually in the past 10 years. The report asserted that countries need to make their emission reduction goals 5 times greater in order to limit warming to 1.5°C, the threshold scientists believe is a dangerous line to cross for climate change.

Even if all the countries involved in the Paris Agreement brought emissions down to the levels they initially pledged to meet, the report noted, the world would still be on track for 3.2°C warming since the start of the Industrial Revolution—three times the present rise. That's 5.76°F, a scenario that would dramatically augment the severity of current wildfires, hurricanes, heat waves, and droughts. Since many of the world's biggest greenhouse gas emitters are not on track to meet their climate reduction pledges, the final warming number could be substantially greater even than this.[12]

A landmark IPCC report in August 2021, dubbed a "Code Red for humanity" by UN Secretary General Antonio Guterres, indicated that global warming is dangerously close to spiraling out of control, humans are "unequivocally to blame, and the deadly heat waves, gargantuan hurricanes, and other weather extremes that are already here will only become more severe."[13]

Despite the increasingly dire warnings from climate experts that major steps must be taken to reduce greenhouse gas emissions, atmospheric CO_2 reached a record level of almost 421 parts per million, about 50 percent higher than pre-industrial levels, in May 2022.[14]

How Climate Change Makes Violence, Terrorism, and War More Likely

Another profound implication of climate change has been analyzed by the Pentagon, US intelligence agencies, and other nations' military organizations. The reality is that climate change will escalate the potential for instability, terrorism, and war by reducing access to food and clean water, and causing tens of millions of desperate refugees to flee from droughts, wildfire, floods, storms, and other disasters wrought by climate change.[15]

Compelling evidence exists that major droughts caused or worsened by climate change helped spark recent civil wars in Darfur[16] and Syria.[17] Syria experienced a very severe drought between 2006 and 2011, which led to widespread crop failures, resulting in many farmers leaving their land for the cities at a time when many refugees fleeing the violence in Iraq were pouring into the country. The instability caused frustration, tension, and anger, which eventually exploded into a civil war that was exploited by jihadists and fanatics, including ISIS.

The negative effects of climate change in Darfur and Syria are especially frightening when one considers that drought and desertification due to climate change are causing chaos in many other countries in the Middle East, as well as central and north Africa, fanning the flames of social revolutions and civil wars.[18] Such unrest poses major security threats to Israel and the West, with drought-induced hunger leaving populations angry, frustrated, and vulnerable to radicalization and recruitment.

Drought, famine, and violence are also causing major migrations, furthering the potential for more chaos, instability, and violence. Unless we take drastic action, it will no longer be correct to consider the disruption, human rights tragedies, and economic costs of destabilization in countries like Syria and Sudan as outliers—they are illustrative of increasingly evident events.

It therefore should not be surprising that the US Pentagon stated as early as 2004 that climate change is a larger threat than even terrorism.[19] "Picture Japan, suffering from flooding along its coastal cities and contamination of its fresh water supply, eyeing Russia's Sakhalin Island oil and gas reserves as an energy source," suggests a Pentagon memo on global warming. "Envision Pakistan, India and China—all armed with nuclear weapons—skirmishing at their borders over refugees, access to shared river and arable land."[20] The former Secretary General of the U.N., Ban Ki-moon, has said that climate change needs to be taken as seriously as war and, further, that "changes in our environment and the resulting upheavals from droughts to inundated coastal areas to loss of arable land are likely to become a major driver of war and conflict."[21] Fighting global climate change may be one way to prevent future wars and genocides, simultaneously increasing energy security and physical security.

OTHER EFFECTS OF CLIMATE CHANGE

The world's temperature has risen significantly in recent years, with the last eight years being the hottest in recorded history.[22] Every decade since the 1970s has been hotter than the previous one, and all twenty-three years of this century are among the twenty-three hottest years recorded since global temperature records started being kept in 1880 (the only other year in the top twenty-one is 1998). The year 2020 tied 2016 as the hottest globally, breaking the records held previously by 2015, and before that by 2014, the first time that there had been three consecutive years of record world temperatures.[23] July 2021 was the warmest month in recorded history.[24]

Just as a person with a high fever suffers from many of its effects, our planet has experienced many negative consequences from the warmer global temperatures.

Severe climate events have always occurred, but climate change has made them more frequent and destructive.[25] As more moisture evaporates in warmer temperatures and warmer air holds more moisture, the potential for heavier storms is enhanced. Sea levels have risen, which exacerbates storm surges, and as the waters are warmer, more energy is added to the storms, meaning they are likely to be more destructive.[26]

A December 2019 report from the World Meteorological Organization was even more frightening, indicating that climate change was accelerating, with climatic conditions likely to get far worse in the near future.[27] Among the worrying trends cited in the report is that seas are warming and rising faster, putting many cities at risk of tidal flooding (there is already "sunny day flooding" in coastal cities like Miami, Florida, due to higher tides).[28] Polar icecaps[29] and glaciers worldwide[30] have been melting rapidly, faster than scientific projections. Glaciers are "reservoirs in the sky," providing vital water for irrigating crops every spring, so their retreat will pose a major threat to future food supplies for the rising world population. They are melting at a pace many researchers did not expect for decades, and Arctic Sea ice has declined so rapidly that the region may have ice-free summers by the 2030s.[31]

To provide a sense of just how rapidly this is occurring, in June 2019 temperatures in Greenland were 40°F above normal, causing the melting in a single day of two billion tons of ice, the equivalent of 800,000 Olympic swimming pools.[32] The Arctic permafrost has begun to thaw seventy years before scientists had predicted it would occur only a few years ago, potentially liberating vast quantities of greenhouse gases that had been trapped underground for millennia. In the spring of 2019, Arctic Sea ice coverage approached record lows.[33]

In addition to these ongoing system-transforming modifications of the planet, hundred-year or once-in-a-lifetime weather events are likely to begin occurring every decade, half-decade, or even annually. Nor will they necessarily happen sequentially. For instance, on March 18, 2019, a deadly cyclone devastated several countries in southern Africa, causing almost a thousand deaths,[34] and catastrophic floods inundated several US Midwestern states, possibly causing a "breaking point for farms, which were already experiencing falling incomes."[35] Different regions of the world will be able to handle crises such as these with relative ease or difficulty; however, no nation state will be able to absorb year upon year of ruinous climatic events and remain stable or prosperous.

Indeed, largely because of huge financial losses from such severe climate events, the same month of the floods in southern Africa and the American Midwest, Munich Re, one of the world's largest reinsurance companies, declared that some properties may soon be essentially uninsurable.[36] The company lost $24 billion in 2010 due to the severe, widespread wildfires in California. Their chief climatologist announced:

> If the risk from wildfires, flooding, storms or hail is increasing, then the only sustainable option we have is to adjust our risk prices accordingly. In the long run it might become a social issue. Affordability is so critical [because] some people on low and average incomes in some regions will no longer be able to buy insurance.[37]

Making the above point even stronger was a UN report in early February 2022 that warned of a "global wildfire crisis," with worsening heat and dryness causing possibly a 50 percent increase in off-the-charts fires.[38]

Still later, on February 28, a newly released UN Intergovernmental Panel on Climate Change report warned that climate change dangers are increasing so quickly that they could soon overwhelm the ability of both humanity and nature to adapt, unless greenhouse gas emissions are rapidly reduced.[39] In the most detailed look yet at the dangers posed by climate change, the report, written by 270 researchers from 67 countries, concluded that countries aren't doing enough to avert climate threats.[40] A *New York Times* article discussed five important takeaways from the report.[41] They are:

1. Climate hazards have worsened significantly in the past decade.
2. If warming isn't slowed, the dangers will multiply.
3. Societies have not done enough to adapt and stay safe.
4. As warming continues, it will be harder and harder to cope.
5. Poor countries face much bigger challenges than rich ones.

As discussed in the following chapter, Israel is especially threatened by climate change.

POTENTIAL TIPPING POINTS

It's clear that urgent preventive action is needed, not least because, as climate scientists warn, the present pace of climate change could speed up dramatically if self-reinforcing positive feedback loops—vicious cycles in the climate system—trigger irreversible tipping points, causing climate change to spin out of control, beyond the reach of any mitigation.[42]

Once the genie is out of the bottle—as massive polar ice sheets begin sliding into the sea, to give one example—there is no stuffing him back in. As Jerry Brown, the former governor of California, a state subjected to many severe climate events, recently commented, "Humanity is on a collision course with nature."[43]

The feedback loops can take several forms. Stronger and more prevalent wildfires will burn more trees, which absorb CO_2. Carbon is released from the burning trees into the atmosphere, which warms it more, exacerbating the potential for additional wildfires and other climatic events. Moreover, much additional energy is needed to rebuild the houses and other structures and cars destroyed by the fires.

Another feedback loop occurs when ice, a reflector of the sun's rays, melts. The darker soil or water revealed underneath absorbs more of the sun's energy, causing more ice to melt, and faster. Yet another example is that as temperatures rise, people use more air conditioning, which means more fossil fuels are burned, resulting in more greenhouse gas emissions, and thus more warming. This in turn leads to more people employing air conditioning, and the cycle continues and intensifies.

I'm afraid the news only gets worse. Prior to the December 2019 Madrid climate conference, scientists warned in the prestigious journal *Nature* that irreversible climate tipping points are more likely and could occur at lower temperature increases than recently thought.[44] Humans were, said the writers, in effect playing Russian roulette with Earth's climate by ignoring the growing risks.[45]

Will Steffen, a climate researcher with the Australian National University and co-author of the cautionary paper in *Nature*, told reporters: "What we're talking about is a point of no return, when we might actually lose control of this system, and there is a significant risk that we're going to do this. It's not going to be the same conditions with just a bit more heat or a bit more rainfall. It's a cascading process that gets out of control."[46]

The scientists warned of nine potential tipping points that are now active: Arctic Sea ice; the Greenland ice sheet; the boreal forests; permafrost; the Atlantic meridional overturning circulation; the Amazon rainforest; warm-water corals; the West Antarctic Ice Sheet; and parts of East Antarctica.[47]

To illustrate how serious these potential tipping points are, if the major ice sheets on Greenland, West Antarctica, and part of East Antarctica collapsed, it would result in around ten meters (about thirty-three feet) of sea-level rise worldwide.[48] If tipping points were reached in rainforests, permafrost, and boreal forests, additional massive amounts of greenhouse gases would be released, amplifying warming, making other tipping points not only more likely, but closer in time.[49]

The study also showed that far from reducing the amount of CO_2 and other greenhouse gases in the atmosphere, the world is adding to them faster than ever. Climatologists have concluded that concentrations of 350 parts per million (ppm) of atmospheric CO_2 is a threshold level for climate stability. The world has not only greatly exceeded 400 ppm,[50] but the CO_2 level is continuing to grow.[51] In May 2022, the atmospheric carbon dioxide level, which had hovered below 285 ppm for thousands of years prior to the Industrial Revolution, surpassed 420 ppm—the highest value in human history.[52] Of course, every year that CO_2 emissions do not decrease, and especially if they increase, it becomes harder to meet any CO_2 reduction targets.

It's sometimes hard to grasp these seismic changes in human terms—the processes seem too vast and impersonal. However, the scope and scale of the effects of climate change cannot disguise the very real consequences to human wellbeing.

HEALTH EFFECTS OF CLIMATE CHANGE

Climate change will lead to a significant spread of illnesses caused by extreme weather, heat stress, and mosquitos, including malaria.[53] According to the World Health Organization (WHO) expert Diarmid Campbell-Lendrum: "WHO considers that climate change is potentially the greatest health threat of the 21st Century. . . . The reason for that is that unless we cut our carbon emissions, we will continue to undermine our food supplies, our water supplies and our air quality—everything that we need to maintain the good health of our populations."[54]

Maria Neira, director of WHO's Department of Environment, Climate Change, and Health, told a news briefing at the December 2018 Madrid climate conference: "Health is paying the price of the climate crisis. Why? Because our lungs, our brains, our cardiovascular system is very much suffering from the causes of climate change which are overlapping very much with the causes of air pollution."[55] Yet, less than one percent of international financing for climate action goes to the health sector, she said, calling this state of affairs "absolutely outrageous."[56]

The Power of Denial

Given the overwhelming evidence that confirms anthropogenic climate change, and the larger number of catastrophic meteorological events accompanying it, why are there still a considerable number of people, including some in power, who remain either skeptical or in denial? When Ipsos MORI, one of the United Kingdom's largest market research companies, carried out a survey of people in twenty countries on the issue.[57] It discovered that only 54 percent of Americans agreed with the statement, "The climate change we are currently seeing is largely the result of human activity." This put the United States at the bottom of their list, ten points below the next lowest countries, Australia and Britain.

The survey also found that whereas 93 percent of people from China agreed with the statement, "We are heading for environmental disaster unless we change our habits quickly," only 57 percent of Americans concurred, again placing the United States last among the nations surveyed.

According to James Hoggan, author of *Climate Cover-Up: The Crusade to Deny Global Warming*, the oil, coal, and other industries that profit from the status quo are willing to go to great lengths to mislead people so they can continue to prosper. Hoggan, who was initially a skeptic about climate change, writes in the preface to his book that the industry's cover-up of climate change threats is a "story of betrayal, a story of selfishness, greed, and irresponsibility on an epic scale, . . . a story of deceit, of poisoning public judgment."[58]

Although the state of denialism is thankfully receding, there are still conservative politicians and commentators who are downplaying the significance of climate change, most notoriously US Republican Senator James Inhofe, who called it the "greatest hoax ever perpetrated on the American people."[59]

No wonder some are confused. On one side you have vociferously opinionated media pundits, bloggers, and politicians like Senator Inhofe (who received close to a million dollars in campaign contributions from the oil and coal industries between 2000 and 2008) and Donald Trump (who has called climate change a Chinese "hoax");[60] on the other are the genuine experts, typically more cautious in their assertions. For sure, a few examples of scientific misbehavior have occurred, unfairly seized upon and exaggerated by climate change deniers. But follow-up investigations have demonstrated that there were no efforts by the scientific community to mislead the public deliberately.[61]

In the end, the situation is too dire and the warning signs too stark for climate change to be a partisan issue associated with the knee-jerk identities of our political parties. Climate threats are, I believe, the greatest moral, environmental, economic, and social justice issue of our time. Every aspect of our lives must be reconsidered: a shift to renewable forms of energy; improved transportation systems; more efficient cars and other means of transportation; the massive reduction of the production and consumption of animal-based foods; and lower population growth. All these, and more, need to be adopted in efforts to lower our greenhouse gas emissions and keep future temperature rises to no more than an additional half—or at the most, one—degree Celsius.

I'm pleased to be able to say that the Jewish voice in favor of mitigating climate change is being heard. On

October 29, 2015, a Rabbinic Letter on the Climate Crisis, signed by 425 rabbis, called for "vigorous action to prevent worsening climate disruption."[62] It is my hope that this initiative will inspire many more rabbis and additional Jews to play major roles in addressing climate threats.

Like many of you, I have a personal stake in the future of Israel and the world—one that is brought home to me whenever I hear of a couple getting married or a baby being born. From 2016 when my wife and I moved to Israel until 2022, four of my grandchildren have married, and each has a child, making us great-grandparents. In 2100, these newborns will be almost as old as I am now. What kind of world will they inhabit? Will they look back at their ancestors and wonder how it was possible that they—we—didn't do more, when the evidence was so stark and compelling, and when we had the means in our hands, and on our plates, to make a difference?

Steps to avert a climate catastrophe are discussed in Chapter 8 on veganism.

6

ENVIRONMENTAL ISSUES
IN ISRAEL

> And I will bring back the captives of My people Israel,
> and they shall build the wasted cities, and dwell therein;
> and they shall plant vineyards, and drink their wine; and
> they shall lay out gardens and eat their fruit. (Amos 9:14)

> It took the [Jews] 2,000 years to end their exile and
> return to the Promised Land. It has taken them only 52
> years to turn the land of milk and honey into a country
> of foaming rivers, carcinogenic water, and dying fish.[1]

Jews are properly concerned about the wellbeing of Israel
and wish her to be secure and prosperous. But what about
security, wealth, and comfort of another kind—the quality of
Israel's air, water, and ecosystems? What about the physical
condition of the eternal holy Land? While not discussed
frequently enough, these and other environmental dangers
and degradations have increasingly become serious issues
that will affect Israel's future.

The State of Israel has accomplished amazing things
in its few decades—in agriculture, education, law, social
integration, technology, education, Torah study, human
services, and academics. But simultaneous neglect and
ruthless exploitation of its land, water, air, and resources
have left Israel ecologically endangered.

Among the contributing factors to Israel's environmental problems are some seemingly positive changes that most Israelis hope will continue: rapid population growth, widespread industrialization, and increased affluence, resulting in a sharp increase in the use of automobiles and other consumer goods. However, the environmental impacts of these factors have been insufficiently considered for many years, mostly because of the need to consider security the top priority.[2]

CLIMATE CHANGE: AN EXISTENTIAL THREAT TO ISRAEL

Israel is especially threatened by climate change. Rising seas could cause the coastal plane, where much of Israel's population and infrastructure are located, to be inundated. Climate experts project that the Middle East as a whole will become significantly hotter and drier, and military experts believe that this makes instability, terrorism, and war more likely.[3]

As early as July 6, 2007, an article in the *Jerusalem Post* had the headline, "Israel Urged to 'Act Now' or Risk Global Warming Tragedy." The article warned that:

*   Temperatures could rise by about 3.3 degrees Celsius from pre-industrial levels, with more intense and frequent heat waves.
*   Annual rainfall could decrease by 20 to 30 percent, with much of the rain coming from severe storms.
*   Melting polar ice caps could cause sea level rises that could inundate the Mediterranean coastal plain, irreparably damaging infrastructure like ports and power plants, as well as residential areas.
*   The southern (Negev) desert could expand significantly northward.

Unfortunately, as with other countries, not enough has been done in Israel to alleviate these threats.

In a report presented at the 2019 United Nations Framework Convention on Climate Change, held in Madrid, Spain between December 2 and December 13, the Israeli Ministry of Environmental Protection projected that the average temperature in Israel will rise by an additional 0.9 to 1.2 °C by 2050, while rainfall will decrease by at least 15 to 25 percent by the end of the century.[4] To indicate how serious these projections are, the average world temperature since the start of the Industrial Revolution has risen about 1.2°C, and Israel already has faced serious water problems during some years.

The gravity of the climate threats to Israel is indicated in a September 16, 2021 article, "How Our Home Is Slowly Becoming Uninhabitable," in the *Jerusalem Post*.[5] Among the frightening points it discussed are the following, based on Israeli Environmental Protection Ministry and other Israeli environmental organization reports:

* There has been an overall warming trend throughout Israel and this may cause longer dry seasons, droughts, dry rivers, urban heat islands, and fires. This, and the expected heavier rains, will require a strengthening of infrastructure to increase the resilience of ecosystems.
* Heavier rainfall in short periods is expected, and this would cause major flooding and land erosion. A fifty-one-year record of rainfall for a two-week period occurred in northern Israel in January 2021.[6]

* It is likely that there will be a 10-percent decrease in precipitation by the end of the century. Water sources will experience increased salinity, making the water more difficult to use, and the water flow from the Jordan River into Lake Kinneret is expected to decrease by 22 percent.
* Israel's sea levels are rising by 10 mm annually, which is expected to affect all of Israel's coastline, with the coastal cliffs being threatened. Since most of Israel's population and infrastructure are in the Mediterranean coastal plain, this is very worrisome.
* Severe climate events can damage food resources, threatening future food security.
* Heat waves and other severe climate events can be especially harmful for young children, elderly people, and chronically ill patients.

Israel has already become significantly hotter, warming up almost twice as fast as the world's average,[7] and the trend is expected to continue. A heat wave scorched Israel for over a week in early August 2021, with temperatures reaching 46°C (115 °F).[8] The Israeli Meteorological Service found that "there has been a clear and sharp spike in heat waves in the country," and that "the coming decades will see lengthy heat waves with temperatures higher than 50 degrees Celsius (122 °F)."[9]

Many Israelis have already died from heat waves.[10]

The already hotter and drier weather in Israel is resulting in more frequent and severe wildfires, unlike anything previously seen in Israel. Some Israeli climate experts are calling the current situation in Israel "the age of mega-fires," warning that recent severe fires should be considered a "wake-up call for Israel."[11] A fire in the Jerusalem Hills in August 2021 was so unprecedented that an Israeli fire official said, "Flames of 50 meters (about 164 feet), red clouds, it looked like the end of the world. In Ramat Raziel you saw a fire whirl, where the fire creates the wind itself, these are things we never saw in the past."

A July 2022 analysis by a special climate crisis committee of the Israel Fire and Rescue Services, including senior firefighting personnel and high-ranking officials at the Public Security Ministry and the Meteorological Service, showed how woefully unprepared Israel is for some climate threats.[12] Among their very frightening conclusions are the following:

* "The climate crisis will lead to an increase in unstoppable massive wildfires in Israel," particularly in populated areas, which will constitute "immediate danger to life and property."
* Israel's firefighting service lacks hundreds of millions of shekels in personnel and equipment needed to effectively respond to the anticipated fires.
* While the fire service says it will require 3,400 firefighters, 150 fire stations, and 657 fire engines in order to respond effectively to the expected massive fires, there are currently only 2,260 firefighters, 126 fire stations, and 582 fire engines.
* Due to these shortages, the firefighting system might collapse because of an inability to handle the frequency and intensity of the fires.
* "Each day that passes without overall preparation . . . leads us to the brink of disaster."

Climate change is increasingly being seen as a strategic threat to Israel.[13] Recently, the Israeli Defense Forces recognized that the climate crisis could increase the instability of the Middle East countries and make terrorism and war more likely.[14] Israel's National Security Council plans to include climate change effects in its annual assessments, particularly their effects on terrorism, IDF readiness, state stability, mass migration, and potential refugees.[15]

OTHER ISRAELI ENVIRONMENTAL PROBLEMS

One could write an entire book about environmental issues in Israel, as current MK Alon Tal has done,[16] or any other country, so just some key points about a few significant Israeli environmental issues will be considered in this chapter.[17]

Air Pollution: Israel faces severe air pollution problems, especially in its major cities—Jerusalem, Tel Aviv, and Haifa—and in its industrial centers, such as Ashdod. The main causes are industrial and automobile emissions. The Israel Union for Environmental Defense (IUED) reported that more Israelis die annually from exposure to air pollution in Tel Aviv and Ashdod alone than in all of Israel from terrorist acts and traffic accidents. Over 15 percent of Israeli children suffer from asthma, mainly caused by air pollution.

Population Density and Lack of Open Space: As discussed in more detail in the chapter on population, Israel is one of the world's most densely populated countries. With over nine million people in a country about the size of New Jersey, Israel's population is denser than most other countries, and most of its population is concentrated in a few urban centers. A major national challenge is safeguarding precious land resources. Because of continued rapid population growth, poor planning, and improper development, gardens, parks, and play areas that are essential to health and quality of life are becoming increasingly scarce.

Waste Disposal: Because of Israel's small land area and increasing amounts of garbage from its rapidly growing population, the country faces a solid-waste crisis. Solid-waste disposal may result in significant and irreversible damage to Israel's groundwater, air, soil, and overall quality of life. Some Israeli environmentalists regard garbage disposal as Israel's number-one environmental problem.

Species Extinction: Many species in Israel are threatened, mainly due to pollution, tourism, and urban sprawl. Among the problems are that there is less land for migrating birds to forage on, habitats for many animal species are being replaced by houses, highways, and other developments, and many coral reefs near Eilat are threatened with extinction.

Death of the Dead Sea: The Dead Sea has been shrinking rapidly. It relies on the fresh water of the Jordan River, but that once-major flow has become just a contaminated trickle because water has been diverted for agricultural and other uses. Due to the major drop in the level of the Dead Sea, large sinkholes have been created that make some nearby areas dangerous.

Dust Storms and Sandstorms: While seldom considered, an increasingly serious problem for Israel and other countries in the Middle East are dust storms and sandstorms. As a recent article put it, "Ignored in comparison to other kinds of natural disasters, the Middle East's dust storms and sandstorms are increasingly impacting people's health and the economies of the region."[18] The article pointed out that such storms have occurred an average of about one a week in some areas of the region during certain periods and that "the phenomenon has been growing in both volume and severity in recent years, and is expected to get worse in the coming years." These storms especially affect children, the elderly, and people with asthma.

During its first fifty years after independence, Israel had many environmental success stories. Swamps were drained to reduce health threats and forests were greatly expanded. Israel made major innovations in water usage, including the development of drip irrigation technology and other conservation measures, as well as the building of desalination plants that provided adequate water for its growing population despite its arid climate.

However, the environmental situation in Israel in 2019 can be summed up by this statement from Israeli environmental activist Alon Tal, arguably Israel's leading environmental expert, co-founder of the Israel Union for Environmental Defense and of the Arava Institute for Environmental Studies, and author of *Pollution in the Promised Land: An Environmental History of Israel:*

> But if I am honest with myself and read the present data dispassionately, the inescapable truth is that these are probably the worst of times for Israel's environment. Streams remain contaminated, and ecosystems are collapsing. Greenhouse emissions continue to spiral

upward. Urban sprawl, characterized by ill-considered construction projects, diminish the landscape and steadily make the country a less pleasant place. Environmental policy tends to be sluggish and uninspired.

Why does Israel have such a disappointing environmental record? Beyond the usual official reliance on spin and propaganda, three explanations illuminate the profound disconnect between governmental rhetoric and actual action. First is a weak and unmotivated Ministry of the Environment. The second involves inadequate regulatory enforcement. And third, there is the matter of Israel's relentless demographic expansion. An overview of just some of the country's recent failures tell the story of missed environmental opportunities, and show what is needed for Israel to do better.[19]

Tal also stated:

Everybody in this country—right, left, religious, secular, Jewish, Arab—we all want to breathe the air and not get sick from the water in our faucet. We all want to be able to go out and take a lovely hike in nature and feel like we're being stewards of this land. That is a consensus. To me, it's absolutely shocking that as a country, we've done such a poor job of it till now. I know we can do better.[20]

Fortunately, there has been much recent progress in Israel in addressing climate change and other environmental problems. The former government, led by Prime Minister Naftali Bennett, made addressing climate and other environmental threats a priority.[21] The then Minister of Environmental Protection Tamar Zandberg is a vegan and very dedicated to addressing environmental threats. An example of her commitment is in her statement:

The climate crisis requires us all to take action, here and now. . . . It is important to present the issue [of climate change] as a unifying issue. It requires society as a whole—the Government and the public—to join forces and fight climate change across the globe.[22]

Alon Tal was an MK in the Bennett-led government and actively promoted environmental initiatives. An example of the much-increased emphasis on environmental sustainability is that all Israeli schools now have to provide instruction about the climate crisis.[23]

Hopefully, future governments will build on the environmental initiatives of the former government, especially as climate and other environmental threats become increasingly apparent.

The Israeli Union for Environmental Defense, (IUED), Society for the Protection of Nature in Israel (SPNI), the Abraham Joshua Heschel Center, Neot Kedumim, and other Israeli environmental groups are increasing their efforts to raise the public's environmental awareness through hikes, lectures, and other educational activities. The IUED seeks to reduce pollution by promoting new legislation and taking polluters to court. (For further information about Israeli environmental groups and publications, see Appendix C.)

As discussed in Chapter 4. Judaism has many powerful teachings on environmental sustainability and resource conservation. It is essential that these teachings be applied now to reduce the many threats to Israel's environment, and indeed its survival.

7

HUNGER

Is this not the fast that I have chosen? To loosen the
chains of wickedness, to undo the bonds of oppression,
and to let the crushed go free. . . . Is it not to share your
bread with the hungry? (Isaiah 58:6–7)

On Yom Kippur, the holiest day of the Jewish year, Jews
fast and pray for forgiveness, a favorable judgment, and
a good year. On this same day, we are told, through the
words of the prophet Isaiah, that fasting, confession of sins,
and prayers are not sufficient; people must also work to end
oppression and provide food for theose in need.

Helping the hungry is fundamental in Judaism. The
Talmud states: "Providing charity for poor and hungry
people is as important as all the other commandments of
the Torah combined." (*Baba Batra* 9a)

The *Midrash* teaches:

God says to Israel, "My children, whenever you give
sustenance to the poor, I impute it to you as though you
gave sustenance to Me. . . ." Does then God eat and drink?
No, but whenever you give food to the poor, God accounts
it to you as if you gave food to Him. (*Midrash Tannaim*)

On Passover we are reminded not to forget the poor. Besides
providing *ma'ot chittim* (funds for purchasing matzah and
other holiday necessities) before Passover for people in

need, during the Seder meal itself, we reach out to them in a more personal way:

> This is the bread of affliction, which our ancestors ate in the land of Egypt. Let all who are hungry come and eat. Let all who are in need come and celebrate the Passover.
> (Passover Haggadah)

Jews are even admonished to feed enemies if they are in need:

> If your enemy is hungry, give him bread to eat.
> If your enemy is thirsty, give him water to drink.
> (Proverbs 25:21)

This is consistent with the rabbinic teaching that the greatest hero is a person who converts an enemy into a friend (Avot de Rabbi Nathan, chapter 23).

It is a basic Jewish belief that God provides enough for all. In our daily prayers, it is said, "You [God] open Your hand and satisfy every living thing with its desire" (Psalm 145:16). Jews are obligated to give thanks to God for providing enough food for us and for all of humanity.

In the *Bircat Hamazon* (grace after meals), Jews thank God, "Who feeds the whole world with goodness, grace, loving kindness, and mercy." The blessing is correct. God has provided enough for all. Nature's bounty, if properly distributed and properly consumed, would sustain all people.

Hundreds of millions of people are hungry today, not because of insufficient agricultural capacity, but because of the proliferation of unjust social systems and wasteful food production methods, including the widespread use of crops to fatten farmed animals.

The Jewish position on the subject of world hunger was eloquently summarized by Rabbi Marc H. Tanenbaum, former national inter-religious affairs director of the American Jewish Committee:

> If one takes seriously the moral, spiritual, and humanitarian value of biblical, prophetic, and rabbinic Judaism, the inescapable issue of conscience that must be faced is: How can anyone justify not becoming involved in trying to help save the lives of starving millions of human beings throughout the world—whose plight constitutes the most agonizing moral and humanitarian problem in the latter half of the 20th century?[1]

WORLD HUNGER TODAY

The following facts about hunger are from World Against Hunger's report, "World Hunger Key Facts and Statistics 2022":

* While more than enough food is produced worldwide to feed the world's population, as many as 811 million people (over 10 percent) still go hungry.
* World hunger is on the rise after steadily declining for a decade, After the proportion of undernourished people in the world declined from 15 percent in 2000–2004 to 8.9 percent in 2019, from 2019 to 2020 the number of undernourished people grew by as many as 161 million, largely due to climate change, conflict, and the COVID-19 pandemic.
* While small farmers, herders, and fishermen produce about 70 percent of the global food supply, they are especially vulnerable to food insecurity,

with rural populations suffering the most from poverty and hunger.

* An estimated 14 million children below the age of five worldwide suffer from severe malnutrition.
* The Ukraine War is making the situation far worse, because far less grain is being exported from Russia and Ukraine, two of the world's largest producers.

WHAT CAUSES HUNGER?

The above-mentioned World Against Hunger report also considers causes of hunger:

* Hunger is strongly interconnected with poverty, which involves interactions among an array of societal, political, demographic, and social factors.
* Another key driver of severe food crises, including famine, is conflict. Hunger and undernutrition are much worse when conflicts are prolonged and institutions are weak. The number of conflicts is on the rise, some worsened by severe climate events. As indicated previously, severe droughts have sparked civil wars in the Sudan and in Syria. In 2020, conflict was the main cause of hunger for 99.1 million people in 23 countries.
* Weather-related events, often caused by climate change, have also impacted food availability in many countries and thus contributed to increased food insecurity. The recent increase in the frequency and severity of heat waves, droughts, wildfires, storms, and floods has had negative effects on food production in many areas.

* Economic downturns have also affected food availability and decreased people's ability to access food, especially in countries dependent on oil and other primary-commodity export revenues.
* Due to the widespread COVID-19 pandemic and the unprovoked, unjustified Russian invasion of Ukraine, food prices worldwide have recently spiked, greatly increasing hunger, especially in the developing countries.
* The effects of animal-based diets and agriculture on hunger will be discussed in the next chapter.

Jeremy Rifkin summarized the anomaly of rich people dieting and poor people starving:

> While millions of Americans anguish over excess pounds, spending time, money, and emotional energy on slimming down, children in other lands are wasting away, their physical growth irreversibly stunted, their bodies racked by parasitic and opportunistic diseases, their brain growth diminished by lack of nutrients in their meager diets.[2]

Extensive hunger and malnutrition in so many parts of the world make rebellion and violence more likely. Professor Georg Borgstrom, international expert on food science, fears that "the rich world is on a direct collision course with the poor of the world. . . . We cannot survive behind our Maginot line of missiles and bombs."[3]

Unless the problem of global hunger is fully addressed and very soon, the outlook for global stability is very poor. Professor Robert Heilbroner, a noted economist, predicted that, in times of severe famine, countries like India would be sorely tempted to resort to nuclear blackmail.[4]

UN Secretary General Antonio Guterres said, "Unless immediate action is taken, it is increasingly clear that there is an impending global food scarcity emergency that could have long term impacts on hundreds of millions of adults and children."[5] He urged countries to rethink their food systems and encouraged more sustainable food practices.[6]

JEWISH RESPONSES TO HUNGER

1. Applying Basic Jewish Values

As indicated in Chapter 3, Jews are urged to practice justice, be compassionate and kind, and work to reduce poverty. These actions can all help to reduce hunger.

2. Involvement

As indicated in Chapter 1, Judaism teaches involvement and concern with the plight of fellow human beings. Every life is sacred, and we are obligated to do what we can to help others. The Torah states: "You shall not stand idly by the blood of your neighbor." (Leviticus 19:16)

Jews rightfully condemn the silence of the world when six million Jews and millions of other people were murdered by the Nazis. Can we be silent when millions die agonizing deaths because of lack of food? Can we acquiesce to the apathy of the world toward the fate of starving people?

Elie Wiesel has pointed out that there can be no analogies to the Holocaust, but that it can be used as a reference point. In that context, we can consider the approximately nine million people worldwide who die each year due to malnutrition and the six million Jews who were slaughtered by the Nazis. True, victims of hunger are not being singled out because of their religion, race, or nationality, but, as was the case for Holocaust victims, they perished while the world continued to go about its business, grumbling about personal inconveniences, indifferent to the plight of the starving people. Since the *Mishneh* teaches that if one saves a single human life, it is as if one has saved an entire world (*Sanhedrin* 4:5), what then if one fails to save a single life? Or nine million?

The Hebrew prophets berate those who are content and comfortable while others are in great distress:

> Tremble you women, who are at ease,
> Shudder you complacent ones;
> Strip and make yourselves bare,
> Gird sackcloth upon your loins. (Isaiah. 32:11)

> Woe to those who are at ease in Zion . . .
> Woe to those who lie upon beds of ivory
> And stretch themselves upon their couches . . .
> Who drink wine from bowls
> And anoint themselves with the finest oils
> But are not grieved at the ruin of Joseph. (Amos 6:1, 4, 6)

Like other people, Jews have frequently experienced hunger. Because of famines, Abraham was forced to go to Egypt (Genesis 12:10), Isaac went to the land of Abimelech, king of the Philistine, in Gerar (Genesis 26:1), the children of Jacob went to Egypt to buy grain (Genesis 42:1–3), and Naomi and her family fled Israel and went to Moab (Ruth 1:1–2). There were also famines in the reigns of King David (2 Samuel 21:1) and King Ahab (1 Kings 18:1–2).

Jews know the agony of great hunger. The Prophet Jeremiah, referring to the time of the destruction of Jerusalem, proclaims: "Happier were the victims of the sword than the victims of hunger, who pined away, stricken by want of the yield of the field." (Lamentations 4:9)

Based on Jewish values and Jewish history, we Jews must empathize with the starving millions of the world. We must be involved by speaking out and working in support of more just, environmentally sustainable agricultural policies. Some traditional Jewish ways to be involved in helping people in need are to pursue justice, practice charity, show compassion, share resources, and simplify our lifestyles.

3. Sharing

Feeling compassion for the poor and hungry is not enough. A fundamental Jewish principle is that those who have much should share with others who are less fortunate. The Talmudic sage Hillel stresses that we must not be concerned only with our own welfare: "If I am not for myself, who will be for me? But if I am for myself only, what am I?" (*Pirkei Avot* 1:14). Indeed, as mentioned above, the Haggadah read at Passover Seders exhorts us to welcome and share with all who are hungry and in need. The act of prolonging one's meal, on the chance that a poor person may come so that one may give him or her food, is so meritorious that the table of the person who does this is compared to the altar of the ancient Temple. (*Brachot* 55a)

Judaism's great emphasis on sharing is also illustrated in the following Chassidic tale:

> The story is told of a great rabbi who before his death was given the privilege of seeing the realms of Heaven

and Hell. First, he was taken to Hell, where he was confronted with a huge banquet room in the middle of which was a large elegant table covered with a magnificent tablecloth and the finest china, silver, and crystal. The table was covered from one end to the other with the most delicious foods that the eyes have ever seen or the mouth tasted. And all around the table, people were sitting looking at the food . . . and wailing.

It was such a wail that the rabbi had never heard such a sad sound in his entire life and he asked, "With a luxurious table and the most delicious food, why do these people wail so bitterly?" As he entered the room, he saw the reason for their distress. For although each was confronted with this incredible sight before him, no one was able to eat the food. Each person's arms were splinted so that the elbows could not bend. They could touch the food but could not eat it. The anguish this caused was the reason for the great wail and despair that the rabbi saw and heard.

He was next shown Heaven, and to his surprise he observed the identical scene witnessed in Hell: The large banquet room, elegant table, lavish settings, and sumptuous foods. And, in addition, once again everyone's arms were splinted so the elbows could not bend. Here, however, there was no wailing, but rather joy greater than he had ever experienced in his life. For whereas here too the people could not put the food into their own mouths, each picked up the food and fed it to another. They were thus able to enjoy not only the beautiful scene, the wonderful smells, and the delicious foods, but also the joy of sharing and helping one another.[7]

Rabbi Jay Marcus, former longtime spiritual leader of the Young Israel of Staten Island, comments on the fact that *karpas* (eating of greens) and *yahatz* (breaking of the middle matzah for later use as the dessert) are next to each other in the order of the Passover Seder service.[8] He suggests that those who can live on simple things like greens, such as vegetables, will more readily divide their possessions and share with others.

To help share God's abundant harvests with the poor, the Torah instructed farmers:

1. A corner of the field always had to be left unharvested; it was the property of the poor (*Pe'ah*). (Leviticus 19; 9–10)
2. If fewer than three ears of corn were dropped during the harvest, they were not to be gleaned, but were to be left for the poor (*Leket*). (Leviticus 19; 9–10)
3. A sheaf forgotten by the farmer could not be retrieved but had to be left for the poor (*Shik'khah*). (Deuteronomy 24:19–21)
4. Every third year a part of the tithe of the harvest had to be set aside for the poor. (*Ma'aser Ani*)
5. On the eve of every holy day, Jews had to put aside a special gift for the poor, *mat'not yad*.

As discussed in the next chapter, veganism is consistent with this Jewish concept of sharing. As Jay Dinshah, late founder and long-time President of the American Vegan Society, stated:

> After all, vegetarianism is, more than anything else, the very essence and the very expression of altruistic sharing . . . the sharing of the One Life . . . the sharing

of the natural resources of the Earth . . . the sharing of
love, kindness, compassion, and beauty in this life.[9]

If Jay Dinshah were alive today, he would likely change
"vegetarianism" to "veganism," since the organization he
founded is now called the American Vegan Society.

The Los Angeles–based Jewish organization Mazon
attempts to help Jews share their joyous events with
hungry people. It urges people to contribute 3 percent of
the money normally spent for weddings, bar mitzvahs, and
other celebrations to the group, which funnels the money
to organizations working to reduce hunger. For contact
information, see Appendix C.

4. Simplifying Lifestyles

Because millions lack sufficient food, it is imperative that
those of us who have so much simplify our lives so that we
can share more with others. A group of major religious
leaders, including representatives of several branches of
Judaism in the United States and Israel, met in Bellagio,
Italy, as long ago as May 1975, to consider "The Energy/
Food Crisis: A Challenge to Peace, a Call to Faith." They
agreed on a statement that included this assertion:

> The deepest and strongest expression of any religion
> is the "styles of life" that characterizes its believers. It
> is urgent that religious communities and individuals
> scrutinize their life style and turn from habits of waste,
> overconsumption, and thoughtless acceptance of the
> standards propagated by advertisements and social
> pressures.
>
> The cry from millions for food brought us together
> from many faiths. God—Reality itself—calls us to

respond to the cry for food. And we hear it as a cry not only for aid but also for justice.[10]

Simpler lifestyles, with less wasteful diets, can be an important first step toward justice for the hungry of the world. Simpler diets do not mean a lack of joy or a lack of fellowship. As Proverbs 15:17 states, "Better a dinner of herbs where love is present than a stalled ox with hatred."

During the Middle Ages, local Jewish councils established "sumptuary laws" for the community. People were forbidden to spend more than a specified amount of money for weddings and other joyous occasions. These laws were designed so that the poor should not be embarrassed for being unable to match the expenditures of the wealthy, and so that a financial strain was not placed on the community as a whole.

Perhaps the spirit of such laws should be invoked today. Can we continue to consume flesh that requires so much grain to be fed to animals at a time when millions of people are starving? Is it not now time for officiating rabbis to specify guidelines that reduce waste and ostentation at weddings, bar mitzvahs, and other occasions? (Several Chassidic Rebbes have already established limits on expenses and on the number of guests at weddings and other religious celebrations within their communities.)

It is a fundamental Jewish belief that God provides enough for every person's needs. In our daily prayers, it is said: "He opens His hand and provides sustenance to all living things" (Psalms 145:16). Jews are mandated to give thanks to God for providing enough food for everyone. In the *Birkat Hamazon* (Grace After Meals), we praise God, "Who feeds the entire world with goodness, grace, loving kindness and compassion." The blessing is, of course, absolutely correct. God has provided enough for all. The bounties of nature, fairly distributed and properly consumed, would sustain all people.

The means are available for each person to enjoy an adequate diet. Every nation could be self-sufficient in producing food. The conditions of inequality and injustice that are causing widespread hunger are outrageous and must be changed. As the Indian independence leader Mahatma Gandhi stated: "The world has enough for everyone's needs, but not everyone's greed."[11] Ways to reduce hunger are discussed further in the Chapter 8 on veganism.

With so much hunger, poverty, and injustice in the world, explicit Jewish mandates to feed the hungry, help the poor, share resources, practice charity, show compassion, and pursue justice, along with the duty imposed on us by God to remember the suffering and deprivation Jews experienced throughout Jewish history, should provide the impetus for Jews, as individuals and communities and in institutions, to be in the forefront of efforts to provide leadership in creating food production and distribution systems that will sharply reduce world hunger.

8

SHOULD JEWS BE VEGANS?

And God said, "Behold, I have given you every herb bearing seed, which is upon the face of the earth, and every fruit tree yielding seed; to you it shall be for food." (Genesis 1:29)

The dietary laws are designed to teach us compassion and to lead us gently to vegetarianism.—Rabbi Shlomo Riskin, Chief Rabbi of Efrat, Israel

What was the necessity for the entire procedure of ritual slaughter? For the sake of self-discipline. It is far more appropriate for man not to eat meat; only if he has a strong desire for meat does the Torah permit it, and even this only after the trouble and inconvenience necessary to satisfy his desire. Perhaps because of the bother and annoyance of the whole procedure, he will be restrained from such a strong and uncontrollable desire for meat.
—Rabbi Solomon Efraim Lunchitz, in *Kli Yakar*

As a vegetarian and later a vegan activist in the Jewish community for over forty years, I believe it is essential that Jews recognize and act on the knowledge that vegan diets are most consistent with basic Jewish teachings and have many benefits.

I hope this chapter helps start a respectful dialogue on whether Jews should be vegans. I think such a dialogue would be a *Kiddush Hashem* (a sanctification of God's name), since it would show the relevance of Judaism's eternal teachings and would help make Jews (and others) aware of the many benefits of non-animal-based diets and of their applicability to creating healthier people and a healthier planet.

SIX WAYS THAT ANIMAL-BASED DIETS VIOLATE BASIC JEWISH TEACHINGS

As I have been arguing for many years, animal-based diets conflict with basic Jewish values in at least six important areas:

1. While Judaism mandates that people should be very careful about preserving our health and our lives, numerous medical studies in respected peer-reviewed journals have linked animal-based diets directly to heart disease, stroke, many forms of cancer, and other life-threatening diseases. Animal-based diets also make future pandemics, with their many negative health effects, more likely.

2. While Judaism forbids *tsa'ar ba'alei chayim*—inflicting unnecessary pain on animals—most farmed animals, including those raised for kosher consumers, are reared on factory farms where they live in cramped, confined spaces and are often drugged, mutilated, and denied fresh air, sunlight, exercise, and any enjoyment of life, before they are consumed.

3. While Judaism teaches that "the earth is the Lord's" (Psalm 24:1) and that we are to be God's partners and co-workers in preserving the world, modern intensive farmed-animal agriculture contributes far more than does plant-based

agriculture to climate change, soil erosion and depletion, air and water pollution, overuse of chemical fertilizers and pesticides, destruction of tropical rainforests and other habitats, and other forms of environmental degradation.

4. While Judaism mandates *bal tashchit*, that we are not to waste or unnecessarily destroy anything of value, nor use more than is needed to accomplish a purpose, the production of meat and other animal products is built on an extremely wasteful pyramid of resources (compared to plant protein production): overuse and waste of grain, land, fresh water, energy (most of it nonrenewable), and other resources.

5. While Judaism stresses that we are to provide for the poor and share our bread with the hungry, over 70 percent of the grain grown in the United States is very inefficiently funneled through animals in order to produce meat, milk, and eggs, while an estimated nine million people worldwide die each year from hunger and its effects. If we raised fewer animals and ate more "bread" ourselves (grains and beans, fruits and vegetables), we could share so much more of the "loaf" with the world's hungry people.

6. While Judaism teaches that we must seek and pursue peace, and that violence can result from unjust conditions, diets high in animal protein monopolize resources, creating a shortage of affordable land, food, water, and energy for those in need, especially in the developing world. This exacerbates the tension between haves and have-nots and may fuel social unrest, violence, and war.

One could say "*dayenu*" (it would be enough) after any one of these arguments. Each one by itself constitutes a serious conflict between Jewish values and current practice that should encourage every conscientious Jew to seriously consider adopting a vegan diet. Combined, the six arguments make an even more compelling ethical case.

So, since animal-centered diets violate and contradict each of these important Jewish mandates—to preserve human health, to attend to the welfare of animals, to protect the environment, to conserve resources, to help feed the hungry, and to pursue peace—it is an important mitzvah for committed Jews (and others) to replace as much of the animal food in their diets as they can. We can do this with nutritionally superior plant alternatives: tofu, stir-fry vegetables, veggie burgers, baked beans, and chickpea curries, as well as lush salads and a variety of fruit, nuts, and seeds.

These arguments and other Torah teachings connected to veganism and related issues are presented in more detail in my books *Judaism and Vegetarianism* and *Vegan Revolution: Saving Our World, Revitalizing Judaism,* and my over 250 articles and 25 podcasts of my talks and interviews, which can be found online at www.JewishVeg.org/Schwartz.

HOW A SWITCH TO VEGANISM CAN HELP STABILIZE CLIMATE

As discussed in Chapter 5, climate change is an existential threat to humanity. Because of increasingly dire warnings by climate experts and a significant increase in the frequency and severity of climate events, climate change is now on people's minds. However, the many connections between typical American (and other Western) diets and climate change have generally been overlooked. Even Al Gore missed this important point when he produced his award-winning film, *An Inconvenient Truth*. So, let's examine how a major switch to plant-based diets can help stabilize climate.

Current modern intensive animal agriculture greatly contributes to the four major gases associated with the greenhouse effect: carbon dioxide, methane, nitrous oxides, and chlorofluorocarbons. The burning of tropical forests to create pastureland and land to grow feed crops for animals releases huge amounts of carbon dioxide into the atmosphere and destroys the very trees that can absorb so much CO_2 and release the oxygen within it. In effect, trees are the "lungs" of our planet. Yet these forests are being cut down or burned on every continent to further animal agriculture.

The highly mechanized agricultural sector, much of which is directed to producing feed for farmed animals, uses enormous amounts of fossil fuel to produce pesticides, chemical fertilizer, and other agricultural resources, as well as transporting the animals and their products. Running the tractors, trucks, and other equipment used to produce feed also contributes to carbon dioxide emissions. In addition, the large amounts of petrochemical fertilizers used to produce feed crops create significant quantities of nitrous oxides. Moreover, the increased refrigeration necessary to prevent animal products from spoiling adds more chlorofluorocarbons to the atmosphere.

During the past twenty years, most climate change discussions have focused on implementing changes in energy use but have given little attention to the impact of our diets. This trend began to change upon publication of a landmark 2006 report by the United Nations Food and Agricultural Organization (FAO) that estimated that livestock production globally is responsible for more greenhouse gas emissions (GHGs), in CO_2 equivalents, than the emissions from all of the world's cars, planes, ships, and all other means of transportation combined.[1]

The FAO report, *Livestock's Long Shadow*, projected that, if human population growth and dietary trends continue, the world's then annual consumption of almost 60 billion farmed land-based animals will double by mid-century. The resulting increase in GHGs would largely negate the reduced GHG emissions from all conservation and improved efficiencies in transportation, electricity, and other sectors. This, in turn, could make it extremely difficult, if not impossible, to reach the GHG reductions that climate experts believe essential in order to avert a climate disaster. While that doubling in population and meat consumption may or may not occur, it is troubling that in the face of livestock's strong role in warming the planet, many countries are encouraging the expanded consumption of animal products.

The FAO explained that animal agriculture's contribution to GHGs is so great because farmed animals, especially cattle and other ruminants, emit methane as part of their digestive processes. During the 10 to 20 years it is in the atmosphere, methane is about 84 times as potent per unit weigh as CO_2 in producing global warming.

The FAO also asserted that: 1) the manufacture of animal products causes about 9 percent of total CO_2 emissions, including the production of pesticides and fertilizer, use of irrigation pumps, extensive refrigeration, and other processes; 2) nitrous oxides are emitted from animals' manure and from chemical fertilizer used to grow feed crops, and these gases are almost 300 times as potent as CO_2 in producing warming; and 3) when rainforests are burned to create grazing land and land to grow feed crops for animals, substantial amounts of CO_2 are released, and trees that would absorb CO_2 are destroyed.

An in-depth analysis, "Livestock and Climate Change" by World Bank Group environmental specialists Robert Goodland and Jeff Anhang, appeared in the November/December 2009 issue of *World Watch* magazine. The authors argue that there are sources of GHGs from the livestock sector that were overlooked, underrepresented, or placed in the wrong sectors in the FAO report. They concluded that the livestock sector is responsible for *at least 51 percent* of all human-induced GHGs.[2]

Goodland and Anhang concluded that it is not methane emissions but land use, including the destruction of tropical forests to produce land for grazing and to grow feed crops, that is the prime source for GHGs attributable to livestock. They call for the replacement of livestock products with plant-based alternatives, stating that this would result in rapid reductions in atmospheric GHGs, mostly because of methane's short half-life, while also greatly reducing ongoing world food and water crises.

Considering the ability to reforest land currently used to raise animals, systems engineer Sailesh Rao, PhD, argues in his paper, "Animal Agriculture Is the Leading Cause of Climate Change," published in the *Journal of Ecological Society*, that shifts toward vegan diets could, in effect, reduce atmospheric greenhouse gases by at least 87 percent, greatly lessening climate threats.[3]

Leading climate specialists have focused increasingly on the role of animal-based agriculture in causing climate change, pointing out that there is no more powerful environmental action that any individual can take than adopting a plant-based diet.

Reinforcing the above analysis is a July 2022 report from the Boston Consulting Group pointing out that the best approach to reducing climate threats is shifting to plant-based meat.[4] The report indicated that for each dollar investment in improving and scaling up the production of meat and dairy alternatives there was three times more greenhouse gas reductions compared with investment in green cement technology, seven times more than green buildings, and eleven times more than zero-emission cars.[5]

Bottom line: a society-wide shift toward vegan diets provides the best chance of averting a climate catastrophe. It would sharply reduce greenhouse gas emissions because of far less cows and other ruminants emitting methane. Even more importantly, it would enable the reforestation of the vast areas now used for grazing and growing feed crops for animals, which would reduce the atmospheric CO_2 from its current very dangerous level to a much safer one.

An excellent, comprehensive analysis of the urgency of a society-wide shift toward vegan diets in order to avert a climate catastrophe is in the 2020 book *Food Is Climate* by Glen Merzer. He points out that the number of trees in the world has been reduced from about six trillion to about three trillion, mainly due to animal-based agriculture.[6] Shamefully, at a time when efforts to reduce greenhouse gas emissions are increasingly urgent, many trees are still being destroyed to create land for grazing and growing feed crops for animals.

The Impact of Animal-Based Diets
on the Environment[7]

In addition to livestock's major contribution to climate change, as discussed above, it is responsible for many other threats to the environment, laying waste to the natural world.[8]

Each year, about a billion tons of precious topsoil are lost to erosion, either through overgrazing or poor or inefficient land use. Over half of all United States rangelands are overgrazed, with billions of tons of soil lost every year. Erosion is leading to lower yields and a reduction in soil fertility worldwide.[9]

Animal agriculture contributes to water pollution in several ways: excessive nitrogen and phosphorus from chemical fertilizers—much of it used (in the United States) to grow such crops as wheat, corn, and soy for animal feed—runs off into waterways, leading to eutrophication;[10] and animal waste from "lagoons" of excrement outside factory farms can leach or overflow into bodies of water, in addition to producing foul odors and flies.[11]

As indicated above, cattle are one of the leading causes of rainforest destruction—whether for grazing or to grow crops to feed to livestock around the world.[12] It has been estimated that over a hundred plant, animal, and insect species are lost every day due to the decimation of their habitats.[13] A May 2019 report by the Intergovernmental Science Policy Platform on Biology and Ecosystem Services (IPBES), written by 145 environmental experts from 50 countries, found that one million of the planet's eight million species are threatened with extinction, largely due to human actions, including animal-oriented agriculture and overfishing.[14] Sir Robert Watson, IPBES chair, concluded:

"The health of ecosystems on which we and all other species depend is deteriorating more rapidly than ever," and "transformative changes" are needed to save the planet.[15]

This loss of biodiversity is a tragedy not only for animals. Half of the world's plant species reside in tropical rainforests, and some may hold secrets to curing some of today's deadly diseases.[16] A further concern is that the decrease of rainforests may reduce rainfall and weather patterns with potentially devastating effects on agriculture in many areas.[17]

As part of a climate change mitigation strategy, such international bodies as the United Nations are urging us to reduce our fossil fuel dependency and conserve energy. Here, too, animal agriculture proves to be both fossil fuel–dependent and energy-inefficient.[18]

The production of meat requires ten to twenty times more energy per edible ton than grain production. Indeed, growing feed crops for farmed animals requires considerable energy for plowing, pumping irrigation water, harvesting, producing pesticides and fertilizer, and transportation. Additional energy is needed to process those crops. Furthermore, the production of a pound of steak (500 calories of food energy) uses 20,000 calories of fossil fuels, most of which are expended to produce feed crops.[19]

Housing animals in huge windowless sheds requires energy for lighting, artificial ventilation, and conveyor belts. Slaughterhouses also require much energy and, because of the need to sluice away blood and viscera, are water-intensive. In fact, animal foods require much more energy for processing, packaging, and refrigeration than do plant-based foods. It requires seventy-eight calories of fossil fuel to produce a calorie of protein obtained from feedlot-produced beef, but only two calories of fossil fuel to produce a calorie of protein from soybeans.[20]

Only 2.5 percent of the world's available water is potable, and only 1 percent is accessible.[21] Around 790 million people, or 11 percent of the world's population, lack access to safe drinking water.[22] Yet, despite the fact that fresh water is being depleted at an alarming rate as glaciers melt and aquifers shrink, the world's commitment to animal-based agriculture continues.

Almost a third of the world's water is consumed in order to produce meat and other animal products,[23] with 56 percent of the water in the United States (or 14 trillion gallons) used to grow crops to feed animals,[24] and between 20 and 33 percent of the world's freshwater consumption is employed for animal agriculture.[25]

Because of the enormous amounts of water needed to produce feed crops for animals or to keep the animals themselves hydrated, an egg requires 53 gallons of water to produce; a pound of chicken, 468 gallons; a gallon of cow's milk, 880 gallons; and a pound of beef, 1,800 gallons.[26]

Just one hamburger requires up to 660 gallons of water to produce, the equivalent of about two months of showers for an individual. The production of one pound of steak uses 2,500 gallons of water, while only 25 gallons are required to produce a pound of wheat.[27] *Newsweek* calculated that "the water that goes into a 1,000-pound steer would float a Naval destroyer."[28]

Manure runoff from industrial farms pollutes groundwater and rivers. In fact, one-third of rivers in the United States have been polluted by animal excrement, fertilizer, pesticides, and other toxic substances.[29]

When we consider all of these negative environmental and climate-change effects, and then add the harmful effects of animal-based diets on human health and global hunger, it is clear that animal-centered diets and the animal agriculture needed to sustain them pose tremendous threats to global survival. It is not surprising that the Union of Concerned Scientists (UCS) ranks the consumption of meat and poultry as the second most harmful consumer activity (surpassed only by the use of cars and light trucks).[30] It is clear that a shift toward veganism is imperative to move our precious but imperiled planet away from its present catastrophic path.

Jeremy Rifkin summarizes well the very negative effects of animal-based agriculture:

> The ever-increasing cattle population is wreaking havoc on the earth's ecosystems, destroying habitats on six continents. Cattle raising is a primary factor in the destruction of the world's remaining tropical rainforests. Millions of acres of ancient forests in Central and South America are being felled and cleared to make room for pastureland to graze cattle. Cattle herding is responsible for much of the spreading desertification in the sub-Sahara of Africa and the western rangeland of the United States and Australia. The overgrazing of semiarid and arid lands has left parched and barren deserts on four continents. Organic runoff from feedlots is now a major source of organic pollution in our nation's groundwater. Cattle are also a major cause of global warming. . . . The devastating environmental, economic, and human toll of maintaining a worldwide cattle complex is little discussed in public policy circles. . . . Yet, cattle production and beef consumption now rank among the gravest threats to the future wellbeing of the earth and its human population.[31]

ANIMAL-BASED DIETS CONTRIBUTION TO HUNGER[32]

Perhaps the greatest scandal associated with hunger is that, although we have an abundance of cereal crops that could be fed to human beings, a large percentage of soy, corn, oats, and wheat is grown to feed farmed animals instead of people. Indeed, the average person in the United States consumes almost five times as much grain (most of it indirectly, in the form of animal foods) as a person in a developing country. About 70 percent of the grain grown in the U.S. is fed to animals destined for slaughter.[33] Half of its arable land is devoted to feed crops or grazing,[34] with 95 percent of corn being directed to animal feed.[35] What makes this especially shameful is that foods high in fiber and complex carbohydrates and devoid of cholesterol and saturated fat are converted into unhealthy animal products with the opposite characteristics.

An animal-based diet also wastes a colossal amount of land. It requires about 3.5 acres per person, whereas a vegan diet requires only about a fifth of an acre. For instance, it takes about a hundred calories of grain to deliver twelve calories of chicken or three calories of beef. Meanwhile, protein conversion rates are 9 percent for pork, 21 percent for poultry, and 3 percent for beef.[36]

This shocking waste and loss of food—and the finite resources, such as topsoil, water, phosphorus, and land that go into its production—are exacerbated by a global system that encourages raising animals or feed crops for export dollars. In spite of dedicating so much of its land and other resources to raising farmed animals, the United States is, as of 2020, the world's largest importer of beef.[37] For example, although Honduras suffers widespread poverty and malnutrition, it exports large amounts of beef to the United States.[38] In Central America, over half of the agriculturally productive land is used for animal production, for the wealthy and for export. A switch from animal-centered diets would free land and other resources that could be used to grow nutritious crops for people.

In addition to all the waste and loss of water and land in food production, an enormous amount of food is wasted and lost after it has been grown. According to Feeding America, 72 billion pounds of food are wasted annually in the United States, even though 37 million Americans go hungry. That food is worth $218 billion; wastes 21 percent of fresh water; and occupies a fifth of landfill area.[39] So great is the amount of food lost (left in the fields to rot, unable to make it to market because of poor roads, lack of refrigeration, or because no one is there to pick it) or wasted (thrown away as leftovers, or because it's not considered suitable for sale) that it alone is responsible for at least 6 percent of global greenhouse gas emissions. To put it another way, food waste is three times more GHG-intensive than aviation, and if it were its own country, food waste would be the world's third greatest emitter, behind the United States and China.[40]

Animal products are part of that wasteful food chain—especially when, for instance, in the case of cow's milk, a glut in production means it becomes financially inefficient to bring milk to market; or the market itself collapses and there is too much supply.[41] However, animal products represent their own particular waste and loss because of the choices to grow food to feed animals rather than people. In fact, a 2018 study found that the opportunity costs of animal-based diets exceeded all food losses because that lost food could have fed 350 million people.[42]

These facts indicate that the food being fed to animals in the affluent nations could, if properly distributed, potentially end both hunger and malnutrition throughout the world. A switch from animal-centered diets would free up land and other resources, which could then be used to grow nutritious crops for people. This new approach would also promote policies that would enable people in the developing countries to use their resources and skills to raise their own food.

With so much hunger in the world, explicit Jewish mandates to feed the hungry, help the poor, share resources, practice charity, show compassion, and pursue justice, as well as the lessons from many experiences of hunger in Jewish history, point to veganism as the diet most consistent with Jewish teachings about hunger.

At a time when there is more than enough food produced annually to feed all of the world's people if it were fed directly to them rather than to animals, the current widespread hunger is a true scandal.

CONCLUSION

The aims of vegans and environmentalists are very similar— to simplify our lifestyles, show regard for the earth and all forms of life, and apply the awareness that "the earth is the Lord's." In view of the many negative effects of animal-based agriculture on the earth's environment, resources, and climate, it is becoming increasingly clear that a shift toward vegan diets is imperative to move our precious but imperiled planet away from its present catastrophic path.

Since Jews are a small minority of the world's population (about 0.2 percent), even if every Jew became vegan (a very unlikely scenario), the effect on the climate and other environmental crises would be negligible. However, as Isaiah 49:6 declares, Jews are mandated to be a "light unto the nations," and being vegan is one way to carry this out. The power of a positive example should not be underestimated. It's my view that if many Jews became vegans, or at least sharply reduced their consumption of meat and other animal foods, and if veganism and related issues became a major focus of Jewish life, members of other religions would notice and might also shift toward veganism. This could spur secular people to reduce their consumption of meat. A positive feedback loop could result, with veganism being accepted as the most rational diet, with many positive benefits to individuals and the world.

Our mission must include the lightening of the immense burden of human diets on animals, on the environment, and on the world's poor and hungry. To do so is to demonstrate the relevance of Judaism's eternal teachings to the problems of the world today. I sincerely hope that we—and the rest of the world—begin making the necessary changes before it is too late. There is no Planet B or effective Plan B.

POPULATION

We're nearing the moment when the quantity of life will harm the quality of life. You can't talk about standard of living without also talking about quality of life— the ability to go out and enjoy nature without being surrounded by mobs of people; to have a seat on the train and not stand in the aisle with hundreds of passengers; and then there's the question of employment for young people: With so many children being born, what employment will we have to offer them, especially in an age where AI [artificial intelligence] is replacing human labor in many fields?[1]

We have already discussed climate change, environmental threats both worldwide and in Israel, and hunger. Population plays a significant role with all of these issues, so it is important to consider this topic.[2]

Population growth is one of the critical problems that the world faces today. It is largely due to an increase in life expectancies because of improved standards of living, as well as advances in sanitation and medical technology. There is now widespread concern about the world's ability to provide enough food, energy, housing, employment, education, and health care for the increasing global population, while simultaneously protecting our environment, quality of life, and political freedoms.

For many years, the world's population grew exponentially, doubling in as few as 35 years during the mid-20th century. While throughout most of the world's history, the population was under one billion people, the exponential growth led to a population of 7.837 billion in 2021.[3] It is now growing at a much slower rate, but is still expected to reach 8.848 billion in 2035 and 9.688 by 2050,[4] leveling off to about 11 billion by the end of this century.[5] This is far less than it would be if exponential growth continued, but still represents more than a 40-percent increase from the 2021 population. This would make it much harder for humanity to avert a climate catastrophe and other environmental threats.

JEWISH TEACHINGS ON POPULATION

Judaism has many teachings on the importance of having children, but, as discussed later, it also has teachings about limiting procreation in times of great dangers, such as is occurring today.

The first *mitzvah* of the Torah is the duty of procreation. On the sixth day of creation, God created human beings, male and female, and blessed them and commanded them: "Be fruitful and multiply, and replenish the earth" (Genesis 1:28). Later, after the Flood, this mandate was repeated to Noah: "Be fruitful and multiply, and replenish the earth" (Genesis 9:1).

The blessing of fertility was extended to Abraham and Sarah (Genesis 17:16). Through Isaac, Abraham was promised by God that he would be blessed with descendants as numerous as the stars of heaven and as the sand on the seashore (Genesis 15:5). This blessing was repeated to Jacob, in the early years of his life (Genesis 28:14) and also later (Genesis 35:11).

The principal blessing that Torah personalities conferred on their children and grandchildren was that of fertility. This was true of Isaac's blessing to Jacob (Genesis 28:3), Jacob's blessing to Manasseh and Ephraim (his grandchildren) (Genesis 48:16), and Jacob's blessing to Joseph (Genesis 49:25).

The following is one of many Talmudic passages that stress the importance of having children:

> Rabbi Eliezer stated: "He who does not engage in the propagation of the race is as though he sheds blood; for it is said, 'whoever sheds man's blood, by man shall his blood be shed,' and this is immediately followed by the text, 'And you, be you fruitful and multiply.'" Rabbi Jacob said: "[One who does not propagate], it is as though he has diminished the Divine image; since it is said, 'For in the image of God He made man,' and this is immediately followed by, 'And you be fruitful.'" Ben Azzai said: "It is as though he sheds blood *and* diminishes the Divine image, since it is said, 'And you, be you fruitful and multiply.'"[6]

Every human life is sacred and every new life brings God's image anew into the world. Hence Judaism has always regarded marriage and procreation as sacred duties and divine imperatives. People are to populate the earth, for the world that God created is "very good" and people should follow God's commandment to be fruitful and multiply "with the intention of preserving the human species."[7]

Judaism is never content with general formulations. It always provides specific indications of how commandments are to be carried out. Hence the *Mishnah* considered the question of how large a family one needs in order to satisfy the injunction to have children:

> A married man shall not abstain from the performance
> of the duty of propagation of the race unless he already
> has children. As to the number, *Beit Shammai* (the school
> of Shammai) ruled: two males, and *Beit Hillel* ruled: a
> male and female, for it is stated in scripture, male and
> female He created them. (*Yebamot* 61b)

According to the Talmud, for *Beit Shammai*, the model for
the sufficiency of two sons was Moses, since he had two
sons. The disciples of Hillel base their opinion on the story
of the first humans (Adam and Eve). The prevailing *halachic*
opinion agrees with *Beit Hillel*.

Although the rabbis considered it meritorious for Jews
to have large families, they looked at birth control more
favorably after a couple had a son and a daughter. However,
rabbis generally encouraged couples not to limit themselves
to two children. This is consistent with Maimonides'
injunction:

> Even if a person has fulfilled the commandment of "be
> fruitful and multiply," he is still enjoined not to refrain
> from fruitfulness and increase as long as he is able, for he
> who adds a life in Israel [is as he who created a world].[8]

Other statements in the Jewish tradition which show the
great importance placed on raising a family include:

* To refrain from having children is to impair the
  divine image. (*Genesis Rabbah* 34:14)
* One who brings no children into the world is like a
  murderer. (*Yevamot* 63b)
* A childless person is like one who is dead. (*Nedarim* 64b)
* Was not the world created only for propagation?
  (*Hagiga* 2b)

In his *Sefer Hamitzvot*, Maimonides comments on the purpose of the first *mitzvah*: "God has commanded us to be fruitful and multiply with the intention of preserving the human species" (Commandment 212).

The *Sefer HaChinuch* (Book of Education) also cites having children as a fundamental positive mitzvah, because without it, none of the other mitzvot could be fulfilled. The Talmud teaches that when one is brought to judgment, one of the first questions asked is, "Did you undertake to fulfill the duty of procreation?" (*Shabbat* 31a). The importance of reproduction in order to populate the earth is also indicated by the prophet Isaiah (45:18): "For thus says the Lord, the Creator of the heavens: He is God, He fashioned the earth and He made it, He has established it; He did not create it to be waste; He has fashioned it so that it will be inhabited."

As indicated above, Jewish teachings that are consistent with limiting population growth are discussed below.

CURRENT ISRAELI POPULATION ISSUES

Unless otherwise indicated, material in this section is from a January 4, 2021 article in *Haaretz*, "Israel's Population Is Growing at a Dizzying Rate. Is It Up for the Challenge?"[9]

Israel's population is growing at a rate of two percent annually, which is four times the average 0.5 percent rate of other developed countries. If that rate continued, Israel's population would double in about 35 years and quadruple in 70 years—clearly an unsustainable situation.

Israel's Central Bureau of Statistics believes that Israel's rate of population growth will slow down, but also projects that Israel's 2021 population of 9.2 million people will reach 15.7 million by 2050—a 70-percent increase over its current population—and up to 20 million by 2065, more than double what it is now.

While almost all the developed countries are increasing at a rate below the replacement level, with the rate for maintaining their population size (2.1 children per woman) and the problems of having an aging and shrinking population, Israel is facing problems that are more typical of developing countries with high birthrates.

Israel is already one of the most densely populated countries in the world, and is projected to become even more so. Israel currently ranks fourth in population density among OECD countries, after only Belgium, South Korea, and the Netherlands. It is projected to be second only to South Korea by 2030, and to become the most crowded of all the almost 200 of the world's nations by 2065, with the exception of Bangladesh. Since much of Israel includes the very sparsely populated Negev desert in the south, it is especially densely populated in some areas in its center and north.

Alon Tal, former head of the Tel Aviv University School of Public Policy and a member of the Knesset while Naftali Bennett was prime minister, is leading efforts to slow Israel's population growth. As discussed previously, he is one of Israel's leading environmentalists, author of *Pollution in a Promised Land*, and founder of both the Israeli Union for Environmental Defense (IUED) and the Arava Institute for Environmental Studies (AIES). While a member of the Knesset, he promoted environmental awareness and actions.

Tal formed one of the few organizations addressing Israel's rapid population growth, *Zafuf* (Crowded): The Israel Forum for Demography, Environment, and Society. The organization's goal is to increase public awareness of overpopulation and to persuade decisionmakers to take actions to avert an impending population crisis.[10]

Tal's book, *The Land Is Full*, discussed how overpopulation is causing many problems, including longer commutes due to increased traffic, crowded classrooms, long waits for medical attention, sharply rising costs for housing due to a residence shortage, and slower legal services.

Tal spoke about his book on many TV shows, and gradually discovered that "people began to understand the issue, and became aware that we need to step up in order to change something."[11] He stressed that "Israel is going to double in size in the next 30 years, and it is not going to be pretty. We have to do whatever we can to preserve some quality of life in this country."[12]

In June 2022, Tal projected that Israel will be the West's most crowded country by 2050, growing to 17.5 million residents.[13] He stated:

> The State of Israel will become the most crowded Western country, with over 800 people per square kilometer. We are familiar with the reality, and know that protecting open spaces isn't enough. I want to know what the Israel Planning Administration and the Construction and Housing Ministry are doing to translate their statements into reality. The open spaces are disappearing at a dizzying rate of 24 square kilometers per year, and the pace will increase along with the growth in population.[14]

Special Committee on Addictions, Drugs and the Challenges Facing Young Israelis Chairman Ram Shefa (Labor) commented:

> We all have to understand that we're in an existential crisis. We are young people who are worried about what will be

here in 30 years. The mass media doesn't understand the severity of the situation. Instead of crowding the cities, people are taking over agricultural green areas. Our job is to cause a change in awareness and to influence legislation, so that the Environmental Protection Ministry can make the changes that it needs to make.[15]

Professor Manuel Trajtenberg, who headed the government committee formed in the wake of the 2011 social justice protests in Israel, argues that Israel is already paying a high price for its tremendous population density. He believes that since Israel will not be able to increase its infrastructure and housing to match the two-percent increase in population, there is an ongoing decrease in the level of services.

Trajtenberg projects that Israel's per capita GDP would double by 2050 if its natural growth would decrease from its current level of two percent a year to the average rate for developed countries of 0.5 percent. He is very critical of the government for encouraging a high birth rate by granting child allowances, while inadequately providing for children once they are born, sending them to overcrowded and lackluster schools, and not providing for free preschool.

In an essay in the *Zafuf* forum, he writes:

> The lack of consistency in government policy in this area is appalling: On the one hand it grants universal child allowances, which are ineffective and convey a message of promoting larger families, while on the other hand it shirks responsibility for providing services for these children and easing the burden on their parents While these young families are having a large number of children, the government refrains or retreats from providing the services that will make this possible without leading these families into a dire financial situation.

Israel's population growth is concentrated mainly in the weaker and less educated socioeconomic groups, the Arabs, with an average of three children per woman, and especially the ultra-Orthodox, with an average of seven children per woman. These two population groups have the lowest income in Israel and the lowest rate of participation in the workforce and are often poorly educated.

Population Issues Related to Jews Today

Many Jews believe that one of the critical challenges today is the issue of Jewish survival in the Diaspora. For many years they have argued that the low Jewish birth rate, along with high rates of intermarriage and assimilation, pose a grave danger to the survival of the Jewish people.

Jews have responded to arguments by advocates of zero population growth in several ways:

*   Since Jews constitute less than one-tenth of a percent of the world's population, the Jewish contribution to world population growth cannot matter significantly.
*   Since six million Jews—one-third of the Jewish people—were killed in the Holocaust, Jews have a special obligation to bring children into the world to replace their numbers.
*   Jewish population in 2022 is still less than it was before the Holocaust
*   Jews have made special contributions to the world, far beyond their very small proportion of the world's population, in areas such as science, the arts, education, business, and politics. Hence increasing

the number of Jewish children might well increase the general level of accomplishment in the world.

* It is also important that Judaism survive because the world badly needs the Jewish messages of peace, justice, and righteousness.

Some advocates of maintaining or increasing the Jewish population have attacked the premises of the zero population growth movement. They argue that rapid population growth, while a very serious concern, is not the prime cause of the world's problems. They are caused more by injustice, greed, and high consumerism. But these critics have often ignored the facts that millions are dying annually due to hunger and its effects, that half the world's people suffer from poverty, illiteracy, malnutrition, and disease, and that the world's ecosystems are being increasingly threatened. They also put great faith in technology as a solution to global problems, not taking into account that many of today's problems have been caused or worsened by the misuse of technology over many years.

It should be pointed out that there are many encouraging signs for future Jewish survival and security:

* Some segments of Judaism, such as the Orthodox and Chassidim, are growing in numbers; they tend to have high fertility rates and seldom intermarriage, assimilate, or defect from Judaism. These groups may be replenishing Jewish population, matching losses among the rest of the Jewish population.
* There has been a tremendous increase in the number of Jewish day schools in the United States.

* The many yeshivas for high school and college students make the U.S. a potential new center of Talmudic learning.
* There are currently more yeshivas and yeshiva students in Israel than in any time or place in Jewish history.
* There are many *ba'alei* and *ba'alot teshuvah* (returnees to traditional Jewish observance) in the U.S., Israel, and other countries. These people generally bring a renewed dedication and involvement to Judaism.
* There has been evidence of renewed Jewish commitment among some Reform Jews, a large number of whom assimilated in previous generations. New Reform prayer books contain more Hebrew and increasingly include such concepts as mitzvot. In recent decades, the Reform movement has affirmed Jewish peoplehood, encouraged *aliyah* (moving to Israel), and asserted that Jews have a stake and responsibility in building the state of Israel. However, recently in the U.S., Reform Jewry is diminishing to the extent that they and the Conservative movement have closed training colleges.
* Jewish programs on college campuses have been developing rapidly. Many Jewish college students are having positive encounters with Judaism, despite increased antisemitism on many college campuses.
* Thousands of scholars are researching *Yiddishkeit* (Jewish tradition). Hebrew literature and Jewish scholarship are flourishing in Israel.

Thus, in many ways, as a counter to the assimilation of many Jews, there has been a marked improvement in the quality and intensity of Jewish life in the last generation.

It should be pointed out that there have been many false prophecies in the past projecting Jewish disappearance. The late Professor Simon Rawidowicz pointed out that Jews are "the ever-dying people," with each generation since early in Jewish history believing that it might be the last one.[16]

It is interesting to note that the patriarchs Abraham and Isaac each had only two children, and in each case one of them (Abraham's son Ishmael and Isaac's son Esau) left the faith.

JEWISH TEACHINGS THAT SUPPORT LIMITING POPULATION GROWTH

Despite Judaism's strong emphasis on procreation discussed above, there are justifications in Jewish sacred writings for aspects of the zero-population growth philosophy. While in Egypt, Joseph had two sons during the seven years of plenty, but no additional children during the following seven years of famine. The renowned Biblical commentator Rashi interprets this to mean that when there is widespread hunger, one should not bring additional children into the world.[17]

According to the Talmud, Noah was commanded to desist from procreation on the ark, since it contained only enough provisions for those who entered the ark.[18] It can be argued that when Adam and later Noah were commanded to "Be fruitful and multiply," the earth was far emptier than it is today. Now that the earth is "overfilled," as indicated by the poverty, malnutrition, and squalor faced by so many of the world's people, as well as the many environmental challenges, perhaps Jewish tradition should come to a new understanding of this commandment.

The Jewish tradition teaches that those who have no biological children can give "birth" in other ways. For example, the Talmud states that if someone teaches Torah to his friend's child, "it is as if he gave birth to him" (Sanhedrin 19b), as it is written: "These are the offspring of Aaron and Moses . . ." (Numbers 3:1). The Talmud points out that the verses that follow list only the sons of Aaron, yet the Torah calls them the "offspring" of both Moses and Aaron. This is because Moses taught them Torah, and through his teaching, according to the Talmud, he became their spiritual parent.

Another example is the following Talmudic statement (*Sanhedrin* 19b): "Whoever teaches his friend's child Torah, it is as if he created him, as it is written [concerning the disciples of Abraham and Sarah]: 'the souls they made in Haran' (Genesis 12:5)." In Haran, Abraham and Sarah served as teachers and guides to the spiritually searching men and women of their generation and brought them to God and the Abrahamic tradition. Rashi, in his commentary on the words, "the souls they made," says that they brought people "under the wings of the *Shechinah*—the Divine Presence."[19] Their teachings gave new life to these searching souls, and from the perspective of the Torah, these are "the souls they made in Haran." Many greats in the Torah world had no children. These include the last Lubavitcher Rebbe, the Chazon Ish, and the great Israeli Bible teacher, Nechama Leibowitz. But they certainly had thousands of spiritual offspring.

There would thus seem to be some rationale for Jews to advocate some version of zero population growth. But we should look more deeply into the issue. Are current crises due primarily to too many people or are there other, more important causes?

Perhaps what the world needs today is not zero population growth (ZPG), but zero population-impact growth (ZPIG).[20] For it is not just the number of people that is important, but how much they produce, consume, and waste. Affluent nations have an impact on the environment extremely disproportionate to their populations. The United States, with about 4.25 percent of the world's population, consumes a far higher percent of resources and energy. It has been estimated that an average American has up to 50 times the impact of an average person in the developing countries, based on resources used and pollution caused. This means that the US 2021 population of 332.3 million people[21] has an impact on ecosystems equal to over 16 billion people in the developing world, or over twice the world's 2021 population of about 7.837 billion people.[22]

Most people connect current widespread hunger and resource scarcities in the world today to overpopulation. Yet, numerous studies have concluded that there is currently enough food in the world to feed all the world's people adequately—the problem lies in waste, injustice, and inequitable distribution.[23]

For example, as discussed previously, in the U.S. about 70 percent of the grain goes to feed the nine billion animals destined for slaughter in the country each year, while over 10 percent of the world's people are chronically malnourished.

Poverty, injustice, and inequality also contribute to continued population growth. The developing countries do not provide unemployment benefits, sick leave, or retirement pensions. Hence, children become the only form of security in periods of unemployment, illness, and old age.

They are also regarded as economic assets, since by the age of seven or eight, children are net contributors to their families—fetching water and firewood from distant places, looking after younger children, cooking and cleaning, thus freeing adults for other jobs. Furthermore, infant death rates are still relatively high in the underdeveloped world, so many children are desired in order to ensure that some will survive to provide security in one's old age.

Because of these conditions, family planning programs by themselves are ineffective in lowering birth rates. It is necessary to improve people's educational opportunities and their economic and social conditions, so that they will not feel the need for more children to provide economic survival and old-age security. With an improved economic outlook, people start to limit their families, as has occurred in the U.S. and in the more affluent countries of Europe. However, unless the world changes its present unjust and inequitable social, political, and economic conditions, the world's population will continue to grow, along with global hunger, poverty, illiteracy, unemployment, and violence.

There need be no inconsistency between Jewish survival and global survival, in the area of population growth. A Jew can have a large family and still help reduce famine and poverty in the world by working for conservation and justice. A family of five that has an impact equal to the consumption and pollution caused by five or ten families in a developing country, such as Bangladesh or Nigeria, does far less harm (in using resources and causing environmental damage) than a family of three with an impact equal to fifty such people.

A Jew who has few or no children can work for Jewish survival by striving to increase Jewish commitment through example, teaching, and writing. Judaism teaches that our good deeds can be our "main offspring." The Torah states: "These are the offspring of Noah: Noah was a righteous man . . ." (Genesis 6:9). The verse begins to introduce the offspring of Noah, and before it mentions the names of his children, it tells us that he was righteous. The classical biblical commentator Rashi states that this teaches us that Noah's most important offspring were his "good deeds," and he cites Midrash *Tanchuma* that states: "The main offspring of righteous people are their good deeds."

There are ways that the Jewish community can work for Jewish survival other than exhorting Jews to have large families:

* Providing programs to make Judaism more challenging and exciting. For example, involvement in some of the issues discussed in this book might entice alienated Jews to return to Judaism and thereby reduce assimilation and intermarriage.
* Improving Jewish education and lowering tuition rates at Jewish schools so that more children can attend.
* Applying "physical fitness for Jewish survival," by teaching Jews the benefits of nutritious meals, proper exercise, and avoidance of tobacco, alcohol, and harmful drugs.

Ways in which Jews can work for better global conditions that would eventually lead to reduced population growth rates are discussed in "Action Ideas" in Appendix A.

Jews can, and should, work for both Jewish and global survival. While reaffirming that every human life is sacred and that every birth brings God's image anew into the world, we should support family planning programs consistent with Jewish teachings and people's cultures and religious beliefs. We should strive to make people aware that rapid population growth is more a *result* of global problems than their root cause.

While helping Jews who wish to have large families, the Jewish community should strive to create a more meaningful, dynamic, and committed Jewish life, and also work for a global society that conserves resources, practices justice, seeks peace, and reduces hunger and poverty, thereby lessening people's need to have so many children. Finally, as we battle for justice and a more equitable sharing of the earth's abundant resources, which are necessary to improve conditions for all the world's people, we should work to make others aware that this is also the most effective way to move the world onto a more sustainable population path.

10

INTERNATIONAL ISSUES

> I saw all the oppressions that are practiced under the sun.
> Behold, the tears of the oppressed, they had no one to
> comfort them! On the side of the oppressors there was
> power. (Ecclesiastes 4:1)

JUDAISM AND INTERNATIONAL CONCERNS

Judaism encompasses both universal and particularistic concerns. Particularistic aspects include observances of the Sabbath and holy days, rules of *kashrut* (kosher eating), and prayer obligations. Jews are taught to be especially concerned about their co-religionists: "All Israel is responsible, one for each other" (*Shavuot* 39a).

We have already discussed many Jewish universal teachings: Every person is created in God's image; every life is sacred and is to be treated with dignity and respect; we should be kind to the stranger, for we were strangers in the land of Egypt; we should show compassion even to enemies.

Additional Jewish universal values include:

* The first covenant God made was with Noah, on behalf of the entire human race, as well as the animal kingdom. (Genesis 9:11)
* Abraham challenged God on behalf of the pagan, evil cities of Sodom and Gomorrah. In an attempt

to save the righteous, he pleaded, "Shall not the Judge of all the earth do justly?" (Genesis 18:25)

* Some of the noblest characters in Scripture are not Jewish. Ruth, a Moabite who later became an Israelite, is presented as a model of an ideal human being, representing the values of kindness, self-sacrificing loyalty, and love. Job, the symbol of the righteous person who maintains his faith in God in spite of unprecedented suffering, is not depicted as a Jew.

* Some of Israel's greatest leaders were descendants of proselytes. This includes King David, who Jewish tradition states will be the ancestor of the future Messiah. The Eighteen Benedictions of the Prayer Book include a special prayer for "righteous proselytes." Hillel, the foremost Talmudic sage of his day, received converts with special eagerness. Some Talmudic sages were converts to Judaism.

* Even of the traditional enemy of the Jewish people, the Edomites, it is said: "You shall not abhor an Edomite, for he is your brother." (Deuteronomy 23:8)

* The prophets stress that Jews have a universal mandate, a charge to improve conditions for all the world's people. Consider, for example, these words of Isaiah:

Thus says God, the Lord . . .
I the Lord have called you in righteousness,
And have taken hold of your hand,
And kept you, and set you for a covenant of the people,
For a light unto the nations;
To open the blind eyes,
To bring the prisoners from the dungeon,

And them that sit in darkness out of the prison house.
(Isaiah 42:6–7)

* Throughout their history, Jews have worked not for individual salvation, but for salvation of the entire world:

On that day, there shall be a highway from Egypt to Assyria. The Assyrians shall join with the Egyptians and Egyptians with Assyrians, and both countries shall serve the Lord. On that day, Israel shall be a third partner with Egypt and Assyria as a blessing on earth; for the Lord of Hosts will bless them, saying, "Blessed be My people, Egypt, My handiwork Assyria, and My very own Israel." (Isaiah 19:23–25)

* Hillel, in his famous formulation, teaches that we must be concerned with other people as well as ourselves: "If I am not for myself, who will be for me? But if I am only for myself, what am I? And if not now, when?" (*Pirkei Avot* 1:14)
* The prophet Malachi (2:10) powerfully expresses Jewish universal concerns:

Have we all not one Father?
Has not one God created us?
Why then do we deal treacherously with one another,
profaning the covenant of our ancestors?

* Amos (9:7) proclaims God's concern for all nations:

"Are you not like the Ethiopians to Me, O people of Israel?" says the Lord.
"Did I not bring up Israel from the land of Egypt, and the Philistines from Caphtor; and the Syrians from Kir?"

* Jeremiah was appointed as "a prophet to the nations" (Jeremiah 1:5). God tells him: "See, I have set you this day over nations and over kingdoms, to pluck up and to break down, to destroy and to overthrow, to build and to plant." (Jeremiah 1:10)
* The Book of Jonah depicts God's concern for the non-Jewish inhabitants of the city of Nineveh, the very same people who later go to war against Israel. Jonah, a Jew, is sent to teach the people of Nineveh to repent and serve God, and is taught, in turn, that God cares for all people, as well as animals.
* The Talmud states: "The pious of all nations shall have a place in the world to come."[1]
* During the festival of Sukkot in the days of the Jerusalem Temple, 70 animal sacrifices were made for the "70 nations" (a term that then represented all sectors of humanity).

The *sukkah* (temporary harvest booth inhabited by Jews during Sukkot) must possess enough of an opening through the top so that the person inside can see the stars and the universe beyond, perhaps to remind us that there are worlds and nations beyond our own, which always deserve consideration.

After a *bracha* (blessing) is recited, the *lulav* (palm branch) that is held during Sukkot, is waved to the north, south, east, and west, and then up and down, to signify that God's sovereignty is universal in all directions. Hence, when we pray for salvation and help, we should have in mind these blessings not only for ourselves, but also for humanity.

Rabbi Haninah, a third-century sage, stated that salvation for the world would come only when the nations accepted the lesson of the *sukkah* and the *lulav*—that no nation can experience prosperity and happiness unless there is harmony among all nations.[2]

The sages declare that any person can accept the Torah:

> The Torah was given in public, openly, in a free place. For had the Torah been given in the land of Israel, the Israelites could have said to the nations of the world: "You have no share in it," but now that it has been given in the wilderness, publicly and openly, in a place that is free for all, everyone willing to accept it may come and accept it. (*Mechilta D'Rabbi Ishmael*)

* A Chassidic wisdom story expresses the universal spirit of Judaism:

> "Why," a student asked, "is the stork called in Hebrew *Chassidah*, which means the loving one?"
> "Because," the rabbi answered, "he gives so much love to his wife and offspring."
> "Then why," asked the student, "if he gives so much love to his mate and his young, is the stork considered *trayfe* (forbidden as food) rather than kosher?"
> "He is considered *trayfe*," the rabbi answered, "because he gives love *only* to his own."[3]

* Rabbi Nachman of Breslov asserted:

> [Our sages taught that] every person must say, "The whole world was created for my sake" (*Sanhedrin* 37a). Therefore, since the whole world was created for my sake, I must always be concerned with improving the world, fulfilling the needs of humanity, and praying for its benefit.[4]

The concept of Jews as a "chosen people" has often been misinterpreted as an expression of exclusivity. But the prophets remind the people that being chosen does not mean divine favoritism, nor does it guarantee immunity from punishment; on the contrary, being "chosen" means being held to a higher standard and thus being more intensely exposed to God's judgment and chastisement:

> Hear this word that the Lord has spoken against you, O people of Israel, against the whole family whom I brought up out of the land of Egypt. You only have I known of all the families of the earth. Therefore, I will punish you for all your iniquities. (Amos 3:1, 2)

> In the end of days it shall come to pass, that the mountain of the Lord's house shall be established on the top of the mountains, and it shall be exalted above the hills. Peoples shall flow unto it, and many nations shall come and say, "Come, let us go up to the mountain of the Lord, To the house of the God of Jacob; So that He may teach us of His ways, and we will walk in His paths." For the Torah shall go forth from Zion, and the word of the Lord from Jerusalem. And He shall judge among many peoples, and rebuke strong nations afar off; they shall beat their swords into plowshares and their spears into pruning hooks; Nation shall not lift up sword against nation; neither shall they learn war anymore. They shall sit every man under his vine and under his fig tree; and none shall make them afraid; for the mouth of the Lord of hosts has spoken it. For all the peoples will walk every one in the name of his god; we will walk in the name of the Lord our God forever. (Micah 4:1–5)

For global harmony, "a law (Torah) must go forth from Zion." Such a "law" has been proclaimed, but the nations have refused to acknowledge it. It is a law that states that there is one Creator of the entire world, that every person, created in God's image, is of infinite worth and should be able to share in the bounties provided by God's earth, and that people and nations must seek and pursue peace, pursue justice, and love others, since they are like themselves. If people and nations took this law from Zion seriously, there would be increased harmony, peace, and sufficient resources for all the world's people.

Micah's words provide a moral blueprint for the world, a covenant rooted in truth and justice that supports the structure of peace. This is explicitly spelled out by a Talmudic teaching:

> Upon three things the world rests, upon justice, upon truth, and upon peace. And the three are one, for when justice is practiced, truth prevails, and peace is established. (*Ta'anit* 4:2; *Megilla* 3:5)

While the prophets believed that individual nations would continue to exist, they were true internationalists who urged, foresaw, and worked towards the creation of proper relations among nations, based on peace, justice, and truth. Their vision represented a farsighted view of national interests, in which love of one's country and loyalty to humanity represent two concentric circles.[5] In ways consistent with Jewish tradition and values, Jews must be in the forefront of those working for greater international justice, so that the needs of all the world's people may be met and so that nations will finally beat their swords into plowshares and their spears into pruning hooks, and so that each person will be able to sit unafraid, "under his vine and fig tree." (Micah 4:4)

Conditions for the World's People Today

When one surveys the conditions for most of the world's people today, one is struck by the extent to which Jewish teachings about justice, compassion, and sharing have been neglected. Unless otherwise indicated, the following facts come from the World Vision's 2021 report, "Global Poverty: Facts, FAQs, and How to Help."[6] They demonstrate the tremendous extent of poverty in today's world, even as the rich are getting richer and many are gaining super wealth:

* According to the World Bank, about 9.2 percent (689 million) of the world's population live in extreme poverty, living on less than $1.90 a day.
* The global COVID-19 pandemic reversed recent years of progress in reducing worldwide poverty, with 97 million people reaching extremely poverty in 2020.
* Over 14,200 children under age five are dying annually from the three interrelated scourges of poverty, disease, and hunger.
* Two-thirds of the world's poor are children and youth. In most areas, more females than males live in poverty.
* Increasingly, extreme poverty is concentrated in sub-Saharan Africa, with about 40 percent of its people living on less than $1.90 a day.
* When considering not just income, but also deprivation in living standards, education, and health, 1.3 billion people, including about 640 million children, in 107 developing countries were "multidimensionally poor" in 2020, according to

the UN Development Program. Almost 85 percent of these multidimensionally poor live in South Asia and sub-Saharan Africa. Multidimensional poverty means that even if a person's income is above the poverty line, there is a lack of electricity, clean drinking water, adequate education, and proper toilet facilities.

The World Vision's 2021 report also considers the negative effects of poverty. These include:

* A poor quality of life, a life of struggle and deprivation.
* Lack of access to quality education because impoverished families need their children to work, parents can't afford school fees, or there aren't nearby quality schools. These factors often lead to a generational cycle of poverty, since without a quality education children grow up being unable to provide for their own children.
* Inadequate medical care, often because the family can't afford a doctor or medical treatment.
* No electricity, or electricity for only part of the day.
* Inadequate shelter.
* Often little to no food on the table, or unhealthy food, so that some important nutrients are not sufficiently obtained. This can result in stunting and wasting that permanently impact their development. This is another factor that can continue the cycle of poverty.
* Inadequate access to clean water and sanitation.
* The spread of preventable diseases and the unnecessary death of children.

World Vision's 2021 report on global income disparities[7] reveals many sharp differences between the wealthy and the poor, and how they have been widened due to the COVID-19 pandemic:

* While the richest 10 percent of the global population currently earns 52 percent of the world's income, the poorest half earns only 8 percent.
* While a person in the top 10 percent earns an average of $122,100, a person in the bottom half will earn only $3,920.
* Wealth gaps are even wider. While the wealthiest 10 percent of the world's population owns 76 percent of all wealth, the poorest half owns just 2 percent.

In addition to the great income disparities between nations, there are also great disparities within nations, including the U.S. Vermont Senator Bernie Sanders has done a lot in his unsuccessful presidential campaigns and beyond. While not necessarily agreeing with all of Sanders' views, I think his economic analysis has much merit and should be considered. Among the challenging facts he brings out are:[8]

* Half of Americans are living paycheck to paycheck, with many very concerned about their ability to feed their family.
* While most Americans have adequate housing, 500,000 Americans are homeless, and additional millions are concerned about being evicted.
* Over ninety million Americans have no, or inadequate, health insurance.

* An entire generation of young people carry extremely high student debt, meaning that their standard of living will likely be lower than that of their parents.
* Wealthy Americans have a life expectancy about 15 years longer than low-income Americans.
* The wealthiest 1 percent of Americans now owns more wealth than the bottom 92 percent.
* The 50 wealthiest Americans own more wealth than the bottom half of American society— about 165 million people.
* While the Coronavirus pandemic caused millions of Americans to lose their jobs and incomes, 650 billionaires saw their wealth increase by $1.3 trillion in one year.
* The gap between the richest Americans and everyone else has been steadily increasing, with a massive transfer of wealth from the middle class and working families to the very wealthiest people. While the wealthiest 1 percent of Americans owned about 7 percent of the nation's wealth in 1978, it had increased to almost 20 percent in 2019.
* Incredibly, the two wealthiest Americans, Elon Musk and Jeff Bezos, now own more wealth than the bottom 40 percent of Americans combined.

Senator Sanders not only spells out the huge income gaps, but he provides a detailed plan of steps to reduce them:[9]

* The minimum wage should be raised from the current "starvation wage" of $7.25 an hour to a living wage of at least $15 an hour, helping lift many people out of poverty.

* Steps should be taken to make it easier for workers to join unions, enabling them to collectively bargain for better wages and working conditions.
* Millions of well-paying jobs should be created by rebuilding our crumbling infrastructure—our roads, dams, bridges, sewers, wastewater plants, culverts, schools, and affordable housing.
* Additional millions of well-paying jobs can be created in combatting climate change, by fundamentally transforming our energy system away from fossil fuels towards renewable energy and energy efficiency.
* As in every other major country, healthcare should be available to all Americans as a human right. Passing a Medicare for All program "would end the absurdity of us paying twice as much per capita for healthcare as do the people of other countries," while tens of millions of Americans lack adequate health insurance.
* Public colleges and universities should become tuition-free, so that all American young people, regardless of income, will have the right to high-quality education—including college.
* Legislation should be passed to make the wealthiest Americans and most profitable American corporations start paying their fair share of taxes.

In summary, it is essential that the universal Jewish values discussed above be applied to help reduce income gaps, create better conditions for the world's people, and create a more just, peaceful, compassionate, and environmentally sustainable world.

Cooperative Concepts in Jewish
History and Tradition

To eliminate or at least sharply reduce the economic inequalities discussed above, it is important that there be a greater emphasis on cooperation and sharing, consistent with the Jewish teachings in this section.

When the Jews wandered in the wilderness after the Exodus from Egypt and in the early years after settling in the land of Israel, the people were strongly egalitarian; there was no hierarchy of kings or rulers. Decisions were reached democratically by the assemblage of one man from each family or tribe. Unfortunately, women had no societal influence then. In addition, ownership of the wealth-producing property was essentially communal. The rights to pasture lands and water were vested in the tribe as a unit, and private property was minimal. Later, in the days of the prophet Samuel, when the people clamored for a king in order to emulate the surrounding nations, God told Samuel to warn the people about what would happen in the wake of such centralization of wealth and power:

> This will be the practice of the king who will rule over you: He will take your sons and appoint them as his charioteers and horsemen, and they will have to run before his chariot . . . or they will have to plow his fields and make his weapons and equipment for his chariots. He will take your daughters as perfumers and bakers; he will seize your choice fields, vineyards and olive groves and give them to his courtiers. . . . He will take a tenth part of your flocks and you will become his slaves. The day will come when you will cry out because of the king whom you yourselves have chosen; and the Lord will not answer you on that day. (I Samuel 8:11–18)

If we substitute "international corporations" for "kings," we can see a similar exploitation today. We see CEOs (the corporate kings) making huge salaries and garnering millions of dollars in bonuses each year, while at the same time they may lay off workers in the name of making even greater profits. The disparity between a CEO's income and the average worker's salary is far greater than ever before. Is this really what God wants?

Division of property was initially part of the Torah's plan to ensure social equality. Originally, the land was distributed among the Israelite tribes, using the principle that "to the more [larger tribe] you shall give the greater inheritance, and to the fewer [smaller tribe] you shall give the lesser inheritance." (Numbers 26:54) This first distribution of land was on the basis of social need, not individual power or privilege.

To avoid conditions whereby, due to bad fortune, a family might be compelled to sell or mortgage its land and thereby suffer for generations, a complete redistribution of land every fifty years was provided, for in the Jubilee law: "In the year of the Jubilee, you shall return every man unto his possession" (Leviticus 25:13). This law protecting property rights in ancient Israel was designed to ensure social equality. Therefore, the Torah's concept of property rights was very different from that of modern capitalism, which tends to lead to great concentrations of wealth perpetuated generation after generation, while poverty also persists from one generation to another.

A literal Jubilee Year would be impossible to carry out today, and everyone's property cannot be confiscated and redistributed every fifty years. But we can still learn the basic principle behind this amazing law: it is not socially responsible to allow vast amounts of wealth to accumulate in the hands of the few, while allowing others to suffer in abject poverty for generations.

The underlying message of the Jubilee Year, as with other "commandments dependent on the land," such as the laws related to leaving the gleanings of the harvest and the corners of the field for the poor, is the principle that "the Earth is the Lord's" (Psalm 24:1). In proclaiming the Jubilee Year, the Torah provides the logic behind this periodic revolution in property rights: "For the land is mine; for you are strangers and settlers with me" (Leviticus 25:23).

In the Torah, a person's rights to property are not those of an outright owner, but rather of a steward who is a co-partner with God in preserving and protecting the earth and seeing that its resources are used for the benefit of everyone. As Rabbi Eleazer of Bertothas says, "Give unto God of what is God's, since you and what you have are God's" (*Pirkei Avot* 3:8). King David expresses a similar idea: "For all things come of You [God] and out of Your own have we given You" (1 Chronicles 29:14).

The Sabbatical Year included the cancellation of financial debts in order to both limit inequality and excessive accumulation of capital. The Torah's prohibition on taking interest for loans served the same goal. Both of these arrangements were later bypassed for pragmatic reasons, but the basic idea behind them is that property should be used for one's own (simple) living and for the common good, not for the enormous accumulation of wealth.

The Jewish view that private property rights are not absolute but are subjected to proper regulation and civic authority and must be guided by the common good, and that property should not be wasted or exploited in damaging ways, but rather used sustainably, is exemplified by the many *mitzvot* obliging Jewish farmers to share with the poor:

* A corner of the field (*Pe'ah*) had to be left unharnessed; it was the property of the poor. (Leviticus 19; 9–10)

* If less than three ears of corn were dropped during the harvest (*Leket*), they were not to be gleaned, but were to be left for the poor. (Leviticus 19: 9–10)

* A sheaf forgotten by the farmer (*Shik'khah*) could not be retrieved but had to be left for the poor. (Deuteronomy 24: 19–21)

* Every third year, a part of the tithe of the harvest (*Ma'aser Ani*) had to be set aside for the poor. (Deuteronomy 14:28)

* Prior to every Purim, M*atanot l'Evyonim,* a special donation for the poor is collected.

* Before Passover, there are large campaigns for *Ma'ot Chittim*, donations to enable poor people to purchase matzah, wine, and other Passover needs.

These principles not only help the poor, they also help the landowner by teaching him to "let go" and say "*dayenu*" (enough), "I did not create this bounty: it ultimately belongs to God." The same is true of any business, not just agriculture.

Shabbat might be the first labor law, mandating a day of rest for everyone. And so are the holidays that require Jews not to work. This was revolutionary at the time of the Torah, and is not trivial today, when many workplaces require employees to be available 24/7, with technology making this possible anywhere and anytime. The long and difficult campaign for an eight-hour workday, which cost some people's lives, is becoming relevant again where in some areas (from agriculture to high-tech and law) people work from the early morning to late at night. The biblical idea that all people, and nonhuman animals, deserve a day of rest each week, and days for worship and communal celebrations, is in some cases under attack in our society.

Another important point to consider is the open hostility of the Jewish tradition toward the arrogantly rich and their "conspicuous consumption," when the desired state is modest, limited, self-restrained living. The prophet Amos rails against such extravagance at the expense of others:

> Woe to those who are at ease in Zion,
> And to those who feel secure
>   on the mountains of Samaria . . .
> Woe to those who lie upon beds of ivory,
> And stretch themselves upon their couches,
> And eat lambs from the flock,
> And calves from the midst of the stall;
> Who sing idle songs to the sound
>   of the harp . . .
> Who drink wine in bowls,
> And anoint themselves in the finest oils,
> But are not grieved on the ruin of Joseph! (Amos 6:4–6)

The last line tells us that it is not the enjoyment of good food and wine per se that the prophet denounces; it is because "those who are at ease in Zion" were "not grieved at the ruin of [the tribes of] Joseph" that had been conquered and decimated by the invading Assyrians. Amos felt it was a terrible sin to indulge in such luxuries while one's fellow Jews had been killed or exiled, lacking the barest necessities of life. As the modern saying goes, we should "live simply that others can simply live."

An element of the Ten Commandments, "You shall not steal," along with the subsequent prohibition of coveting, is a reminder not to make material gain the purpose of our lives. Even when we do not actually steal, we are in a way stealing from the poor when we are overindulgent and wasteful, or when we exploit the resources of the developing countries in order to increase our own country's power and wealth, or when we stand idly by during the starvation and degradation of others when we could do something to help.

Since, as the Torah clearly states, everything belongs to God, the Jewish principle that the rich are obligated to assist the poor, preferably by helping them find work or providing them with a living wage, naturally derives from God's ownership of all. The Hebrew word *tzedakah* means both charity and justice. Why? Because Judaism considers charity to be an act of justice. The Torah teaches that people in need have a right to dignity and succor, to food, clothing, and shelter, with a claim on those who are more fortunate. According to Jewish law, it is unjust for Jews to not give charity to those in need. This can be contrasted with those politicians in the secular world who want to cut taxes for the rich and maintain loopholes for corporations, while making draconian cuts in programs for food, shelter, and medical care for those in need. This goes against Jewish principles.

In addition to laws about charity, the Torah also provides instruction in honest business practices:

> You shall do no wrong in judgment, in measures of length, of weight, or in quantity. Just balances, just weights, a just *ephah* [the standard dry measure] and

a just *hin* [a measure for liquids], shall you have. I am
the Lord your God, who brought you out of the land of
Egypt. (Leviticus 19:35, 36)

The rabbis of the Talmud gave concrete expression to the
many Torah and prophetic teachings regarding justice and
righteousness. They indicate in detail what is proper when
conducting business. Rabbinic literature translates prophetic
ideals into specific laws for the marketplace concerning
duties of employers to employees and of workers to their
employers, as well as suppliers to customers: fair prices; the
avoidance of false weights and measures; proper business
contracts; and fair methods of competition. For example, in
order to preserve the dignity and provide for the basic needs
of poor workers, wages for day laborers must be given on the
day that work is done, not delayed (Deuteronomy 24:10–15).
This principle applies to some extent even today, where field
workers harvesting produce often live hand-to-mouth and
cannot wait for weeks to be paid.

The sages were also very harsh towards attempts to
take away a person's livelihood by unfair competition
(*Sanhedrin* 81a). Their overall view of business ethics can be
summarized by the verses: "And you shall do that which
is right and good in the sight of the Lord" (Deuteronomy
6:18), and "better is a little with righteousness than great
revenues with injustice." (Proverbs 16:8)

The Talmudic sages were also very strict about their
personal ethical standards, as the following story illustrates:

Reb Saphra had wine to sell. A certain customer came
in to buy wine at a time when Reb Saphra was saying
the *Shema* prayer [which cannot be interrupted by
conversation]. The customer said, "Will you sell me

175

the wine for such and such an amount?" When Reb
Saphra did not respond, the customer thought he was
not satisfied with the price and raised his bid. When Reb
Saphra had finished his prayer, he said, "I decided in
my heart to sell the wine to you at the first price you
mentioned; therefore, I cannot accept your higher bid."
(*Sheil'tot, Parshat Vayechi*)

Consistent with these principles, the Talmud, though firmly
recognizing personal property rights, did not consider such
rights to be unlimited. They often restricted them, even
eliminating them in some instances for the common good.
For example, the *halachah* (Jewish law) prohibits profit
related to "fraudulent misrepresentation" (*Baba Metzia* 49b).
It opposes monopolization of basic necessities and bans
hoarding for the purpose of increasing prices (*Baba Batra*
90b). The Talmud prohibits the export of articles of food to
foreign countries if this would increase the domestic price of
these articles (*Baba Batra* 90b). For the common good, the
rabbis even justify the confiscation of private property in
some cases. (*Yebamot* 89b; *Gittin* 36b)

A good example of this is a case in the Talmud
concerning a well of water essential to people in a village.
The rabbis concluded that the title to the well should not
be maintained in trust by any one individual or small
group, but by the entire community, so as to be open and
accessible to all without cost.[10] Judaism points toward
communal possession and control of those social enterprises
that are essential to life. The earth's vast resources should
be developed for the welfare of every person, not for the
enrichment of the few.

Toward a Global Marshall Plan to Reduce Societal Ills and Injustice

Creative new ideas are needed to improve conditions for the world's many disadvantaged people and to reduce terrorism. One approach is that the United States, preferably with other developed nations, including Israel, should lead a global effort to greatly reduce poverty, hunger, illiteracy, illness, pollution, and climate change. One such approach is to put in place a Global Marshall Plan, a proposal of Rabbi Michael Lerner, along with *Tikkun* magazine, which he edits, and the interfaith Network of Spiritual Progressives (NSP), which he directs. Putting this plan into practice would improve the image of the United States and other countries involved and would reduce the potential for terrorism and war.

The global Marshall Plan seeks a new strategy for the U.S., one based on "generosity, not domination in its foreign policy." To help end centuries of war and violence and attempts to dominate others, the Network of Spiritual Progressives is calling for "a fundamentally new approach that emphasizes that generosity and genuine caring for others can be a much more effective and morally coherent approach to human security, peace, and development." The NSP is calling for a new paradigm, a "Strategy of Generosity," that aims to "reestablish trust and hope among the peoples of the world" in order to reduce world poverty and save the global environment from climate change and the many additional current environmental threats. They want to shift a foreign policy based on self-interest to one that considers: "What best serves all the people on this planet and best serves the survival of the planet itself?"[11]

The NSP argues that, because of the interconnectedness of all people on the planet, "the best interests of America and the best interests of our children and grandchildren are best served by working for the best interests of everyone else, and the best interests of the planet . . . ," rather than to frame things in terms of narrow self-interest.[12] They believe that the plan will only work if it is supported for the right reasons, with the "Strategy of Generosity" at the core, and global common good as the primary goal.

The Global Marshall Plan is patterned after the massive project suggested by General George Marshall after World War II to provide aid to Western European countries, with the goal of enhancing the economies of those countries, partially in order to prevent the rise of communist power in that part of the world. This initiative led to similar major relief efforts providing aid to more recently impoverished areas. The NSP initiative builds on these previous efforts and aims to greatly expand them in trying to obtain a healthier, safer, more just, and environmentally sustainable world.

Essentials of the plan developed by the Network of Spiritual Progressives include:

* "Providing enough funding to significantly reduce global poverty, homelessness, hunger, inadequate education and inadequate health care, plus restore the global environment." It is estimated that this would require the world's developed nations to dedicate 1–2% of their Gross Domestic Product (GDP) toward funding this goal every year for the next twenty years. The NSP believes that the United States must play a leading role in this initiative.

* Creating an unbiased, international nongovernmental mechanism for receiving and properly distributing the funds.
* Projects funded by the Plan would be "environmentally sensitive, respectful of native cultures, safeguarded against corruption, protected from manipulation to serve corporate profit motives or the interests of elites, and empowering of the people in each region."
* The funding agency or mechanism "should be governed by a board of ethicists, religious leaders, poets, writers, social theorists, philosophers, economists, scientists, and social change activists all of whom have demonstrated that they give higher priority to the well-being of others than to the well-being of corporations or wealthy elites."[13]

Creating a Global Marshall Plan may seem utopian, but in many ways today we have a choice, as indicated in the title of a book by Buckminster Fuller, *Utopia or Oblivion*. We can continue on the present path, based on greed, nationalism, domination, hatred, and bigotry, with increasingly worsening economic, environmental, and social conditions, which could lead to violence, or we can strive for a more generous, tolerant, just, peaceful, humane, and environmentally sustainable world. The choice between a far better future and a far worse future is in our hands, and the stakes are very great, so we must not fail.

Even if a full global Marshall plan is not produced, an increase in US economic and humanitarian aid to other countries might be a far better way to improve security than increased expenditures on arms.

11

PEACE

"Not by might, not by power, but by my spirit," says the Lord of Hosts. (Zechariah 4:6)

Judaism involves a special obligation to strive for peace. The *Midrash* states that there are many mitzvot (commandments) that require a certain time and place for their observance, but with regard to the mandate to "seek peace and pursue it" (Psalms 34:15), we are to seek it in our own place and pursue it everywhere else (*Leviticus Rabbah* 9:9). The famous Talmudic sage, Hillel, states that we should "be of the disciples of Aaron, loving peace and pursuing peace." (*Pirkei Avot* 1:12)

Concerning the special duty of Jews to work for peace, the sage's comment: "The Holy one blessed be He said: 'The whole Torah is peace. And to whom do I give it? To the nation that loves peace!'" (*Yalkut Shimoni, Yithro*)

The *Midrash* employs lavish words in praise of peace:

Great is peace, for God's name is peace. . . . Great is peace, for it encompasses all blessings. . . . Great is peace, for even in times of war, peace must be sought. . . . Great is peace for when the Messiah comes, he will commence with peace, as it is said, "How beautiful upon the mountains are the feet of the messenger of good tidings, who announces peace" (Isaiah 52:7; *Leviticus Rabbah* 9:9). Great is peace, for with peace the Holy One, blessed be He, will announce the Redemption of Israel, and with peace He will console Jerusalem (*Deuteronomy Rabbah* 5:15). See how beloved is peace; when the Holy One, blessed be He, wished to bless Israel, He could not find a vessel great enough to contain their blessings, except for peace. (Ibid.)

The whole Torah was given for the sake of peace, and it is said, "all her paths are peace." (Proverbs 3:17; *Gittin* 59b)

It is significant that many of the most important Jewish prayers conclude with a supplication for peace. These include the *Amidah* (silent prayer, also known as the *Shmoneh Esrei*, which is recited three times daily), the *Kaddish*, the *Birkat Hamazon* (Grace After Meals), and the Priestly Blessing.

In spite of Judaism's adamant opposition to idolatry, peace is so important that the rabbis taught:

Great is peace, for even if the Jews were to practice idolatry, and peace prevailed among them at the same time, God would say, "I cannot punish them because peace prevails among them." (*Genesis Rabbah* 38:6)

Judaism emphasizes the pursuit of justice and harmonious relations between nations to reduce violence and the prospects for war. The Prophet Isaiah proclaims:

And the work of righteousness shall be peace; and the effect of righteousness quietness and confidence forever. (Isaiah 32:17)

Yet there are many sections in the Hebrew Scriptures that justify war under certain conditions and discuss rules for combat. War was universally accepted (and often still is) as inevitable, often as a last resort, and therefore a legitimate foreign policy instrument.

God commanded the Israelites to conquer the land of Canaan through warfare and to destroy or evict the inhabitants. After the Exodus from Egypt, God is praised as a "Man of War" (Exodus 15:3). The Israelites are told: "For the Lord, your God, is He Who goes with you, to fight against your enemies, to save you" (Deuteronomy 20:4). The books of Judges, Samuel, and Kings report many armed battles, some involving widespread destruction.

However, the general tone of Jewish tradition shudders at war and its instruments. God is often pictured as ultimately despising war and intending its elimination: "And I will break the bow and the sword and the battle out of the land, and will make them to lie down safely" (Hosea 2:20); "God makes wars to cease unto the end of the earth; He breaks the bow, and cuts the spear in sunder; He burns the chariot in the fire" (Psalms 46:10).

The Talmudic sages forbade the use of instruments of war for ornamentation or for anything connected with sacred services. Concerning the Sabbath laws, the Mishnah states:

> [On the Sabbath] a man may not go out with a sword, a bow, a shield, a club, or a spear; and if he went out [with such as these] he is liable to a sin offering. Rabbi Eliezer says, "They are merely decorations." But the sages say, "They are nothing but shameful." (*Shabbat* 6:4)

The Talmud regards the sword as the opposite of the Torah: "If the sword is here, there cannot be the book; if the book is here, there cannot be the sword" (*Avoda Zarah* 17b). To the Talmud, the true hero is not the person with many conquests:

> One who conquers his impulses, it is as if he conquered a city of heroes. . . . For the true heroes are the masters of Torah, as it is said, "mighty in power are those who obey God's Word." (*Avot de Rabbi Nathan* 51:27)

The Talmudic sages taught: "Who is mighty? One who controls his passions" (*Pirkei Avot* 4:1), as it is said: "Better is the long-suffering than the mighty." (Proverbs 16:32)

The Torah forbids the use of metal tools in the construction of the Holy Altar. "And if you make Me an altar of stone, you shall not build it of hewn stones; for it you lift up your sword upon it, you have profaned it" (Exodus 20:22). Consistent with their abhorrence of war, the sages comment on this verse as follows:

> Iron shortens life, while the altar prolongs it. The sword, or weapons of iron, is the symbol of strife, while the altar is the symbol of reconciliation and peace between God and man, and between man and his fellow. (*Sifra Kedoshim* 11:8)

Because of his many violent battles, King David was denied the opportunity to build the Temple. He was told:

> You have shed blood abundantly, and you have made great wars. You shall not build a house unto My name, because you have shed much blood upon the earth in My sight. Behold, a son shall be born to you who shall be a man of peace; and I will give him rest from all his enemies round about, for his name shall be Solomon (peaceful), and I shall give peace and quiet to Israel in his days. He shall build a house for My name. (I Chronicles 22:8–9)

Despite the great yearning throughout the Jewish tradition for peace, Jews have had to fight wars throughout history, up to our own day. The prophets realized the horrible results of battle. The following words of Jeremiah (4:19–27), written over 2,000 years ago concerning the conquest and despoiling of Jerusalem, could have been written about the aftermath of a modern war:

> My innards, my innards! I writhe in pain!
> The chambers of my heart!
> My heart moans within me!
> I cannot hold my peace!
> Because you have heard, O my soul,
> the sound of the horn,
> The alarm of war.
> Destruction follows upon destruction;
> For the whole land is spoiled . . .
> I beheld the earth,
> And, lo, it was waste and void;
> And the heavens, and they had no light.
> I beheld the mountains, and lo, they trembled.
> And all the hills moved to and fro.
> I beheld, and, lo, there was no man,
> And all birds of the heavens were fled.
> I beheld, and, lo, the fruitful field was a wilderness,
> And all the cities thereof were broken down
> At the presence of the Lord,
> And before His fierce anger . . .
> For thus says the Lord:
> "The whole land shall be desolate."

The Jewish tradition does not mandate pacifism, nor peace at any price, although some Jews became pacifists based on Jewish values. The Israelites frequently went forth to battle, and not always in defensive wars. But they always held to the ideal of universal peace and yearned for the day when there would be no more bloodshed or violence, and when the instruments of war would be converted into tools of production:

And they shall beat their swords into plowshares,
And their spears into pruning hooks;
Nation shall not lift up sword against nation,
Neither shall they learn war any more.
But they shall sit every man under his vine and
under his fig tree;
And none shall make them afraid;
For the mouth of the Lord of hosts has spoken. (Isaiah
2:4; Micah 4:3–4)

However, throughout most of history, the world's people have too often beaten their plowshares into swords and their pruning hooks into spears.

CAUSES OF WAR

Judaism teaches that violence and war result directly from injustice: "The sword comes into the world because of justice delayed, because of justice perverted, and because of those who render wrong decisions." (*Pirkei Avot* 5:11)

The Hebrew word for war, *milchama*, is derived from the word *locham*, which means both "to feed" as well as "to wage war." The Hebrew word for bread, *lechem*, comes from the same root. This has led the Sages to point out that lack of bread and the search for sufficient food make people more inclined to wage war.[1] Since the seeds of war are often found in the inability of a nation to provide adequate food for its people, failing to reduce hunger throughout the world, and feeding tremendous amounts of grains to animals destined for slaughter instead of feeding them directly to starving people, can create conditions leading to war.

Former Oregon Senator Mark Hatfield has stated:

> Hunger and famine will do more to destabilize this world; it's more explosive than all atomic weaponry possessed by the big powers. Desperate people do desperate things. . . . Nuclear fission is now in the hands of even the developing countries in many of which hunger and famine are most serious.[2]

Richard J. Barnet, former director of the Washington-based Institute for Policy Studies and author of *The Lean Years*, an analysis of resource scarcities, believes that the anger and despair of hungry people can lead to violence and spreading conflicts.[3] "Just as scarcity of food can lead to war, so can scarcity of sources of energy. A prime current threat to peace is the perceived need for affluent countries to obtain sufficient oil to keep their economies running smoothly."

The Persian Gulf area, where much of the world's oil is produced, has been the site of much instability and competition, resulting in the Gulf War in 1990.

REDUCING PROSPECTS FOR WAR

Judaism emphasizes that justice and harmonious relations among nations reduce prospects for violence and war. The prophet Isaiah stated: "And the work of righteousness shall be peace; and the effect of righteousness, quietness and confidence forever" (Isaiah 32:17). The Psalmist observed: "When loving-kindness and truth have met together, then righteousness and peace have kissed each other." (Psalms 85:11)

The Talmudic rabbis stress that justice is a precondition for peace: "The world rests on three things: on justice, on truth, and on peace. And all three are one, for where there is justice, there is also truth, and there is peace." (*Ta'anit* 4:2; *Megilla* 3:5)

According to the Jewish tradition, progress toward more just conditions, less waste, and more equitable sharing of resources will reduce the chances of war and violence. This should encourage those working to change economic and production systems that result in waste and exploitation and keep the majority of the world's people in poverty.

JEWISH TEACHINGS ON THE TREATMENT OF ENEMIES

Judaism has very powerful statements about how one should regard and treat one's enemies:

> Rejoice not when your enemy falls,
> And let not your heart be glad when he stumbles. (Proverbs 24:17)

> If your enemy is hungry, give him bread to eat,
> And if he is thirsty, give him water to drink. (Proverbs 25:21)

God feels compassion even for the enemies of the Jewish people:

> In the hour when the Israelites crossed the Red Sea [while the waters drowned the Egyptians], the ministering angels wanted to sing a song of praise before God. But He said to them: "My handiwork is drowning in the sea, and you want to sing a song before Me!" (Sanhedrin 29b)

On *Pesach* (Passover), which commemorates the Exodus from Egypt, Jews temper their celebration of our freedom because Egyptians died during the Israelites' liberation. This is reflected in two Passover observances:

* At the Seder table, one drop of wine is spilled at the recitation of each of the ten plagues, to reduce our joy (since wine symbolizes joy).

* The complete *Hallel*, hymns of praise to God (taken from Psalms 113–118), is recited on only the first two days of Passover. On the rest of the holiday, only part of *Hallel* is said (because the crossing of the sea and drowning of the Egyptians took place on the last days). By contrast, on the harvest festival of Sukkot, the entire *Hallel* is recited during the entire week, because everyone, Jew and Gentile alike, can rejoice in the produce of the land.

Judaism does not believe that another person or nation need be considered a permanent enemy. Under the right conditions, positive changes can occur: "Who is the mightiest of heroes? He who makes his enemy into his friend."[4] Judaism believes that forbearance to adversaries can lead to understanding and eventually to reconciliation. Two examples: "Say not, I will pay back evil" (Proverbs 20:22); and "When a man's ways please the Lord, he makes even his enemies to be at peace with him." (Proverbs 16:7)

The following story epitomizes the Jewish stress on converting an enemy into a friend. Samuel ibn Naghrillah (also known as Shmuel ha-Nagid), an eleventh-century Spanish Jewish poet, was vizier to the king of Granada. One day a certain man cursed Samuel in the presence of the king. The king commanded Samuel to punish the offender by cutting out his tongue. When Samuel treated his enemy kindly instead, the curses became blessings. When the king saw that Samuel had not carried out his command, he asked why not. Samuel replied, "I have indeed torn out his angry tongue and given him instead a kindly one."[5]

By treating an enemy as a human being created in God's image, entitled to respect and sometimes in need of help, we can often obtain a reconciliation. Based on a biblical verse, a Talmudic sage expounds the following lesson:

> Rabbi Alexandri said: Two ass-drivers who hate each other are traveling on the road. The ass of one of them falls under its burden and his companion bypasses him. But then he says to himself, "It is written in the Torah: 'If you see the ass of him that hates you lying under its burden, you shall forebear to pass by him; you shall surely release it with him'" (Exodus 23:5). He immediately turns back and helps his fellow to reload. The other ass-driver then begins to meditate in his heart, saying, "This man is really my friend and I did not know it." Both then enter an inn, and eat and drink together.[6]

Philo, the renowned Jewish philosopher who lived in Alexandria, Egypt in the first century of the Common Era, comments on the same biblical passage. He indicates that, by fulfilling this mitzvah, you will benefit yourself more than your enemy: "he gains help [with unloading his animal], you gain the greatest and most precious treasure: true goodness. And this will often be followed by a termination of the feud. He is drawn toward amity by your kindness. You, his helper, with a good action to assist your counsels, are predisposed to thoughts of reconciliation."[7]

The Talmud teaches: "If two people claim your help, and one is your enemy, help him first" (*Baba Metzia* 32b). This is based on the importance of converting an enemy into a friend.

Significantly, history shows that even staunch foes often later establish positive relations. Germany and Japan, both bitter enemies of the United States during World War II, are now considered important trading and military allies of the U.S. The "demonization of enemies" is incompatible with both Jewish values and the lessons of recent world history.

Jewish Teachings on Non-Violence

Although Jewish religious texts frequently deal with war, Judaism does not glorify war for its own sake. The underlying attitude of Jewish tradition is an abhorrence of violence and an affirmation of the obligation to work and make sacrifices for the ultimate goal of peace.

The prophets speak of the futility and limited benefit of unnecessary and inappropriate warfare:

> For thus says the Lord God, the Holy One of Israel:
> In sitting still and rest shall you be saved,
> In quietness and in confidence shall be your strength;
> And you would not.
> But you said: "No, for we will flee upon horses";
> Therefore shall you flee;
> And: "We will ride upon the swift;"
> Therefore shall your pursuers be swift. (Isaiah 30:15, 16)

> Because you have trusted in your chariots
> And in the multitude of your warriors,
> Therefore the tumult of war shall arise among your people,
> And all your fortresses shall be destroyed.... (Hosea 10:13, 14)

> His delight is not in the strength of the horse,
> Nor is his pleasure in the legs of a man.
> But the Lord takes pleasure in those who fear him,

In those who hope in His steadfast love. (Psalms 147:10–11)

The prophets proclaim that Israel should not depend solely on military arms and alliances, but rather, "Zion shall be redeemed by justice, and her returnees, by righteousness." (Isaiah 1:27)

In an extreme circumstance, Jeremiah even urges the leaders of Judah to submit to Babylonian invaders (who he believed had been sent to carry out God's punishment) without resisting, so that the Jewish people would live and continue to perform God's commandments:

> And I spoke to Zedekiah, King of Judah according to all these words, saying: "Bring your necks under the yoke of the King of Babylon, and serve him and his people and live. Why should you die, you and your people, by the sword, by the famine, and by the pestilence, as the Lord has spoken concerning the nation that will not serve the King of Babylon? And hearken not unto the words of the [false] prophets that speak unto you, saying: 'You shall not serve the King of Babylon,' for they prophesy a lie unto you. . . .
>
> Hearken not unto them; serve the king of Babylon, and live; why should this city become desolate?" (Jeremiah 27:12–14, 17)

While Judaism recognizes the duty of each person to protect his own life and to defend others from violence, it specifically prohibits the shedding of *innocent* blood:

> Murder may not be practiced to save one's life. . . . A man came before Rabbi Yehuda HaNasi (Judah the Prince) and said to him, "The governor of my town has ordered me, 'Go and kill so and so; if not I will slay you.'" Rabba answered him, "Let him rather slay you than that you

should commit murder; who knows whether your blood
is redder? Perhaps his blood is redder." (*Sanhedrin* 74a)

Even in a clear-cut case of self-defense, Judaism condemns
the use of excessive violence. The Talmud stresses that if
a person being pursued could definitely save himself by
maiming a limb of the pursuer, but instead kills him, the
pursued is guilty of murder (Ibid.).

Even when war is considered necessary, Judaism tries
to minimize violence. When the Hebrews laid siege to a
city in order to capture it, "it may not be surrounded on all
four sides, but only on three in order to give an opportunity
for escape to those who would flee for their lives."[8] Even in
what was considered a just war for defensive purposes, each
soldier had to make a sin offering, in recognition that any
killing is an offense against God.

To emphasize the value of peaceful relations, the
Talmudic teachers reinterpret Biblical texts to remove
their violent aspects. The best example is the life of King
David, the great hero of ancient Israel. The Bible describes
David's character defects and misdeeds in his use of
power. The Talmudic sages, however, stress his creative
and contemplative abilities rather than his aggressive
characteristics. They prefer to consider him a pious, humble
man who spent his time in Torah study and writing psalms,
rather than a military hero.

The Talmud similarly recasts the lives of the Jewish
patriarchs. Whereas the Bible tells of Abraham leading
forth 318 "trained men" to smite those who had captured
Lot (Genesis 14:14), in the Talmud these men are considered
scholars (*Nedarim* 32a). While Jacob refers to the portions
he amassed "with my sword and my bow" (Genesis 48:22),

the rabbis interpret Jacob's "sword" to be "prayer" and his "bow" to be "supplication."[9]

Even the character of festivals is modified by the rabbis in order to emphasize spiritual, rather than military, power. Originally, Chanukkah celebrated the military victory of the Maccabees over the tyranny of the Assyrian Greeks. The Talmud de-emphasizes the military aspects of the victory and stresses the holiday's religious aspect. Not one word of rabbinic literature extols the Maccabean battles. For example, when the Talmud describes the "miracle which was wrought," it refers to "the oil in the cruse which burned eight days," rather than to the might of the Hasmoneans (Maccabean army) (*Shabbat* 23b).

One of the Talmudic rabbis' favorite statements was: "Be of the persecuted rather than the persecutor" (*Baba Kamma* 93a). The following statement summarizes their outlook:

> They who are reviled, but revile not others, they who hear themselves reproached but make no reply; they whose every act is one of love and who cheerfully bear their afflictions; these are the ones of whom scripture says: "They who love Him are as the sun going forth in his might." (*Yoma* 23a; *Shabbat* 88b; *Gittin* 36b)

Nonviolence has often found support in Jewish history. Rabbi Yohanan ben Zakkai, a revered teacher of the first century of the Common Era, is the great hero of Jewish peaceful accommodation. When Rome was besieging Jerusalem, he saw the futility of further Jewish resistance to Roman power. He secretly left Jerusalem and met with the leader of the Roman army. When the Roman general saw his great wisdom, he stated that Rabbi Yohanan could have any wish that he desired. Rabbi Yohanan ben Zakkai chose to establish a school in Yavneh for the study of the Torah. Under his leadership and that of the many brilliant teachers who followed him, a national disaster that could have ended the Jewish people was converted into a new movement for perpetuating Judaism.

From the Roman destruction of the Temple in 70 CE until the establishment of modern Israel, the Jews as a people never waged war. Without a government, army, or geographical territory to defend, Jews and Judaism survived not through armed might, but through keeping faithfully to the Jewish religion and way of life.

War is frequently not a solution, but often results in new and greater problems. The great military leader Napoleon once said to his Minister of Education, "Do you know, Fontanes, what astonishes me most in this world? The inability of force to create anything. In the long run, the sword is always beaten by the spirit."[10]

In a similar spirit, Chassidic Master Rabbi Nachman of Breslov asserted: "Many foolish beliefs that people once held, such as forms of idol worship that demanded child sacrifice, etc., have disappeared. But, as of yet, the foolish belief in the pursuit of war has not disappeared. . . . What great thinkers they [scientists who design certain weapons] must be, what ingenuity they must possess to invent amazing weapons that kill thousands of people at once! Is there any greater foolishness than this—to murder so many people for nothing?"[11]

Another Jewish argument against warfare concerns today's tremendously powerful and destructive weaponry. A nuclear war would destroy not only soldiers, but civilians, either immediately or later (due to radiation). Modern nuclear weapons have the potential of putting an end to humanity, as well as all other life on Earth. Judaism is very scrupulous about not shedding innocent blood and about limiting destruction; shouldn't Jews be in the forefront of people striving for peace today?

Yet, can a Jew responsibly reject all possibility of violence? Haven't we obligations to defend others as well as ourselves? Can we simply remain passive before terror, tyranny, and injustice? Shall we not defend human values when they are threatened? Can Israel, for example, fail to be militarily strong in the face of antagonism from many of its neighbors? Sometimes war is necessary, and a call must ring forth summoning the people to their inescapable duty:

> Proclaim this among the nations,
> Prepare war;
> Stir up the mighty men;
> Let all the men of war draw near,
> Let them come up.
> Beat your plowshares into swords,
> And your pruning hooks into spears;
> Let the weak say, "I am strong."
> Make haste and come, all you nations round about,
> And gather yourselves together;
> Cause Your mighty ones to come down, O Lord! (Joel 4:9–11)

A pragmatic position consistent with Jewish values today is what Rabbi Albert Axelrad, former longtime Hillel Director at Brandeis University, has called the "pacifoid" position.[12] He defines this as one who is "like" or "resembling" or "near" pacifist—that is, a person who works like a pacifist in pursuing peace—but accepts the need to fight if there is no alternative. This would include allied resistance to Hitler in World War II, defending Israel against attack by Arab countries today, and responding to acts of terror.

It must be noted that the pacifoid position is not "passivism"—lack of involvement. Jews must act in nonviolent ways when attempting to change unjust conditions. There have been many such examples in Jewish history. Perhaps the first recorded instance of civil disobedience is that of the midwives Shifra and Puah who ignored Pharaoh's command to kill all male babies and saved the Israelite boys (Exodus: 1:15–21). The rabbis state that their action was praiseworthy because the law was genocidal and therefore did not have to be obeyed.

The great medieval philosopher Maimonides held that Jewish law clearly allowed for civil disobedience under certain conditions:

> Oe who disobeys a king's mandate, because he is engaged in the performance of one mitzvah or another, even an insignificant one, is relieved of guilt . . . and one need not add that if the command itself involves the violation of one of God's mandates, it must not be obeyed![13]

May a Jew be a conscientious objector to particular military service, based on Torah values? The answer is yes. In 1970 the Synagogue Council of America, an umbrella group of Orthodox, Conservative, and Reform rabbis and congregational groups, stated in a letter to the director of the Selective Service System (US military draft) that Jews may claim conscientious objection to war based on their understanding of the moral imperatives of the Jewish tradition:

> Jewish faith, while viewing war as a dehumanizing aberration and enjoining a relentless quest for peace, recognizes that war can become a tragic, unavoidable

necessity. Judaism is therefore not a pacifist faith in the sense that this term is generally used.

However, this fact does not preclude the possibility of individuals developing conscientious objection to war based on their understanding of and sensitivity to the moral imperatives of the Jewish tradition. In other words, Jewish faith can indeed embrace conscientious objection, and Jewish religious law makes specific provision for the exemption of such moral objectors. It is entirely proper for individuals claiming such conscientious objector's status to be questioned about the sincerity and consistency of their beliefs, provided they are not singled out to meet requirements not applicable to members of other faiths. It is entirely improper, however, to reject such applications on the false ground that Judaism cannot embrace conscientious objection.[14]

The Rabbinical Assembly (RA) (Conservative) made similar statements in 1934 (reaffirmed in 1941),[15] as did the Reform rabbis' Central Conference of American Rabbis (CCAR) in 1963.[16] In 1971, the multi-denominational Synagogue Council of America expanded on previous statements to assert that selective conscientious objection to war is consistent with Judaism:

Judaism considers each individual personally responsible before God for his actions. No man who violates the eternal will of the Creator can escape responsibility by pleading that he acted as an agent of another, whether that other is an individual or the state. It is therefore possible, under unusual circumstances, for an individual to find himself compelled by conscience to reject the demands of a human law which, to the individual in question, appears to conflict with the demand made on him by a higher law.[17]

What about people who are not pacifists but feel that a certain war is wrong? This became a profound ethical question when many Americans refused to fight in the Vietnam War because they felt that it was illegal and immoral. Jewish tradition, which places great stress on the individual conscience, is consistent with the selective conscientious objector status.

We must always question the basis and likely results of any potential resort to arms. Some questions that might be raised include: Is this really best for the people of this country? For the people of the world? Is there no other way to settle our disputes? Is this conflict necessary to preserve our ideals and values, or is it to serve special interests? Are all the facts known, or have we only heard one side of the issue? Who stands to gain from this war? Could changing our lifestyles to become less wasteful and thus less dependent on imported resources reduce the need to go to war? Will this war really solve the problem? Has the possibility of fruitful negotiation been fully exhausted?

Peace is Judaism's greatest value. War is one of humanity's greatest threats. Hence, it is essential that Jews be actively involved with others in trying to establish harmony between people and nations, and in working toward the time when "nations shall not learn war anymore." (Isaiah 2:4)

12

SEEKING PEACE FOR ISRAEL

> Until Israelis and Palestinians are able to listen to
> each other, hear each other's anguish and anger and
> make cognitive space for one another's hopes, there is
> no way forward.—Rabbi Lord Jonathan Sacks, former
> chief rabbi of the United Hebrew Congregations of the
> Commonwealth[1]

> Pray for the peace of Jerusalem; may those who love her
> prosper. May there be peace within her walls, prosperity
> within her palaces. For the sake of my brethren and
> friends, I shall speak of peace within her midst. For the
> sake of the House of the Compassionate One, our God, I
> will seek her good. (Psalms 122:6–9)

This chapter considers why a just, comprehensive,
sustainable, mutually agreed–upon resolution of Middle
East conflicts is essential, and would have many benefits for
Israel, the U.S., and, indeed, the entire world.

I want to first indicate that I am fully and painfully
aware of past intransigence in the Arab world. I know that
hatred of Jews and Holocaust denial are taught in many
Muslim schools, and that some governments and violent
groups like Hamas refuse to acknowledge Israel's right to
exist. The many outrageous acts of terrorism by Palestinians
must be condemned and steps to prevent them must be
continued. However, since I am a Jew speaking primarily
to fellow Jews, I want to focus on what I believe we, as Jews,

should be doing to work for peace. Instead of each side demonizing the other, we need to seek common ground and ways to overcome obstacles to peace.

AN IMPORTANT ISRAELI PEACE GROUP: *OZ V'SHALOM/NETIVOT SHALOM*

Rather than offering only my own opinions on peace issues in Israel, as an American Jew who has lived in Israel only since 2016, I will base my analysis largely on the views of the Israeli Orthodox peace group *Oz V'Shalom/Netivot Shalom* (the Movement for Judaism, Zionism and Peace) and the views of retired Israeli security and military experts.

The phrase *oz v'shalom* literally means "strength and peace," and that makes a very important point. Pursuing peace is not an indication of weakness. Israel can and must remain strong while, at the same time, seeking peaceful solutions to conflicts.

Oz V'Shalom was founded in 1975 to present an alternative, more moderate expression of religious Zionism. They later merged with *Netivot Shalom* (Paths of Peace), which was formed after the 1982 war in Lebanon, in which a disproportionate number of religious students, who combined their military duty with studies at *Hesder* yeshivas, were killed. This, in turn, caused their teachers and others to question the direction that Zionism was going, and take a stronger stance for peace.

The name *Oz V'Shalom* was taken from Psalm 29:11: "God will grant His people strength (*oz*); God will bless his people with peace (*shalom*)." The name *Netivot Shalom* was taken from Proverbs 3:17: "[The Torah's] ways are pleasant, and all her paths (*netivot*) are peace." The two organizations combined because both are Orthodox groups committed to promoting the ideals of justice, tolerance, and pluralism–concepts central to Jewish tradition and law. For the sake of brevity, I shall refer to them collectively as *Netivot Shalom*. While the organization is less active now, primarily due to lack of funds, I think it is important to consider their views as an Orthodox Israeli group that promotes reconciliation and peace based on Jewish values.

This movement originally began with a group of Orthodox Jewish academics who were alarmed by the growing militarism and intolerance they saw in much of the religious Zionist community. They became aware that religious fundamentalism was gaining throughout the region on both the Arab and Jewish sides and represented a major threat to coexistence. They believed that any effective counterargument in the religious community must also be based on authentic Jewish tradition, and they were convinced that the established religious Zionist camp had drifted away from the values that had been its initial foundation. Unfortunately, this tendency has only increased since the 1970s.

As a religious Zionist peace organization, *Netivot Shalom* is in a unique position to counter fundamentalist and extremist political arguments that they believe have placed the value of possessing the Land of Israel ahead of other vital Torah values, such as human life, justice, and peace—concerns that have always been central to Jewish law and tradition.

Because they are committed to Jewish tradition and law, while at the same time supporting peace, equality, and coexistence, *Netivot Shalom* is able to enter into a dialogue with both the secular left and the religious right. They seek to effect a fundamental change within the entire national religious community and throughout Israeli society by endeavoring, in the words of their mission statement, to:

* Demonstrate support for the peace process on the basis of political reality and justice;
* enhance Jewish unity and pluralism among Israel's religious and secular communities;
* promote coexistence and support for equality for Israel's Arab minority;
* advocate political rights for Palestinians and work toward the establishment of a Palestinian state.

Netivot Shalom argues that the Jewish people's special relationship towards the Land of Israel should not override the preservation of Jewish lives (as well as others). Consistent with the teachings in the previous chapter, they view the pursuit of peace as a central religious value, and believe that Jews have a religious obligation as a nation to seek and pursue peace. They believe that Jewish law clearly requires us to establish a fair and just society, and that attempting to achieve coexistence between Jews and Arabs is not merely an option, but an imperative.

Netivot Shalom sees the pursuit of peace as a political necessity, a religious duty, and an ethical obligation. They understand political reality and the necessity to require territorial compromise as part of any plan to achieve lasting peace between Israel and the Palestinians. The State of Israel's survival and success take precedence over the desire to maintain control over *Eretz Yisrael Hashleimah*, "Greater Israel," including the West Bank (the historical *Yehudah* and *Shomron*, or *Judea* and *Samaria*). Therefore, they advocate making the painful concession of giving up parts of the Land of Israel so that the State of Israel may live in peace with her neighbors. They believe that a peace settlement based on territorial compromise is necessary to realize the values of religious Zionism, which are the preservation of the Jewish character of Israeli society and the maintenance of the highest ethical standards. And they stress that their daily lives and the political life of Israel must be guided by the biblical verse, "And you shall do what is right and good in the eyes of God" (Deuteronomy 6:18), and the Talmudic principle *mipnei darchei shalom* ("for the sake of peace"). (*Baba Metzia* 32b)

Netivot Shalom believes that lasting peace can only be achieved when the basic needs and aspirations of both Israelis and Palestinians are met, with each side acting in consideration of the ideals and constraints of the other. They quote Rabbi Joseph B. Soloveitchik, a leading modern Orthodox rabbinic authority of the twentieth century:

> Saving the life of a single Israeli young man takes precedence over the entire Torah. The Jewish law regarding saving lives must be taken into account when dealing with politics. There are now many who call for giving up not an inch of the land of Israel, who think not, that for our intransigence we may pay a dear price in human lives. The notion that the Messiah must come at the high cost of human blood opposes the breath and spirit of Jewish law. . . . In matters of territories, politics, *and* saving lives, the recognized experts are the army and the Israeli government. If they find that it is possible to give up territories without endangering lives in the community or the state's very existence, then they [the secular authorities] must be listened to.[2]

Netivot Shalom also points out that continuing to rule over a nationally conscious Arab population is a threat to the internal welfare and ethical character of Israel. They stress that if Israel continues the way she has been going, she will soon be faced with the choice of either annexing Judea and Samaria permanently and giving its inhabitants full citizenship (which would result in an Arab majority and destroy Israel's Jewish character), or continuing to oppress an entire population as second-class citizens and being considered an apartheid state (which would destroy Israel's ethical character). Neither of these is a viable option. Both would be the end of Israel as a Jewish, democratic, honorable nation (as some key Israeli political leaders and security experts have also warned, which will be discussed later).

So, while acknowledging that it takes two sides to make peace, *Netivot Shalom* believes that Israel is responsible for forging and advancing a vision of a Jewish state and for acting in pursuit of that vision. They see the choice as between:

* A Jewish state governed by Biblical values, just laws, and reason–*or* a garrison state characterized by chauvinism, institutionalized injustice, and xenophobia;

* a democratic society, flourishing within smaller borders, in which the Arab minority enjoys full human dignity and civil rights–*or* all of *Eretz Yisrael* [the land of Israel, including the West Bank] at the price of repressing the political freedom of millions of Palestinian Arabs;

* mutual recognition and co-existence between Israelis and Palestinians–*or* escalating destruction and loss of life.[3]

As *Netivot Shalom* outlines these stark choices, it becomes clear that it is long past time that we move beyond the current impasse and start using our wisdom and resources to seek a long-lasting solution that will be of enormous benefit for Israel, the Jewish people, the Palestinian people, and all of humanity.

Why Peace Is Extremely Important for Israel

Peace in the Middle East is critically necessary for Israel's future, and Jewish communities should make the pursuit of peace one of our highest priorities. Some reasons include:

Time is not on Israel's side.

As discussed before, unless there is a two-state resolution, Israel will face a future situation when Arabs will be a majority, or close to one, in Israel and the West Bank. Israel would then face the very difficult choice of either giving West Bank Palestinians the right to vote, which would mean the end of Israel as a Jewish state, or not doing so and being looked on by much of the world as an apartheid state. Of course, neither of these choices would be good for Israel.

The unstable situation and the widespread hatred and violence in the Middle East could result in a wider war with devastating consequences for Israel and many other nations.

Another war in the area could be especially destructive for Israel, since Hamas and Hezbollah have been stockpiling missiles and other increasingly lethal weapons. Furthermore, the major wildfire near Haifa in early December 2010 should provide a warning of the potential grave dangers to Israel if her forest areas were set afire by enemy missiles, especially at a time when these areas are often very dry from lack of rain.

In January 2011, Colonel Dan Zusman, who was in charge of defending about 1.5 million Israelis in the Tel Aviv area, said on IDF (Israeli Defense Forces) radio that "missiles and rockets from all fronts will reach Tel Aviv in the next round. . . . We are talking about dozens of missiles of different kinds that will hit Tel Aviv and, therefore, the estimate is that there will be hundreds of dead, destruction of buildings, and destruction of infrastructure."[4]

Unfortunately, since then the situation has become far worse and every major Israeli city would be threatened in a future war, God forbid. In a full-scale war, Hezbollah could fire 1,500 rockets daily, with dozens of long-range rockets targeting central Israel per day.[5] While most of the rockets would be intercepted by the Iron Dome or would fall in empty areas, even if only a small percent hit buildings in Israeli cities, it would have severe negative effects on Israelis' lives.

Failure to resolve the Israeli–Palestinian conflict can make Israel increasingly diplomatically isolated.

While Israel has scored major diplomatic victories recently with the Abraham Accords,[6] involving peace agreements with the United Arab Emirates, Bahrain, Morocco, and Sudan, the vast majority of countries oppose Israel's continued occupation of Judea and Samaria, especially bearing in mind the recent acts of violence by some Jewish settlers.

In 2012, the UN General assembly approved the de-facto recognition of a Palestinian state, with 138 votes in favor and only 9 votes against, with 41 abstentions. On December 16, 2014, the European parliament passed a resolution in favor of Palestinian recognition.[7] While the resolution is only symbolic, it stated that the European Parliament "supports in principle the recognition of Palestinian statehood and the two-state solution, and believes these should go hand in hand with the development of peace talks, which should be advanced." Similar resolutions previously passed by the British, French, Irish, and Portuguese parliaments requested that their respective governments recognize a Palestinian state immediately.

Israel's isolation was indicated by a cover article in the May 22, 2015 *Jewish Voice* (NY): "Israel Targeted for International Isolation by the EU, Vatican and FIFA." The article discussed efforts by a group of influential former European leaders to have the European Union step up its efforts in support of a Palestinian state and to consider promoting a deadline for the negotiation of a two-state solution; the recent Vatican recognition of a two-state solution; and efforts by the Palestinian Football Association to have FIFA (Fédération Internationale de Football Association), world soccer's governing body, suspend Israel, which would prevent Israel from participating in international soccer competitions. Fortunately, the appeal to the FIFA was withdrawn, but future such efforts are likely if current conditions are not changed.

Probably the best indication of Israel's diplomatic isolation is how often the U.N. condemns Israel, far more than all the other almost 200 nations combined.[8]

In addition, the campaign to "boycott, divest from, and sanction" Israel (BDS) is growing on many US campuses and among groups in Europe. While I am, as indicated above, a strong supporter of a two-state solution, I oppose the BDS campaign because many of its supporters oppose Israel's existence or support a one-state solution, which would mean the end of Israel as a Jewish state or as a democratic state. However, support for BDS may grow as long as the world sees Israel as an occupier.

Along with many Israeli security experts, I believe that the best way to reduce Israel's isolation is through a settlement of her conflict with the Palestinians and surrounding Arab nations, followed by cooperative efforts to improve economic, environmental, and social conditions in the area.

Although there are many causes of antisemitism, and it is never justified, one major source for antisemitism today may be the ongoing Israeli–Palestinian and Arab conflicts.[9]
When Palestinians experience, or view on television, Palestinians being detained at security checkpoints and other examples of what they regard as humiliation, it builds resentment against all Israelis and Jews in general. There was a significant increase in antisemitism during and shortly after the Israeli wars in Gaza in January 2009 and 2014.

As I write this in June 2022, there have been recent reports of widespread antisemitism in many parts of the world.[10] An American Jewish Committee 2021 report titled "The State of Antisemitism in America" reported the following examples of the rise of antisemitism:[11]

* One in four American Jews say they have been targets of antisemitism in the past year.
* About 40 percent of American Jews have changed their Jewish-related behavior or appearance because of fear of antisemitism.

SEEKING PEACE FOR ISRAEL

* About 40 percent of all Americans personally witnessed antisemitic incidents.
* Eighty-two percent of American Jews believe antisemitism has increased during the last five years.

Although, unfortunately, antisemitism will never be completely eliminated, a just, comprehensive, sustainable settlement of the Israeli–Palestinian disputes could be a major factor in reducing it. Also, when Muslims worldwide so often see pictures on their TV screens that emphasize the worse aspects of Israel's occupation, it makes terrorism and future conflicts more likely, which will negatively affect not only Israel, but Jews throughout the world. An end to the occupation would also mean an end to broadcasting these types of images.

Of course, there is never an excuse for antisemitism and Israel is doing many positive things, including carrying out humanitarian work in many areas and providing medical help even to her enemies. Unfortunately, antisemitism will continue no matter what Israel does, but properly resolving the conflicts between the Israeli and the Palestinians, and additional Arab neighbors, should be considered in terms of reducing antisemitism.[12]

Israel needs a comprehensive, sustainable, secure peace resolution to effectively address her major economic, social, and environmental problems.

Israel has a large and growing poverty gap. According to a flyer, "Fighting Poverty in Israel," from the anti-poverty and anti-hunger group Meir Panim, which operates 14 completely free restaurants throughout Israel and delivers meals daily to the elderly and homebound, "over 1.75

million Israeli citizens suffer from hunger; two of five Israeli children live below the poverty line; over 817,200 children face the daily challenge of hunger; and 186,700 of Israel's elderly citizens are completely destitute."

The educational and healthcare systems have suffered in recent years because so much of the Israeli budget necessarily goes for security. High school class sizes are increasing to as many as 40 students in some cases. As university budgets are slashed, many departments, especially in the humanities, have been closed. Many Israeli scholars have sought jobs in other countries because of decreases in funding for education and research, creating a serious "brain drain."

A 2022 report by Israel's Ministry of Health showed how serious Israel's health problems are compared to other countries, basing comparisons on data from the Organization for Economic Cooperation and Development (OECD):[13]

* Israel has an average of three hospital beds per 1,000 people compared to the OECD average of 4.4 beds per 1,000.
* Compared to an OECD average for the number of doctors per 1,000 people of 3.69, Israel has just 3.29.
* Israel is significantly short of nurses, with only five per thousand people, ranking only above Mexico, Greece, and Latvia, while the OECD average is 9.4 per 1,000.

Israel badly needs peace in order to address its many domestic problems. Almost a fifth of Israel's budget goes to defense, and this is likely to increase as new weapon systems are introduced in response to security threats.[14] Meanwhile, social services are often being reduced and the percentage of middle-class Israelis has significantly decreased.

Israel needs peace in order to effectively address an impending climate crisis and many other environmental threats.

As indicated previously, climate experts are saying that climate change could spin out of control with disastrous effects within a few decades, unless drastic changes are soon made. A recent warning in a report about climate threats from the Intergovernmental Panel on Climate Change, a UN organization consisting of climate experts from 70 nations, was so severe that UN Secretary General Antonio Guterres called it a "Code Red for Humanity."[15]

Israel is especially threatened by climate change. As discussed in Chapter 6, the hotter, drier Middle East predicted by climate experts makes terrorism and war more likely, and the coastal plain that contains most of Israel's population and infrastructure could be inundated by a rising Mediterranean Sea.

If the climate crisis is not properly addressed, nothing else will matter. It is essential that the world focus its attention on saving the global environment, but this will be more difficult if there is continued instability and violence in the Middle East. Of course, this is also true of the world's other trouble spots.

As also discussed in Chapter 6, Israel faces many other environmental problems that are not being adequately addressed, largely because so much attention and resources are devoted to security concerns. Far more people die annually from air pollution in Israel than from terrorism and traffic accidents combined. Some Israeli rivers are badly polluted. There is a shortage of open space. Less than 10 percent of Israel's garbage is recycled. The flow in the Jordan River is less than a tenth of its normal amount, and most of it near its entrance to the Dead Sea is sewage. Since the Jordan River is the main source of replenishment for the Dead Sea, it is rapidly shrinking, resulting in many large sinkholes that threaten the tourist industry in the area. Additionally, Israel is woefully unprepared to respond to the increasingly severe and frequent wildfires that climate experts are predicting.[16]

Once again, a resolution of Middle East conflicts would enable Israel to respond more effectively to these problems.

Because of the many concerns about security issues, Israel's progressive forces have been considerably weakened.

When people are primarily concerned about terrorism and other security issues, it is hard for a politician who is concerned about the environment, poverty, education, and other social issues to obtain a receptive hearing. During the 2008 national election, *HaYeruka*, Green political party led by top Israeli environmentalists Alon Tal and Eren Ben Yemini, that emphasized environmental and social issues received less than one percent of the vote. This was so discouraging that there has been no separate "Green" Party in later elections.

Israel's progressive parties, Labor and Meretz, have a very small share of the 120 Knesset members. There are polls showing that Meretz might not obtain the 3.25 percent vote necessary to be part of future Knessets.

In a column in the *Jerusalem Post,* Larry Derfner wrote that when he tries to explain Israel to Americans, he asks them to imagine 80 percent of their fellow citizens being Republicans.[17]

Threats to Israel's security rightly occupy Jews' attention, but they also divert attention from other issues of great importance.
When I try to engage Jews on the need to apply Jewish values to the solution of current global threats, I am often told, "All I care about is Israel." Many US Jews support Republican politicians because they think they are better for Israel, agreeing with their very hawkish positions, ignoring their very conservative stance on the environment, climate change, social security, taxes, job creation, and other issues, as well as Republican efforts to suppress voting of certain groups and to take other actions that are detrimental to democracy.

None of these negatives matter to many Jews, as long as politicians are perceived as being "good for Israel," which generally means supporting Israeli hawkish politicians. Jews have a special mission to be a "light unto the nations" (Isaiah 49:6), but it is very difficult to accomplish this goal when so much attention and resources must be expended in combatting terrorism and to maintain a strong military force.

Failure to achieve a settlement of the Israeli–Palestinian conflict damages Israel's image worldwide.
A poll commissioned by the BBC in December 2010 and January 2011 asked over 28,000 people in 27 countries around the world: "Please tell me if you think each of the

following countries is having a mainly positive or mainly negative influence in the world."[18] For Israel, the results were 21 percent positive and 49 percent negative. Of the 27 countries involved in the survey, the majority of people in 22 of them saw Israel in a negative light.

A 2013 BBC poll[19] showed the following: The U.S. was the only country with the majority (just 51 percent) with a mostly favorable view of Israel; the average for the world with the mostly favorable view of Israel was just 20 percent; many countries had very low percentages of their people with mostly favorable views of Israel: Japan (3), Spain (4), Germany (8), United Kingdom (14), Greece (15).

Of course, many of the negative views about Israel are due to misleading and false media reports, but a just settlement of her conflicts would greatly improve Israel's image.

Increasing violence by some radical West Bank settlers has caused widespread criticism. In an especially troubling case, twenty such settlers viciously attacked Israeli human rights activists who were helping Palestinians planting trees. This led seven US Jewish organizations to release an open letter to then Israeli Prime Minister Naftali Bennett, then Israeli Foreign Minister Yair Lapid, and then Israeli Defense Minister Benny Gantz, calling on them to take "unequivocal action" to stop "ongoing terrorism and political violence committed by Jewish Israeli extremists in the West Bank against Palestinians, Israeli civilians, and IDF soldiers."[20] The letter was signed by the Anti-Defamation League, the Central Conference of American (Reform) Rabbis, the Israel Policy Forum, the National Council of Jewish Women, the (Conservative Movement's) Rabbinical Assembly, the Union for Reform Judaism, and the United Synagogue of Conservative Judaism. They wrote:

> We urge the entire Israeli government to unite in strong condemnation against these acts, to work decisively to hold those responsible accountable and to confront the growing threats posed by these extremists with the determination and seriousness that this grave situation requires.

The letter stressed the damage done by such incidents to Israel's "image and relations with the United States government, American people, and American Jewry," in addition to Israel's status as a democracy.[21]

Benefits for Israel if peace is finally reached would potentially include open borders, an end to boycotts, international cooperation, and free movement of persons, products, and services across borders—all of which could lead to major economic growth.
Peace would reduce the need for military expenditures in all the countries involved in the conflict. Billions of dollars would become available for economic development to improve the quality of life for everyone. Peace would open transportation connections, air travel, maritime relations, and better telecommunications. More outside investments would be attracted, leading to more jobs and greater prosperity.

A resolution of the Israeli–Palestinian conflict would serve as a model for other trouble spots in the world.
At a time when military conflicts are becoming increasingly destructive and when so many human needs are unmet, as nations spend large percentages of their wealth on weapons, it is essential that there be a reduction in wars and violence. If Israelis and Palestinians–two peoples who have been at war for decades–can make peace, it could demonstrate that peace is possible everywhere.

Prospects for Middle East Peace

Based on the many reasons given above, it is essential that there be a comprehensive, sustainable, and just resolution of the Israeli–Palestinian conflict. Of course, this depends on actions and compromises by the Palestinians as well as by Israelis. Friends of Israel can win many debates by pointing out negative things that the Palestinians have done in the past, and Palestinians feel that they can do the same about Israel. However, the important thing now is not to harp on past negatives and reasons why it is hard to negotiate with the other side, but to find common ground and solutions.

A key question I often ask with regard to Israel's future is, "How will Israel avert renewed violence and increased diplomatic isolation, effectively respond to her environmental, economic, and other domestic problems, and remain both a Jewish and a democratic state without a proper resolution of her conflict with the Palestinians and the surrounding Arab nations?" I have raised the question often in recent years in personal conversations, in comments posted after online articles, and in letters to editors.

Nobody has been able to disagree with my assumptions or effectively respond to my question. However, two responses that I often received were to the effect that, "Yes, but what can we do—we have no partner for peace," and, "Yes, but as bad as that would be, giving back land as part of a peace agreement would be even worse." The last answer was often combined with statements like, "Arabs can't be trusted," or "the Palestinians won't be satisfied until they have all the land."

Few in the Orthodox community see any hope for a peace agreement. My assertion is based on many personal conversations with members of Orthodox synagogues I have attended, responses to the hawkish and conservative guest speakers there, and articles and letters in the conservative papers with mainly Orthodox audiences, *The Jewish Press, The Jewish World, NY, The Jewish Connection,* and *The 5 Towns Jewish Times.* Prospects for peace are certainly not good now (July 2023), but for the many reasons given above, it should become a top priority for Israel and the world.

Statements for Peace by Former Israeli Prime Ministers
Over the years, many Israeli prime ministers, who were initially hawkish, came to the conclusion that Israel must make painful territorial compromises in order to seek a peaceful resolution. They include Yitzhak Rabin, Ariel Sharon, and Ehud Olmert.

In January 2006, Olmert said: "The choice is between allowing Jews to live in all parts of the land of Israel and living in a state with a Jewish majority [which] mandates giving up parts of the Land of Israel. We cannot continue to control parts of the territories where most of the Palestinians live."[22]

Former Prime Minister Ariel Sharon told the Likud Party in May 2003: "The idea that it is possible to keep 3.5 million Palestinians under occupation is bad for Israel, bad for the Palestinians, and bad for the Israeli economy."[23]

Former Prime Minister Yitzhak Rabin made the following statements:[24]

* I enter negotiations with Chairman Arafat, the leader of the PLO, the representative of the Palestinian people, with the purpose to have coexistence between our two entities, Israel as a Jewish state and Palestinian state, entity, next to us, living in peace.

* I would like Israel to be a Jewish state, and therefore not to annex over 2 million Palestinians who live in the West Bank and the Gaza Strip to Israel, which will make Israel a bi-national state.
* I believe that it is my responsibility as the prime minister of Israel to do whatever can be done to exploit the unique opportunities that lie ahead of us to move towards peace.

Views of Israeli Military and Security Experts

Commanders for Israel's Security (CIS) is "a non-partisan movement comprising the overwhelming majority of available retired IDF generals and their Mossad, Shin Bet (Security Agency) and Police equivalents," who are "united in the conviction that a two-state agreement with the Palestinians, as part of a regional security framework, is essential for Israel's security as well as for its future as the democratic home of the Jewish People."[25]

Their vision is:

> Israel as a secure democratic state with a solid Jewish majority for generations, conducting itself in accordance with the spirit and values of Israel's Declaration of Independence.
>
> To realize this vision. Israel must advance a security-based separation from the Palestinians and pursue peaceful relations with pragmatic countries of the region, all with a view of resolving the Israeli–Palestinian conflict and contributing to regional stability.
>
> The eventual agreement with the Palestinians should be based on the principle of two states for two peoples and account for Israel's security needs.

In 2013, an Israeli Academy Award–nominated documentary, *The Gatekeepers*, provided valuable insights on Israel's security situation. What made it special is that its Israeli director Dror Moreh interviewed all of the six then-living retired heads of the Shin Bet, Israel's security service, and they all responded with great candor about their experiences combatting terrorism and striving to help maintain Israel's security. These six men knew much about the Israeli–Palestinian conflict from personal experience, so their opinions should be carefully considered.

The six strategic experts were critical of Israel's continued occupation of the West Bank and feel that Israel should be doing more to help resolve the Israeli–Palestinian conflict in order to provide Israel with a decent future. Here are just a few quotations from some of the former Shin Bet directors who appeared in the documentary:[26]

* Yaakov Peri: "I know about plenty of junctures since 1967 when in my view . . . we should have reached an agreement and ran away from there." In discussing his growing tired of pulling suspects from their beds in the middle of the night and watching the anguish of their wives and children, he points out: "These are not easy moments. They get etched deep [in your psyche]. And when you retire from the agency, you become a bit of a lefty."
* Avraham Shalom, on Israeli policy becoming primarily about punishing the Palestinians, concludes: "We became cruel . . . to the occupied population in the guise of fighting terrorism."
* Amit Ayalon: "The tragedy . . . [is] that we win every battle, but we lose the war."

There are other examples of key Israeli security experts and others coming to conclusions similar to the retired Shin Bet directors. According to the Israeli National Security Project,

> The roster of former Israeli security officials who support the two-state solution to the Israeli-Palestinian conflict is long and varied. It ranges from those on the left to those on the right to those without any partisan affiliation. It includes senior political figures, such as former presidents, prime ministers, and defense ministers; seasoned bureaucrats; and apolitical experts, such as heads of think tanks. It includes some of the highest decorated soldiers the state of Israel has known, as well as civilians who have served in the highest capacities within Israel's intelligence agencies.[27]

Outline of Steps Toward a Peace Agreement

Gershon Baskin is a long-time peace activist in Israel and founder and former Israeli CEO of the Israel/Palestine Center for Research and Information (IPCRI), a joint Israeli–Palestinian public policy research think-tank on Middle Eastern conflict issues. His group proposed policy options to decision makers about the peace process. Baskin is also a weekly columnist for the *Jerusalem Post* and was an elected member of the leadership of the Green Movement political party, *HaYeruka*. In his July 5, 2010 *Jerusalem Post* article, "Encountering Peace: And We Shall Dwell in Peace," Baskin discussed key points on the potential for peace that are still relevant even over a decade later:[28]

* The basics of an agreement are well understood for what is "the most researched conflict in the history

of conflicts and there are more detailed plans on how to resolve even the minutest of details in this conflict than any other." Every possible issue in the conflict has been explored in depth by Israeli and Palestinian negotiating teams.

* Until now, the peace process has been a failure, and time is running out, as current options may no longer be available in the near future.

* A majority of Israelis and Palestinians say that they want peace and are ready to make painful compromises, but they both also feel that there is no partner on the other side.

* Failure to make peace would be catastrophic for both Israel and the Palestinians, since "The survival of the Jewish people on our land, of the Zionist enterprise in its entirety is based on our ability to extricate ourselves from the occupation of the Palestinian people and to make peace on the basis of two states for two peoples."

* Since there is a lack of trust on both sides, based on a long history in which many agreements have been broken, there must be a reliable third party that will monitor implementation and verify that all aspects of all agreements are being fully implemented. A reliable third party must be able to act immediately with full transparency when there are breaches, "to call the parties to task, to demand explanations and to insist on implementation."

* It is essential that [the U.S.] become actively and directly involved and that intense, direct negotiations monitored by a leading American mediator be held to reach an agreement that both

sides can live with and that leaders on both sides will support enthusiastically.

* [Israeli leaders] must, in effect, look Israelis in the eye and describe to them the necessary conditions for a peace agreement, including that the Palestinian state will include about 96 percent of the West Bank, with the Palestinians given land inside Israel in exchange for the 4 percent of the West Bank that Israel will annex as part of the agreement, and that Jerusalem will be the capital of both countries. Because of mutually acceptable land swaps, about 80 percent of the settlers in the West Bank and East Jerusalem will remain in place as part of Israel.

* President Abbas must also look into the eyes of his people and tell them that they will not be able to return to their lost homes inside Israel, but that they have the potential to build a model state using the latest technologies, create the first successful, working democracy in the Arab world, and have the best school system in the region.

OTHER CONSIDERATIONS

Some other considerations about a possible resolution of the Israeli–Palestinian conflict include:

* Several polls have shown that most Israelis, American Jews, and Palestinians favor a two-state solution. The problem is that both sides feel that they have no partner in efforts to obtain peace, so

confidence-building measures from both sides are essential.

* The terrorist group Hamas, whose charter favors the elimination of Israel, has stated several times that it would abide by a negotiated settlement obtained by the Palestinian Authority if it was also supported in a referendum of Palestinians.[29] Of course, no matter what promises are given, steps to ensure Israeli security must be taken.

CONCLUSION

There is an important choice that Israel and its supporters must now face between: 1) continuation of the status quo, in which case conflicts, diplomatic isolation, and current socio-economic problems will continue and worsen, and Israel may face the difficult choice of remaining a Jewish state or a democratic state; or 2) recognizing that the alternative to such a bleak and depressing future is to make seeking peace Israel's highest priority.

The achievement of peace between Israel and the Palestinians and Arab states will not be easy, but working toward it is essential to a decent future for Israel and puts into practice essential Jewish values and mandates: to seek and pursue peace (Psalms 34:14), to turn enemies into friends (*Avot d'Rebbe Natan* 23:1), and to work cooperatively for justice (Deuteronomy 16:20), as well as the preservation of God's world. (Genesis 2:15)

Fortunately, there are signs of movement among some Palestinians who have recognized that terrorism is counterproductive to their cause and have started to build the infrastructure and economic and security conditions that can form the basis of a future Palestinian state.

Among the many blessings, what a just Mideast peace would bring is that it would enable Israel to strive to fulfill completely her true moral mission as a model of justice, compassion, and, most importantly, *shalom*. Then the vision of Isaiah can be fulfilled: "It shall come to pass in the latter day . . . that out of Zion shall go forth Torah, and the word of the Lord from Jerusalem." (Isaiah 2:2, 3)

13

SHOULD PRAYER INSPIRE ACTIVISM?

> Prayer is meaningless unless it is subversive, unless it seeks to overthrow and to ruin the pyramids of callousness, hatred, opportunism, and falsehoods. The liturgical movement must become a revolutionary movement, seeking to overthrow the forces that continue to destroy the promise, the hope, the vision.—Rabbi Abraham Joshua Heschel[1]

Based on Rabbi Heschel's challenging statement above, prayers should help transform people and inspire them to actively strive to create a more humane, compassionate, just, peaceful, and environmentally sustainable world. But unfortunately, the opposite is too often the case.

A study published in 2005 by the Pew Forum on Religion and Public Life found that while Jews generally are more liberal than any other American religious group, there are significant differences between Jews who regularly attend religious services and those who don't. The study found that Jews who attend synagogue services at least once a week were twice as likely to support the war in Iraq and to define themselves as politically conservative than were Jews who seldom or never go to synagogue.[2]

I was a member of an Orthodox synagogue in Staten Island from 1968 to 2016 and since then one in Israel. My experiences there have been the most important in shaping my views about the failure of synagogue services to inspire people to become more actively involved in relating Jewish values to society's ills. I appreciate the many prayer leaders for their great skill and dedication to keep the *minyanim* (prayer services) moving along without a hitch. Day by day, week by week, the services are carried out very well. But as for the long-range goals of preserving our planet, feeding its people, ending its wars, there is little awareness or efforts to connect the powerful messages in the prayers to current issues.

As I attended Shabbat (Sabbath) services in my modern Orthodox synagogue, and now in my retirement village in Israel, I often think about the tremendous collective wisdom, skills, and generosity among the many *daveners* (worshippers), and what an important impact their abilities and positive traits could achieve if addressed toward climate change—the most urgent, immediate problem facing the world today—as well as other critical societal threats. I believe that God would welcome that kind of involvement along with, and inspired by, our prayers. But the *davening* does not seem to impel worshippers to apply the challenging words of the prayers toward improving the precious world that God has given us.

Of course, I am not recommending that Jews (or others) attend religious services less often. Rather, I would like to see them put into practice the lessons contained in the *siddur* (prayerbook) and other Jewish holy books about God's compassion and other Jewish teachings in their lives.

SOME JEWISH PRAYERS THAT ADDRESS
THE ENVIRONMENT AND ANIMALS

The Jewish prayers remind us in many places of Judaism's tremendous concern for the environment and for animals, with many implications for activism. If we would only listen to the implications of the prayers we recite, they would be a spur to action that would help revitalize Judaism and ultimately help to shift our world from its current dangerous path.

For example, the *Baruch Sheh'amar* prayer, recited daily in the morning prayers, says: "Blessed is the One [God] Who has compassion on the earth; blessed is the One Who has compassion on the creatures [human and nonhuman]." What a far better world it would be if, consistent with the key Talmudic principle that we are to imitate God's qualities, more Jews understood that these statements in the *siddur* obligate us to help feed the hungry, protect the environment, and work to end the current widespread mistreatment of people and other animals.

In the Shabbat services, God is called *Rachum* (the Merciful One) and A*v Ha-Rachamim* (Father of Mercies). Since we are to emulate God, we should also be merciful. The Talmud states that Jews are to be *rachmanim b'nei rachmanim* (merciful children of merciful ancestors) and that one who is not compassionate cannot truly be of the seed of Abraham, our father (*Bezah* 32b). It also states that Heaven grants compassion to those who are compassionate to others and withholds it from those who are not. (*Shabbat* 151b)

In the important *Ashrei* (Psalm 145), recited three times daily, the Psalmist states (verse 9) that "God is good to all, and that God's mercies are over all of God's works [including both people and other animals]." According to Rabbi Dovid Sears, in his book *The Vision of Eden: Animal Welfare and Vegetarianism in Jewish Law and Mysticism*, this verse is "the touchstone of the rabbinic attitude toward animal welfare, appearing in a number of contexts in Torah literature." Referring to the Talmudic teaching that we are to emulate God's ways, he states: "Therefore, compassion for all creatures, including animals, is not only God's business; it is a virtue that we too must emulate. Moreover, compassion must not be viewed as an isolated phenomenon, one of a number of religious duties in the Judaic conception of the Divine service. It is central to our entire approach to life."[3]

THE WHOLE OF CREATION IS TO PRAISE GOD

Ashrei is followed by a number of psalms extolling God that begin and end with *halleluyah*—literally "praise God!" The final psalm in that grouping ends with, "Let all souls praise God. Halleluyah!" The Hebrew word for "soul" used here is *neshamah,* a word that is etymologically related to the word for breath. Based on this connection, some translations render the sentence as "Let *everything that has breath* praise God," which would certainly include nonhuman animals as well as people.

Perek Shira, "A Chapter of Song," is a mystical hymn dating from the fifth–seventh centuries that is found in many traditional *siddurs*, although not generally part of religious services today. It portrays all living creatures and parts of nature, such as forests and oceans, singing their individual songs in praise of the Creator. The universe is filled with hymns as cows, camels, horses, mules, roosters, chickens, doves, eagles, butterflies, locusts, spiders, flies, sea creatures, fish, frogs, and many more creatures offer songs of praise to God.

Several Shabbat morning prayers also reinforce this concept:

* The beautiful *Nishmat* prayer begins with, "The soul [or breath] of every living being shall bless Your Name, Lord, our God; the spirit of all flesh shall always glorify and exalt Your remembrance, our Ruler."
* Shortly after the *Barchu* call to prayer, the *Hakol Yoducha* prayer indicates that "All will thank You and all will praise You . . . all will exalt you. . . ." The Artscroll *siddur* commentator states: "Thus every facet of the universe will join in thanking and lauding God."
* The *Keil Adon* prayer that is generally sung on Shabbat by the chazzan (prayer leader) and congregation together, indicates that God "is blessed by the mouth of every soul."

Ideally, all of nature should be singing praises of God in a celestial chorus. It is hard to see this happening today though, when so many animals are so cruelly treated on factory farms and other settings, and so much of nature is being rapidly destroyed in the name of progress. One cannot help but wonder how many animal voices are now missing from that chorus.

An appreciation of nature can make our prayers more meaningful. Unfortunately, most Jews today do not get out to see nature through hikes and other activities as much as we should, myself included, now that we have become urbanized and spend so much time using technical gadgets for communication and recreation. Not only Jews, but our whole society in general, are suffering from what has recently been called "nature deficit disorder."

As Rabbi Heschel states, we should be looking on the world with a sense of "awe, wonder, and radical amazement."[4] He also points out that the greatest threat to religion is taking things for granted. The special *brachot* (blessings) to be recited when, for example, we see a rainbow or a fruit tree blossoming for the first time each year, as well as on more common occasions such as eating particular foods, are designed to slow us down and make us appreciate those experiences. They should remind us that, as a song in the Rogers and Hammerstein musical *Flower Drum Song* puts it, "A hundred million miracles are happening every day. And those who say they don't agree are those who cannot hear or see."

IMPORTANT ENVIRONMENTAL MESSAGES

There is a very powerful environmental lesson in the book of Deuteronomy that is recited twice daily during services as the second paragraph of the *Shema*, one of Judaism's most important prayers:

> And it will come to pass that if you continually hearken to My commandments that I command you this day, to love the Lord your God, and to serve God with all your heart and with all your soul—then I will provide rain for your land in its proper time, the early rains and the later rains, that you may gather in your grain, your wine and your oil. I will provide grass in your fields for your

cattle and you will eat and be satisfied. Beware lest your heart be seduced and you turn astray and serve other gods and bow to them. Then the wrath of God will blaze against you. God will restrain the heaven so that there will be no rain and the ground will not yield its produce. And you will swiftly be banished from the goodly land that God gives to you.

The message seems clear. If we put God's teachings into practice and take care of the earth as we are commanded, then we will have blessings of prosperity and peace. However, if we turn to false modern gods, such as materialism, egoism, hedonism, and chauvinism, and put these traits before our wise *mitzvot*, then we will be cursed with many environmental and other societal problems. If Jews would take this message to heart—a message that is recited morning and evening by religious Jews as well as at bedtime by many—and apply it toward working for a better world, what a wonderful difference that could make!

Another important prayer, the *Aleinu*, which is recited near the end of every synagogue service, tells us what our role should be: *L'takein olam b'malchut Shaddai*, "to perfect the world under the reign of the Almighty." This is the basis of the Jewish mandate for *tikkun olam*, to heal, repair, and properly transform the world. If this challenging message were taken seriously and applied on a daily basis, what a far better world it would be. As indicated in Appendix C, there are Jewish groups already applying this message, but far more needs to be done.

A Personal Synagogue Experience That Affected My Life

I had a personal experience that illustrates how an inspiring moment at a synagogue service can make a difference. In the early 1970s, I was asked to be the third vice president of my synagogue, with the responsibility of seeing that the youth programs ran smoothly. At the time, I was busy with family and professional responsibilities, and I felt alienated to some extent by the lack of social consciousness of many people in the synagogue. After some soul searching, I decided to not accept the position.

Then came Yom Kippur, during which we recite the *al chet,* a long list of communal sins. Suddenly I was faced with the "*al chet* [for the sin] of casting off responsibility." I thought back to my reasons for refusing the youth program position. Was I casting off my responsibility? Yes, indeed—I was. So, I decided to accept the position and make sure that Jewish values, such as *gemilut chesed* (doing acts of kindness), were an essential part of the synagogue's youth activities. Every year since then, I try to pay special attention to that specific *al chet* and to ask myself, "Are there any responsibilities I am casting off by taking the easy way out?"

Teachings That Can Enhance Prayer Experiences

The following are some anonymous (as far as I know) statements about prayer and activism from a handout I received many years ago as part of a High Holidays (Rosh Hashanah and Yom Kippur) package of inspirational material. To this day, I still find them helpful, and review them annually during these important holidays:

* Pray as if everything depends on God and act as if everything depends on you.

* Prayer does not change God, but it changes [them] who pray.

* Our prayers are answered not when we are given what we ask for, but when we are challenged to be what we can be.

* True worship is not a petition to God; it is a sermon to ourselves.

* Prayer is answered when it enables us to act as God desires.

"RELIGIOUS BEHAVIORISM" OR ACTIVE INVOLVEMENT?

Unfortunately, as indicated before, worship services don't always inspire people to greater activism in working for a better world. Many people (often including me) settle for what Rabbi Heschel called "religious behaviorism." They recite the prayers mechanically, without really considering how the holy words can inspire us to change our communities and ourselves and face up to local and global problems. For some Jews, attendance at prayer services is often a social event, based more on tradition and habit than on a desire for genuine communion with God or a desire to be inspired to greater awareness and activism.

It is my hope that more rabbis, educators, and other Jewish leaders will use sermons, classes, articles and other strategies to help *daveners* better absorb and apply the many powerful messages in the eternal Jewish prayers.

Involvement in trying to improve the environment and conditions for the world's creatures can also make the *davening* experience more meaningful. As Rabbi Heschel states, "Prayer and prejudice cannot dwell in the same heart. Worship without compassion is worse than self-deception; it is an abomination."[5] Prayers and social justice activities ideally complement each other.

Rabbi Heschel's approach is consistent with an approach that Rabbi Arthur Waskow, director of the Shalom Center, stresses: to apply this challenging teaching of Rabbi Heschel that one should carry on politics as if it were prayer and carry out prayer as if it were politics.[6] After marching with the Reverend Martin Luther King in the second civil rights march from Selma to Montgomery, Alabama, Rabbi Heschel said, "I felt as if my legs were praying."[7]

If more Jews took this approach and strove to put the messages in the prayers into practice, this could release a great potential to help revitalize Judaism. It could move our imperiled planet toward a more just, humane, and environmentally sustainable path, toward a time when "no one shall hurt nor destroy in all of God's holy mountain." (Isaiah 11:9)

14

REVITALIZING JUDAISM

> Little does contemporary religion ask of man. It is ready
> to offer comfort; it has no courage to challenge. It is
> ready to offer edification; it has no courage to break the
> idols, to shatter callousness. The trouble is that religion
> has become "religion"—institution, dogma, ritual. It is
> no longer an event. Its accceptance involves neither risk
> nor strain. (Abraham Joshua Heschel, *The Insecurity of
> Freedom* 1)

> We must cultivate a sense for injustice, impatience with
> vulgarity, a capacity for moral indignation, a will to
> readjust society itself when it becomes complacent and
> corrupt. (Ibid. 49)

> What young people need is not religious tranquilizers,
> religion as a diversion, but spiritual audacity, intellectual
> guts, power of defiance. Our task is not to satisfy
> complacency but to shatter it. Our duty is confrontation
> rather than evasion. (Ibid.)

Trying to meet the challenges in the three quotations above
can help revitalize what Rabbi Heschel expressed below as
the central role that Judaism must play in helping to solve
contemporary problems:

> Our civilization is in need of redemption. The evil, the
> falsehood, the vulgarity of our way of living cry to high
> heaven. There is a war to be waged against the vulgar,
> against the glorification of power, a war that is incessant,
> universal. There is much purification that needs to be

done, ought to be done, and could be done through bringing to bear the radical wisdom, the sacrificial devotion, the uncompromising loyalty of our forefathers upon the issues of our daily living.[1]

Many Jews today are appropriately concerned about Jewish survival and the flourishing of Jewish culture and learning. And, as indicated in Appendix C, many Jewish groups are indeed applying Jewish values to today's critical issues. However, much more needs to be done in the face of the many threats to the world today.

Unfortunately, many Jews today seem to be paying insufficient attention to the words of Jewish prophets and sages that resound with their passionate concern for justice, peace, and righteousness. There is little active involvement or protest against injustice, but instead, much complacency and conformity.

Many Jews have forgotten the mandate to strive to perfect the world. Today the synagogues and pronouncements of rabbis have often become irrelevant to the critical issues that face the world's people. God requires justice, compassion, involvement, and protests against evil, but our synagogues have too often focused instead on ritual and on parochial (narrow) concerns.

A person who takes Jewish values seriously would be alienated by much of what occurs in Jewish life today. As Rabbi Heschel stated, "One is embarrassed to be called religious in the face of religion's failure to keep alive the image of God in the face of man."[2] Many idealistic Jews have turned away from Judaism because Judaism's teachings urging active involvement in the crucial challenges of today are not adequately disseminated and practiced.

For observant, caring Jews, the acts of helping those in need and caring for the world are not voluntary options but responsibilities and Divine commandments. These are not only individual responsibilities, but also obligations for the entire Jewish community—obligations, in fact, to the entire world. Our tradition understands this principle as a covenant—an agreement that binds us to God. In this covenant, we assume the task of working to repair the world and, in return, receive the Divine promise that the world will be redeemed. The Jewish message is not only one of responsibility, but also one of hope.

It is a shame that some Jewish leaders and institutions have forgotten that the practical expression of justice, in our own community and toward all communities, has been and must continue to be a major emphasis of Jewish living. It is a tragedy that the Jewish community has generally failed to apply our rich theology to the preservation of the environment. Too often the Jewish establishment has been silent while our world is increasingly threatened by climate change, our air is bombarded by poisons that threaten life, our rivers and streams are polluted by industrial wastes, our fertile soil is eroded and depleted, and the ecological balance is endangered by the destruction of rainforests and other essential habitats.

The Jewish community must become more actively involved. We must proclaim that it is a desecration of God's Name to pollute the air and water, to slash and burn forests, to mistreat animals, and to wantonly destroy the abundant resources that God has so generously provided. We cannot allow whatever other needs or fears we may have, however legitimate, to prevent us from applying fundamental Jewish values to the critical problems of today.

It is also unfortunate that many Jews seem almost totally unaware of the rich legacy of the Jewish tradition and its focus on justice for both the individual and society. Indeed, Judaism provides a pragmatic path for implementing its progressive ideas. The Talmud and other rabbinical writings are filled with in-depth discussions, advice, and legal decisions on how to apply the principles of the prophets to everyday situations. Judaism also offers the richness and warmth of an ancient historical community, a meaningful inheritance for each Jew.

Religious practitioners frequently mischaracterize God's demands. Instead of crying out against immorality, injustice, deceit, cruelty, and violence, they too often condone these evils through silence, while instead emphasizing mostly ceremonies and ritual. As discussed in the previous chapter, to many Jews today, Judaism involves occasional visits to the synagogue or temple, prayers recited with little feeling, rituals performed with little meaning, and socializing. But, to the prophets, worship accompanied by indifference to evil is an absurdity, an abomination to God (Isaiah 1:13). Judaism is mocked when Jews indulge in or condone empty rituals side-by-side with immoral deeds. One example was the abuses of both nonhuman animals and human workers that were found at the world's largest kosher slaughterhouse in Postville, Iowa in 2008.

With some important exceptions, Jews today have too often failed to speak out against an unjust, immoral society. While claiming to follow the ethical teachings of the prophets, many Jews have equivocated and rationalized their inaction. As indicated previously, Rabbi Heschel blames religion's failure to speak out and be involved in critical current issues for its losses:

Religion declined not because it was refuted but because it became irrelevant, dull, oppressive, insipid. When faith is completely replaced by habit, when the crisis of today is ignored because of the splendor of the past, when faith becomes an heirloom rather than a living fountain, when religion speaks only in the name of authority rather than with the voice of compassion, its message becomes meaningless.[3]

THE CHALLENGING TEACHINGS OF RABBI NATHAN LOPES CARDOZO

One of the most ardent exponents of the need to revitalize Judaism is Rabbi Nathan Lopes Cardozo, dean of the David Cardozo Institute and author of many books on Judaism. The messages below are from his potentially transformative book, *Jewish Law as Rebellion: A Plea for Religious Authenticity and Halachic Courage*:

* The purpose of Halacha is to disturb, to not only comfort the troubled but also to trouble the comfortable. But, "Halacha has become nearly passe . . . jailed in compartmentalized and awkward boxes." (35)

* Our yeshivas are failing to properly educate students, having retreated from creative thinking and instead teaching students what to think, rather than how to think. "We are in need of a radically different kind of yeshiva: one in which students are presented with serious challenges to Halacha" (41). But "we are instructing our students and children to obey, to fit in, to conform, and not to stand out." (42)

* "Judaism needs to be instilled with greater spiritual vitality and religious vigor" (64). But today's Jewish community generally involves conformism, with independent thought and difference of opinion condemned.

* "Orthodox Judaism has become over-codified and is on its way to becoming irrelevant" (59). Many young Jews are searching for an authentic Jewish life, but are turned off by a Judaism that they find monotonous, standardized, and external, and not a response to a search for meaning.

* While Jews are to live with a sense of radical amazement, seeing the hand of God in all of life, "Halachic living is severely impeded by observance becoming mere habit." (173)

* While there is a Jewish obligation to be a "light unto the nations," universal issues are generally being ignored as most present-day Halacha is self-centered, with very few halachic authorities addressing current national or global crises. Searching Jews are finding an absence of a sense of mission or concern for the rest of humanity, animals, and the planet.

* To combat the above problems, Judaism desperately needs bigger, bolder ideas.

SUGGESTIONS FOR REVITALIZING JUDAISM

For the reasons indicated above, I think it is essential that steps be taken to revitalize Judaism. Some suggestions are below. I hope that others will build on these suggestions and come up with additional possibilities. Please email me at VeggieRich@gmail.com with suggestions.

Am I the best person to indicate how Judaism can be revitalized? Far from it. However, as with other issues discussed in this book, I am trying to promote a respectful dialogue on this issue, and I hope my suggestions will provide a starting point for such a dialogue.

Following up on Rabbi Cardozo's plea for bigger and bolder ideas in Judaism, I suggest the following, consistent with previous chapters in this book:

* Responding to climate threats should become a major focus in Jewish life today since climate experts are warning that we may soon reach an irreversible tipping point when climate change spins out of control with catastrophic consequences.

* Veganism and related issues should be put on the Jewish agenda since animal-based diets violate basic Jewish teachings on health, compassion, sharing, justice, environmental sustainability, and other values. In addition, shifts away from animal-based diets are essential to efforts to avert a global climate catastrophe.

* Since, contrary to Jewish teachings, animals are widely abused today, Tu BiShvat, "The New Year for Trees," should be used as a model to renew the ancient Jewish "New Year for Animals," which was initially used for tithing of animals for sacrifices. It should be transformed into a day devoted to increasing awareness of Judaism's teachings on compassion to animals and how far current realities are from these teachings.

Responding to Rabbi Cardozo's loving, respectful, and challenging critique of Jewish life today by making such changes would help revitalize Judaism and help bring many currently alienated Jews back to Jewish involvement.

BUILDING ON JEWISH PROGRESSIVE TEACHINGS

Judaism is in many ways a radical religion, in terms of the Jewish teachings on compassion, justice, peace, environmental activism, and other issues that were discussed in previous chapters. However, our Jewish schools and synagogues seem to be creating mainly conservative graduates, people unwilling to apply Jewish values to help shake an unjust status quo.

I believe that in this time of violence, injustice, bigotry, selfishness, and materialism, there should be greater stress on Judaism's powerful, radical teachings. Some examples, most of which have been discussed in previous chapters, include:

* "Justice, justice shall you pursue." (Deuteronomy 16:20)
* "Seek peace and pursue it." (Psalms 34:14)
* "Be kind to the stranger for you were strangers in the land of Egypt." (indicated in some form 36 times in the Torah)
* "Love your neighbor as yourself." (Leviticus 19:18)
* *Bal tashchit* (You shall not waste). (Deuteronomy 20:19–20)
* Be a "light unto the nations." (Isaiah 42:6)
* If I am only for myself, what am I? (*Pirkei Avot* 1:14)
* If not now, when? (*Pirkei Avot* 1:14)

These and other challenging Jewish quotations should become watchwords in synagogues, Jewish schools, Jewish institutions, and Jewish homes. This would help return Judaism to our radical roots and help Jews apply Jewish teachings to societal problems.

USING THE JEWISH FESTIVALS AS A SPUR TO ACTIVISM

Many important Jewish teachings are reflected in Jewish holidays. Rabbi Irving Greenberg has written: "The Holy Days are the unbroken master code of Judaism. Decipher them and you will discover the inner sanctum of your religion. Grasp them and you hold the heart of the faith in your hand."[4]

Let's consider some ways of motivating Jews to greater involvement by relating Jewish holy days, discussed below in order of calendar appearance, to current societal issues:

Shabbat: The important environmental benefits of Shabbat as a day of rest from constant use of gadgets and efforts to increase one's wealth should be stressed. As Rabbi Abraham Joshua Heschel stated in his classic book *The Sabbath* (28),

> To set aside one day a week for freedom, a day on which we would not use the instruments which have so easily been turned into weapons of destruction, a day for being with ourselves, a day of detachment from the vulgar, of independence of external obligations, a day on which we stop worshipping the idols of technical civilization, a day on which we use no money, a day of armistice in the economic struggle with our fellow men and the forces of nature—is there any institution that holds out a greater hope for man's progress than the Sabbath?

Rabbi Samuel Dresner, a student of Rabbi Heschel, asserted that the Sabbath Day should represent armistices in battles between people and society, people and nature, and people with themselves. We are not to even pick a flower on Shabbat, not only because we should not harvest things, but also because we are to be at peace with everything, like in the Garden of Eden, so we do not make or destroy things on the Sabbath.

I always welcome Shabbat with joy as a chance to recharge my batteries, renew family discussions, catch up on my reading and, of course, commune with God. I sometimes wonder how I would manage without Shabbat. I get some of my best work done on Saturday evenings after a restful Shabbat, perhaps partly because my subconscious mind opens blockages that I can't bypass when I am inundated with email messages and busy with many activities during the week.

Certainly, we must maintain the sanctity of Shabbat and other Jewish holy days, but we should also use these days to help us renew our strength for greater involvement during the other days of the week. I also agree with Rabbi Arthur Waskow that the entire world needs a Shabbat, or perhaps an entire Sabbatical Year, to pause from efforts to constantly produce and amass more and more goods, to reassess where we are heading and stop the practices that are so harmful to the environment.

Rosh Hashanah: On this day that commemorates the creation of the world, we should consider how the wonderful world that God has created is so imperiled by climate change and other environmental threats, and vow to work with others in turning things around in the New Year. In praying for a healthy year for ourselves and our loved ones, we should recognize that having a vegan diet is the best way to reduce the risks of disease.

Yom Kippur: On this Day of Atonement and repentance, we should consider how we can repent and atone for all the ways we have negatively impacted the environment and vow to work to restore and improve it. We should consider the prophetic messages of Isaiah that the true purpose of fasting is to sensitize us to the importance of ending oppression and reducing hunger and the message in the Book of Jonah about the importance of repentance and moving away from harmful ways.

Sukkot: This harvest festival could include sermons and discussions on Jewish teachings about food and reducing hunger. The discussion of the cycles of sun, wind and water in Ecclesiastes, which we read on the Shabbat of Sukkot, could be the basis of discussions on renewable energy.

Chanukah: the importance of non-conformity and fighting for one's beliefs should be stressed, with the victory of the few (the Maccabees) against the far stronger Syrian-Greeks as an example.

Tu BiShvat: Another approach to using a Jewish holiday to increase environmental awareness and hopefully activism is to consider Tu BiShvat, the "birthday of the trees," as a "Jewish Earth Day." Since all the traditional foods served at Tu BiShvat Seders are plant foods, it is a good chance to consider Jewish teachings on veganism. When the holiday falls on Shabbat, it could be an environmentally themed Shabbat, with a Tu BiShvat Seder serving plant-based foods, especially fruits from trees that grow in Israel, environmentally oriented sermons, talks, panel discussions, and debates, nature walks, and other appropriate activities. If Tu BiShvat falls during the week, it provides a good opportunity for school children to get close to nature by taking hikes, planting trees, studying relevant texts, reading and writing appropriate material, singing songs, and engaging in other ways that help them appreciate our deep connection to nature.

Passover: This holiday's theme of freedom from oppression could be the basis of discussions about the importance of democracy and civil liberties.

Shavuot: On this holiday that commemorates the giving of the Torah to the Israelites, we could consider the many Torah teachings about justice, compassion, peace, environmental sustainability, and other positive values.

Tisha B'Av: On this sad day that commemorates the destruction of both ancient Temples in Jerusalem, we should recognize that today it is not just a holy Temple and Jerusalem that are threatened with destruction, but the whole world, and work to avert an impending unprecedented climate catastrophe and major environmental and other threats.

In summary, every Jewish holiday provides valuable material to increase awareness and sensitivity about Jewish teachings on many important current issues. I relate Shabbat and all of the Jewish festivals and other sacred days to veganism and vegetarianism in my articles in the holiday section at JewishVeg.org/Schwartz. Similar articles can be written relating the sacred events to other environmental and social justice issues.

BUILDING JEWISH VALUES INTO BAR AND BAT MITZVAH CEREMONIES AND OTHER JEWISH EVENTS

Bar and Bat Mitzvah ceremonies are a big part of the lives of Jewish children. Such occasions can end up as chances for materialism and hedonism, especially as the boys and girls attend many parties of friends and classmates in addition to their own in a relatively short time, but they also provide an opportunity for young Jews to reflect on and apply important Jewish values.

A group that tries to help infuse such occasions and other events with Jewish values is Areyvut, which is the Hebrew word for responsibility. They emphasize that Jews should feel responsible for other Jews and for working toward a better community and a better world.

Areyvut's mission is to infuse the lives of Jewish youth and teenagers with the core Jewish values of *chesed* (kindness), *tzedakah* (charity), and *tikkun olam* (social action). Areyvut offers Jewish day schools, congregational schools, synagogues, community centers, and families a variety of opportunities to empower and enrich their youth by creating innovative programs that make these core Jewish values real and meaningful to them.

Areyvut's fundamental belief is that sparking a passion for service in the young inspires a lifelong commitment to charity, kindness, and social justice. Therefore, Areyvut creates programs that reach out to Jewish youth, building on their individual interests and putting their experiences into a meaningful Jewish and communal context. They encourage young people to engage in both hands-on service and philanthropy, in the belief that all of God's gifts should be used to improve our world. They also believe that community service benefits—and changes—both the recipient and the provider of the service. Their target audience is middle and high school students from all denominations of Judaism, all types of Jewish education, and all levels of Jewish communal affiliation.

Among Areyvut's many programs are *Bnai Mitzvah* and *Chesed* Fairs—hands-on and community service fairs for schools, synagogues, and community centers to educate students about the many different ways they can make a difference in their community.

More information about Areyvut and its programs can be obtained by visiting www.Areyvut.org.

Considering Long-Range Goals

Short-range, day-to-day, week-to-week goals are necessary for the proper functioning of synagogues. But they are not sufficient. To make Judaism more dynamic and meaningful, long-range goals must also be considered.

A short-range goal is to have daily *minyanim* for prayer services. A long-range goal is to make the daily *minyanim* more meaningful to those who attend. The significance of the prayers and their relevance to each person's life and to efforts to obtain a better world, as discussed in the previous chapter, should be considered.

Having a weekly Shabbat service is a short-range goal. A long-range goal is to involve the participants, to inspire and transform them, to help them improve their lives by their weekly synagogue experience.

Reading the Torah in the Synagogue is a short-range goal. Making Torah values part of our lives is a long-range goal. All too often, people listen to the Torah as they might listen to a talk in a foreign language—there is little understanding. Even when the words are understood, there is little effort to relate to the values being expressed.

Reading the *haftorah* (the weekly prophetic portion) is a short-range goal. A person must be selected each week for this task. However, seldom is the long-range task of becoming *b'nei nevi'im* (descendants of the Biblical prophets) considered. Moses said, "Would that all the Jewish people would be prophets" (Numbers 11:29). But, even with the weekly reading of a portion of the prophetic literature, one seldom finds prophetic voices in Judaism today.

Youth activities to keep children active during services is a short-range goal. A long-range goal would be to have youth activities that teach Jewish children values, such as compassion, kindness, and justice. Children all too often get programmed into the same kinds of apathy and mindless activities as adults.

A short-range goal is to work for a better Synagogue, to see that the day-to-day needs are met. A long-range goal would be to apply Jewish values in working for a better synagogue, community, city, nation, and world. All too often, Judaism is confined to the four walls of the sanctuary. The world needs, perhaps more than ever before, Jewish values and Jewish involvement.

A short-range goal would be to work on a particular aspect of Judaism—conducting a Seder, building a sukkah, lighting Chanukah candles. Long-range goals would be to use these activities as inspirations for universal ideals—to feed the hungry, work for a peaceful world, reduce poverty, and clean up the environment.

A short-range goal is to work for Israel's security, to contribute money, to help it meet its social and economic needs. A long-range goal would be to work to help make Israel increasingly what it must become: a holy people, a light unto the nations, a witness for God, an echo of eternity.

A short-range goal is study, the holding of regular classes on the Torah and other aspects of Judaism. A long-range goal is study that leads to action, the type of study that shows what Judaism says about current issues, such as pollution, hunger, energy, poverty, and peace, and provides the knowledge and inspiration to help Jews apply these values.

Short-range goals are essential. They must be met if Judaism is to survive. But there must also be far greater consideration of long-range goals to revitalize Judaism and help make it relevant to today's critical issues.

GETTING STUDENTS MORE INVOLVED

Many studies have shown that students learn more from active involvement than from lectures. Here are a few suggestions about involving students to help imbue them with Jewish values and teachings:

* High school students could be asked to submit papers—perhaps as part of an essay contest—that consider how Jewish teachings could be applied to address current issues such as climate change,

energy conservation, hunger, poverty, peace, health, animal rights, veganism, and many more.

* Debate teams could also be set up, and students could learn the value of researching positions they don't personally agree with. The chapters in this book and many other books can be used as starting points for debating many topics for and against. Many Jews today are afraid to expose their children to opposing views. They shouldn't be. The Talmudic rabbis were not afraid of intense debate, and even preserved the ideas that were voted down, so we could learn from the process. Judaism is a strong religion that has stood the test of time; it can certainly withstand the questioning of today's teenagers. Students should learn that there is not necessarily one correct answer to an issue, and that they should respect others' opinions, even while disagreeing with them

* Having guest speakers with a wide variety of opinions, consistent with Jewish law and values, would create much interest in a wide variety of current issues.

* Students could be encouraged to come up with their own questions and issues that they would like to investigate. Use of the Internet gives students wonderful opportunities to explore current issues.

* When older students are learning to lead the *davening* in preparation for adulthood, there should be an effort to relate the prayers to the issues that they are addressing in their research, discussions, and debates. For example, what are the implications of the verse, "Blessed is the One [God] who has

mercy on all the creatures," or "God is good to all, and His compassion is over all His works"? How would these verses apply to the way we treat animals and the environment? The same could be done with many other statements in the *davening*. We should be making a conscious effort to connect the words with our actions in the world.

Much of my own Jewish philosophy comes from Rabbi Abraham Joshua Heschel, whom I often quote in this book. Unfortunately, relatively few Jews are familiar with his writings nowadays. I regard him as the ideal Jew, as he not only took Jewish prayer and ritual seriously and wrote beautifully on such a wide variety of issues, but also put Jewish teachings into practice in active involvement in many social issues, including supporting freedom for Soviet Jews, working for civil rights, and opposing what he regarded as an immoral war in Vietnam.

I strongly believe that if many more Jews read Rabbi Heschel's many books and essays and, more importantly, tried to live by them, we would have a far more sensitive and dedicated Jewish community, whose involvement in societal issues would lead to a revitalized Judaism and a far better world. So, I strongly suggest that teachers assign and students read some of his books and use them as a basis of discussions.

In summary, there are many creative ways to help revitalize Judaism, and I hope that wiser people than myself will build on the ideas in this chapter and suggest additional ideas, so that Judaism becomes more of what it was always meant to be—a light unto the nations, a kingdom of priests, a holy people, God's witnesses.

15

SUMMARY AND CONCLUSIONS

In this hour we, the living [post-Holocaust Jews], are "the people of Israel." The tasks begun by the patriarchs and prophets and continued by their descendants are now entrusted to us. We are either the last Jews or those who will hand over the entire past to generations to come. We will either forfeit or enrich the legacy of ages.—Abraham Joshua Heschel[1]

I am a Jew because the faith of Israel [the Jewish people] demands no abdication of my mind.

I am a Jew because the faith of Israel asks every possible sacrifice of my soul.

I am a Jew because in all places where there are tears and suffering the Jew weeps.

I am a Jew because in every age when the cry of despair is heard the Jew hopes.

I am a Jew because the message of Israel is the most ancient and the most modern.

I am a Jew because Israel's promise is a universal promise.

I am a Jew because for Israel the world is not finished; men will complete it.

I am a Jew because for Israel man is not yet fully created; men are creating him.

I am a Jew because Israel places man and his unity above nations and above Israel itself.

I am a Jew because above man, image of the divine unity, Israel places the unity that is divine.—Edmond Fleg, "Why I Am a Jew"[2]

WHAT A WONDERFUL PATH JUDAISM IS!

* Judaism proclaims a God who is the Creator of all life, whose attributes of kindness, compassion, and justice are to serve as examples for all our actions.

* Judaism stresses that every person is created in God's image and therefore is of supreme value.

* Judaism teaches that people are to be co-workers with God in preserving and improving the world. We are mandated to serve as stewards of the world's resources to see that God's bounties are used for the benefit of all.

* Judaism asserts that nothing that has value may be wasted or unnecessarily destroyed (*bal tashchit*).

* Judaism stresses that we are to love other people as ourselves, to be kind to strangers, "for we were strangers in the land of Egypt," and to act with compassion toward the homeless, the poor, the orphan, the widow, and all of God's creatures.

* Judaism urges efforts to reduce hunger. A Jew who helps to feed a hungry person is considered, in effect, to have "fed" God.

* Judaism mandates that we must seek and pursue peace. Great is peace, for it is one of God's names, all God's blessings are contained in it, it must be sought even in times of war, and it will be the Messiah's first blessing.

* Judaism exhorts us to pursue justice, to work for a society in which each person has the ability to obtain, through creative labor, the means to lead a dignified life.

* Judaism teaches that God's compassion is over all of His works, that the righteous individual considers the wellbeing of animals, and that Jews should avoid causing pain to animals (*tsa'ar ba'alei chayim*) and, indeed, to all of God's creation.
* Judaism stresses involvement, nonconformity, resistance to oppression and injustice, and a constant struggle against idolatry.

Producing a Better World by Applying Jewish Values

This ancient, marvelous, ever-evolving Jewish outlook, applied to the planet's gravest problems, can help shift the planet away from its present perilous course to produce a far better world. Strategies to obtain a better world include:

* There should be a central focus in Jewish life on the preservation of our natural environment and the improvement of economic and social conditions. Synagogues, yeshivas, Jewish community centers, and other Jewish institutions should increase the awareness of Judaism's powerful messages about justice, peace, compassion, environmental sustainability, and other values, and how these teachings can be applied to the problems of today. Hopefully other religions will note and apply their own teachings in these efforts.
* We should seek a fairer tax system, with a reduction of major tax breaks for the wealthiest Americans and highly profitable corporations. The increased tax revenues should be used to finance a major effort to rebuild our decaying infrastructure, produce

more renewable energy, improve our educational systems and research capacities, and make other necessary investments that will create jobs, increase tax revenue, and help improve the economy, while providing dignity and confidence to workers.

* We should promote major changes in response to the overwhelming consensus among climate scientists that climate change is happening, that it poses a grave threat to life on Earth and human civilization, and that we, humanity, are both a major cause and are the only potential solution. Preventing the climate catastrophe that many climate scientists are predicting should be a major focus in all aspects of Jewish life today. As discussed in Chapter 5, the only possibility of averting a climate catastrophe is through a society-wide shift toward vegan diets.

* A Global Marshall Plan should be established, led by the United States along with other developed nations, including the European Union nations, the U.K., and Israel, to sharply reduce world poverty, hunger, illiteracy, pollution, disease, and other societal problems. This would improve the image of the U.S. and Israel, potentially reducing future acts of terrorism and war.

* There should be a major effort to resolve the Israeli–Palestinian and other conflicts throughout the world, for the great benefit of all the people involved, and so that more money, time, and attention can be applied to addressing today's many global challenges. Israel cannot avert renewed conflict and increased diplomatic isolation, effectively respond to her serious economic, environmental, and other

domestic problems, and remain both a Jewish and a democratic state without an enduring Middle East peace. While recognizing the many obstacles related to Palestinian statements and actions, we should encourage increased efforts to reach a resolution of the disputes. The U.S. and other nations should support Israel in every attempt to achieve a comprehensive, just, and sustainable peace.

* There should be a widespread effort to increase awareness that a large-scale shift toward plant-based diets would provide numerous benefits, including significantly improving human health and reducing climate change, deforestation, desertification, rapid species losses, soil erosion, and many other environmental threats. There is no way that the world will be able to avoid an unprecedented climate catastrophe and meet increasing needs for food, energy, water, and other resources without a major societal switch toward vegetarian, and preferably vegan, diets, along with other positive changes.

* We should stress that plant-based diets are the most consistent ones with basic Jewish teachings on preserving health, treating animals with compassion, protecting the environment, conserving natural resources, helping hungry people, and seeking and pursuing peace.

* A commission of highly respected religious leaders, environmentalists, educators, politicians, and other experts should be formed to investigate and report on the best approaches to reduce current threats and greatly improve conditions worldwide.

Of course, it will not be easy to carry out the strategies listed above. However, we must recognize the seriousness of the threats we face today, and that "business as usual" is no longer an option. Unprecedented changes in thinking and action must be made very soon and Jews, along with others, must play a major role in increasing awareness of the urgency of these changes in order to avoid a catastrophic future. This should be a priority in all aspects of Jewish life. Failure to apply Jewish values to address current threats will result in a very dismal future, with increased poverty, hunger, terrorism, war, pollution, and severe climate events.

Many Jews today justify their lack of involvement with the world's problems by stating that Jews have enough troubles of their own and that we can leave it to others to involve themselves in "non-Jewish" issues. Certainly, Jews must be actively involved in battling antisemitism, working for a secure and just Israel, and engaging with numerous other Jewish needs and obligations. But can we divorce ourselves from active involvement with wider problems? Are efforts to obtain justice, peace, environmental sustainability really "non-Jewish" issues? Don't Jews also suffer from polluted air and water, resource shortages, the effects of climate change, and other societal threats? Can we ignore issues critical to the future of our community, nation, and world? When people are poor, hungry, oppressed, disease-ridden, and victimized by violence, does not our Jewish tradition mandate that we respond, and is it not also very much in the self-interest of our own safety and advancement?

It is essential that Jews, along with others, actively apply Jewish values to current critical problems. We must be "God's loyal opposition" to injustice, greed, and immorality, rousing the conscience of humanity. We must shout "no" when others are whispering "yes" to injustice. We must involve Judaism in the universal task of "comforting the afflicted and afflicting the comfortable." We must act as befits "descendants of the prophets," reminding the world that there exists a God of justice, compassion, and kindness. Nothing less than global survival is at stake.

As indicated by the list of activist Jewish groups in Appendix C, there are many dedicated Jews who recognize that Judaism has splendid values that can play major roles if applied to today's critical issues. It would be very helpful if many more Jews educated themselves on the issues and got more involved in applying Jewish values in efforts to improve the world.

There is a battle worldwide between the forces seeking harmony, tolerance, common ground, and solutions and the forces of fear, obstruction, hatred, bigotry, and demonization of people who are different in views, nationality, or religion. This book is a calling to join with the many, although yet too few, activist Jews serving our Covenant with God, with actions that respond to God's call for our partnering in building a more caring humanity and a better existence for all God's creatures.

The world is moving on a very perilous path due to its failure to take seriously religious values that have a direct impact on society at large, such as justice, kindness, compassion, peaceful relations, and concern for the environment. We must act to inform and influence Jews (and others) to become involved and to protest to help move the world to a more sustainable path before it is too late.

The afternoon service for Yom Kippur includes the prophetic reading of the book of Jonah, who was sent by God to the city of Nineveh to urge the people to repent and change their evil ways in order to avoid their destruction. The people of Nineveh listened and changed their actions— but will we? Today, the whole world is like Nineveh, in danger of annihilation and in need of repentance and redemption. Each one of us must be a Jonah, with a mission to warn the world that it must turn away from greed, injustice, and materialism in order to avoid a global catastrophe.

As I did the research and writing for this book, I saw Israel increasingly isolated, facing what former Israeli Defense Minister Ehud Barak called a looming "diplomatic tsunami." I saw the United States and many other countries facing difficult economic conditions, and signs of climate change occurring more frequently. And I saw many Jews and others in denial about such issues or backing very conservative policies and politicians. As I saw these things, the importance of this book became increasingly clear to me. I hope that people will respond with an open mind and a desire to apply the arguments I have presented in pursuit of a more sustainable future. I very much hope that many respectful dialogues result, and that they lead to solutions to current problems.

I hope that the book will help revitalize Judaism (and perhaps other religions, based on our example), improve Israel's security and wellbeing, reduce antisemitism, address climate change and other environmental threats and, in general, lead to a far better future world.

* * * * *

SOME QUESTIONS TO PONDER

I would like to conclude this book with some questions that I have been pondering and trying to raise for many years about current Jewish life. Knowing my limitations and need for improvements, these questions are addressed at least as much to me as to anybody else. I ask these questions with great love and respect because I hope they will lead to positive changes that will be a *Kiddush Hashem* (sanctification of God's Name).

* Are we defining Judaism in too narrow a fashion? Shouldn't a definition of a religious Jew include a passion for social justice, a moral sensitivity, a strong feeling for ethics and morals?

* Is attending synagogue services more important than what happens there? Are we transformed by our services to become better people, to do something about the injustices and indignities suffered by our fellow humans?

* Have we forgotten who we are and what we stand for and Who we represent? Have we forgotten our roles—to be God's servants and witnesses, a light unto the nations, a holy people, descendants of the biblical prophets, the original champions of social justice?

* Are we too complacent, too ready to believe that we need not change? The patriarch Abraham began the history of Judaism by a radical break with the past, by smashing the idols of his society. Are we ready, too easily, to accept modern idols of conformity, materialism, secularism, and permissiveness?

* Do we realize that the task of religion is to be a challenge to the status quo, to prejudices, and to

a herd mentality, that complacency and taking things for granted are not consistent with Judaism?

* Are we taking our ethical ideals and prophetic teachings seriously enough? If we are implored "justice, justice, shall you pursue" and "let justice well up as waters and righteousness as a mighty stream," why is there so much complacency about poverty, exploitation, corruption at every level of government, and corporate actions that negatively affect our health and safety?

* Why do so few dream of a better world through Jewish Ideals?

* Are we segregating God in our synagogues? If God is sanctified by justice and righteousness, why are we so complacent in the face of an unredeemed, immoral, and unjust world?

* What would the prophets say about our society today? About Judaism in our time? About activities in our synagogues and other Jewish institutions?

* Moses said, "would that all God's people were prophets" (Numbers 11:29), but where is the voice of prophecy in our synagogues and other aspects of Judaism today?

* Have we forgotten, amidst our many study groups, that it is not study that is the chief thing, but action?

* If "to save one life is to save an entire world," why such silence in the face of conditions that lead to the deaths of millions of people annually due to hunger?

* If every person is created in God's image and we all have one Creator, why aren't there greater efforts to

combat racism, antisemitism, sexism, homophobia, and other forms of discrimination?

* Consistent with our prayers to a God of compassion, shouldn't we feel more compassion toward all of God's creatures?

* Considering the many threats to our (and God's) world, from climate change, destruction of tropical rainforests, depletion of the ozone layer, acid rain, rapid loss of biodiversity, soil erosion and depletion, and widespread air and water pollution, and in view of Judaism's strong environmental messages, shouldn't the preservation of the global environment be given greater priority on the Jewish agenda?

* If all Jews put our splendid teachings into practice, can you imagine the effects? Would there be so much crime, violence, distrust, prejudice, and discord, and air, water, and land pollution? Would we have so much "private affluence along with public squalor"? Would we have the misguided priorities that lead to spending so many billions of dollars for the military and not enough for human needs and a better environment?

* When considering what Judaism can and must become, shouldn't we consider the statement that Robert Kennedy often made: "There are those who look at things the way they are, and ask, 'Why?' I dream of things that never were, and ask, 'Why not?'"

* In summary, since Judaism is such a wonderful, challenging, dynamic tradition, why isn't this translated into more Jews' lives today?

I hope this book will help Jews and others respond to these challenging questions and will help revitalize Judaism and enable Jewish groups and individuals to truly apply Jewish values in their lives and communities in efforts to create a more compassionate, just, healthy, peaceful, and environmentally sustainable world.

Appendix A:
Action Ideas

It is not the study that is the chief thing, but the doing.
(Kiddushin 40b)

This book aims to demonstrate that Jewish values can help reduce many of the world's current threats. As the above quotation indicates, it is crucial to put Jewish teachings into practice and help shift the world from its present direction, heading toward potential catastrophes, as discussed earlier.

If you feel that global crises are so great that your efforts will have little effect, consider the following. The Jewish tradition teaches: "You are not obligated to complete the task, but neither are you free to desist from it." (*Pirkei Avot* 2:21) Each of us must make a start and do whatever we can to help improve the world. As stated in Chapter 1, Judaism teaches that a person is obligated to protest when there is evil and, if necessary, to proceed from protest to action. Each person is to imagine that the world is evenly balanced between good and evil, and that their actions can determine the destiny of the entire world (*Tosefta Kiddushin* 1:13).

Even if little is accomplished, trying to make improvements will prevent the hardening of your heart and will affirm your acceptance of moral responsibility. Even the act of consciousness raising is important, because it may lead to future action for change. Here are some things that each person can do:

1. Become well-informed. Learn the facts about global problems and the applicable Jewish values from this and other books (see Bibliography).
2. Inform others. Wear a button. Put bumper stickers where many people will see them. Make and display posters. Write timely letters to editors of local publications. Set up programs and discussions. Become registered with community, library, or school speakers' bureaus.
3. Simplify your lifestyle. Conserve energy. Recycle materials. Bike or walk whenever possible, instead of driving. Share rides. Use mass transit when appropriate.
4. Become a vegan, a vegetarian, or at least sharply reduce your consumption of animal products. As discussed earlier, veganism is the diet most consistent with such Jewish values as showing compassion to animals, taking care of one's health, preserving the environment, sharing with hungry people, conserving natural resources, and pursuing peace.
5. Work with organizations and groups on some of the significant issues discussed in this book. For a list of some key global survival-related organizations and their websites, see Appendix C. If there are no local groups or if you differ with such groups on some important issue, set up a group in your synagogue, Jewish center, or Hillel.
6. Encourage your public and congregational libraries to order, stock, and circulate books on global issues and Jewish teachings related to them. Donate your duplicate copies, request that libraries regularly acquire

such books and subscribe to relevant magazines, and, if you can afford it, buy some to donate.

7. Speak or organize events with guest speakers or create audio-visual presentations on how Jewish values address global issues.

8. Ask rabbis and other religious leaders to give sermons or classes that discuss Judaism's teachings on current global threats.

9. Ask principals of yeshivas and day schools to see that their curricula reflect traditional Jewish concerns with environmental, peace, and justice issues. Volunteer to speak to classes and to help plan curricula.

10. Contact editors of local newspapers and ask that more space be devoted to global issues. Write articles and letters using information from this book and other sources.

11. Try to influence public policy on the issues discussed in this book. Organize letter-writing campaigns and group visits to politicians to lobby for a safer, saner, healthier, environmentally sustainable world.

12. Engage with rabbis and religious educators and leaders on how we should be applying to today's critical issues such Jewish mandates as "justice, justice shall you pursue," "seek peace and pursue it," "*bal tashchit* (you shall not destroy)," and "love your neighbor as yourself."

13. As an outgrowth of Jewish teachings on helping hungry people and conserving resources, work to end the tremendous amount of waste associated with many Jewish organizational functions and celebrations. Respectfully and gently encourage friends, relatives, and institutions to simplify their lifestyles, reduce, and serve less lavish celebratory meals (and put this into

practice at your own celebrations). Request that meat not be served, since production of meat wastes grain, land, and other resources. Refraining from eating meat also expresses identification with the millions of people who lack an adequate diet, as well as the billions of farmed animals slaughtered each year. Reclaim leftover food from *simchas* (Jewish celebrations) to donate to shelters and food kitchens. Recommend to people hosting a celebration that they donate a portion of the cost of the event to Mazon or another group working to reduce hunger.

14. Help set up a committee to analyze and reduce energy consumption in the synagogue. Apply steps taken to reduce synagogue energy use as a model for similar action on other buildings and homes in the community.

15. Set up a social action committee in your synagogue, temple, Jewish center, day or afternoon school, or campus to help people get more involved in educational and action-centered activities. Build coalitions with other social justice groups in the community.

16. Raise the consciousness of your synagogue and other local Jewish organizations and individuals. Ask questions such as those at the end of Chapter 15.

Appendix B: The Making of a Jewish Activist

I am a *ba'al t'shuvah*—meaning "one who has returned"—a Jew who started practicing Judaism late in life. I did not grow up in a religious family and I did not receive a yeshiva education as religious Jewish children generally do today.

Most of my current Jewish learning comes not from formal education, but from extensive reading and conversations with Jews from many different backgrounds, plus Torah classes and lectures over the past few decades.

Like most Jewish boys growing up in New York during the 1940s, I went to a Talmud Torah school a couple of afternoons a week after public school and Sunday mornings in order to prepare for my bar mitzvah. But I was not then particularly interested either in Jewish teachings or societal issues. Rather, like most of my friends and classmates who didn't go to Hebrew school, I was primarily interested in swimming in the nearby Atlantic Ocean, playing handball, baseball, basketball, and other sports with friends, and rooting for the New York Yankees. I would devour every sports section that I could when the Yankees won, but a Yankee defeat would make me very sad. Nowadays I've lost most of my interest in spectator sports. I still support most New York teams, but very seldom spend any time watching them.

One aspect of Judaism that did interest me in my early years was the wisdom teachings contained in a section of the *Mishnah* called *Pirkei Avot*, the "Ethics of the Fathers." This tractate, which contains short, pithy sayings from the early Talmudic rabbis and scholars, is a basic manual on how to be a good Jew. *Pirkei Avot* is still my favorite section of the *Mishnah*, and its passages have helped guide me through life, especially the following:

* You are not required to complete the task, but neither are you free to desist from [doing all that you can]. (2:21)
* Be of the disciples of Aaron [the brother of Moses]: love peace and pursue peace, love all people, and bring them closer to the Torah. (1:12)
* Who is rich? The person who rejoices in his or her portion. (4:1)
* Who is wise? The person who learns from every other person. (4:1)

* * * * *

After graduating from high school in 1952, I wasn't sure what career to pursue, but finally decided to study civil engineering, mainly because that was the field my older brother had chosen. Because I didn't want to go to an out-of-town college and tuition was free at the City University, I attended the City College of New York. Because that campus was far from my home in Far Rockaway, I decided to take advantage of the option of taking my pre-engineer-ing courses for two years at Queens College, which was closer to home.

This decision was a major turning point in my life. Had I gone to City College, initially I would have interacted primarily with engineering students, people interested mostly in mathematical, scientific, and technical courses and concepts. At Queens College, I took liberal arts courses alongside students who had a broader range of views and outlooks.

Because I didn't drive a car at the time, I rode in various carpools to and from the campus. This put me in contact with a wide variety of people and ideas, ranging from very conservative to extremely radical. I started investigating current issues in order to refute some of the radical ideas that I was hearing for the first time. I soon began to recognize the injustices in the world and became imbued with the idea that I should be involved in struggling against these injustices. I began reading books like *The Grapes of Wrath*, and viewing films like *Mr. Smith Goes to Washington*, which inspired me to try to learn more and to strive to improve society.

During this time, my involvement with Judaism diminished to practically nothing. I saw the synagogues and Jewish groups as being primarily concerned with ritual for the sake of ritual, and with maintaining their membership rolls and social status. The Jewish institutions did not seem to be involved with the societal causes of the day and were totally irrelevant to me.

I was now so committed to working to end society's injustices that I seriously considered becoming an English major, in order to write and make others aware of what I was learning. I loved reading novels and reports about historical events and social issues. I yearned to learn more and to apply my knowledge in the struggle toward a more just, peaceful world.

However, family members, fellow students, and college advisors all pointed out how well I was doing in my pre-engineering classes (I had the top grade point average of all the students in the department) and stressed that I would have a much easier time making a living as an engineer than as a writer.

I took their advice and remained in civil engineering, but my feelings about social issues were so strong that I seriously considered not being involved in the world of commerce and business. Instead, I thought about moving to Israel to work on a kibbutz. I saw that system of communal living, cooperative efforts, and desire to serve one's community as a model of an ideal society most consistent with my views at that time. I even planned a trip to Israel immediately after graduating from City College in order to further explore that possibility.

Then, in my final semester, something occurred that represented another major turning point in my life. Because I had the top grade point average in my Civil Engineering class, I was offered a position as an instructor in the Department of Civil Engineering at City College, starting in the spring semester of 1957. I saw this as a great opportunity and quickly accepted the position. This would enable me to help people and to stay out of the business world, which I then regarded as a "rat race" that involved advancing one's career at the expense of others. As a college instructor, I would be able to apply and teach the many concepts I had learned in my studies. I would also be working with material that I had mastered and enjoyed.

I did go to Israel in the summer of 1957, and I did spend some time working on a kibbutz. But my great excitement about my future teaching and the honor I felt at being chosen to be a member of City College's Civil Engineering Department, working side-by-side with teachers whom I greatly admired, reduced my interest in living on a kibbutz. I recall spending my last day in Israel excitedly preparing lecture notes for the course on "Strength of Materials" that I would be teaching shortly after my return.

At the same time, I had a deep love for Israel, which I regarded as a modern-day miracle. Shortly after I returned to the United States, I gave a talk at a "cousin's club" meeting at which I extolled many aspects of life in Israel.

* * * * *

The next major change in my life came when I married Loretta Susskind in 1960 (yes, we have been married now for over sixty years). When I began dating Loretta, she was a social worker at a center in Harlem. We shared an interest in addressing social ills and helping less fortunate people. Loretta came from a more religious family and background than I did. She had continued her Jewish studies beyond the pre-teen Talmud Torah classes and had graduated from Marshalia Hebrew High School. Loretta wanted to introduce Jewish rituals into our family life once we were married. So, she presented me with some books on the Sabbath, the mikvah (Jewish ritual bath), and other Jewish practices.

I read these books somewhat reluctantly at first, and then with increasing interest. I began to see that my ideas about working for a better world were included in the Jewish worldview. I now understood the "task" from which Pirkei Avot says we are not free to desist from as the ongoing process of improving the world. There was plenty of opportunity for a fulfilling spiritual, socially active life within my own tradition!

In fact, I began to see that the whole saga of Jewish history involved a struggle to maintain the Jewish people and its ethical teachings in the face of oppression, widespread antisemitism, hatred, antagonism, and violence.

The more I read, the more I became interested in learning about all aspects of Judaism. In the process, I began to incorporate some Jewish practices into my own life. At first, I didn't attend synagogue services on Shabbat mornings, but would find a nice quiet place outdoors and read Jewish books on a wide variety of topics.

Around this time, Loretta and I purchased a set of five wonderful anthologies: *A Treasury of Jewish Quotations, A Treasury of Jewish Poetry, A Treasury of Jewish Folklore, A Treasury of American Jewish Stories,* and *A Modern Treasury of Jewish Thought.* As I read *A Modern Treasury of Jewish Thought,* I became increasingly thrilled to discover that there were brilliant Jewish thinkers who wrote eloquently about applying Jewish values to the world. I was especially excited by the writings of Rabbi Abraham Joshua Heschel. I relished his radical analysis of Judaism and his honest criticism of "religious behaviorism," which he defined as performing the *mitzvot* (ritual commandments) without any real devotion or any attempt to relate them to the realities of our society. And I loved the powerful but poetic ways that he expressed his challenging ideas.

It was also very important to me that Heschel was both a religious Jew and an activist. He marched with Martin Luther

King, advocated early on for the liberation of Soviet Jews, and spoke out courageously against what I regarded as an illegal, unjust, and immoral war in Vietnam—despite the disapproval of his views and activities from many Jewish leaders.

Through Heschel, I recognized that my earlier rejection of Judaism was not because of any problems inherent in Judaism. Rather, it was because of what the practice of Judaism in the mid-twentieth century had become. As Heschel put it:

> Religion declined not because it was refuted, but because it became irrelevant, dull, oppressive, insipid. When faith is completely replaced by creed, worship by discipline, love by habit; when the crisis of today is ignored because of the splendor of the past; when faith becomes an heirloom rather than a living fountain; when religion speaks only in the name of authority rather than with the voice of compassion, its message becomes meaningless.[1]

I increasingly found that all my social ideals were included within Judaism, and that Judaism provides a structure for leading a meaningful and involved spiritual life—if only people would really practice it. I was very impressed to learn how the Jews had maintained their beliefs and practices in spite of persecutions and harassment in many lands and historical periods. The more I learned, the more I was able to relate Jewish theology to current social issues.

Discovering the writings of Martin Buber further reinforced my emerging belief that it was actually the distortion of religious teachings that I was so much against. I concluded that, to some extent, my religion had been "stolen." Back then in the 1960s, many observant Jews around me seemed to be locked into ritual for its own sake, without seeing or applying the deeper values that could challenge an unjust status quo. People were reading about Moses confronting Pharaoh in the Torah, but few were confronting the oppressors of our own time. Because of my beliefs, I wrote the book, *Who Stole My Religion: Revitalizing Judaism and Applying Jewish Values to Help Heal Our Imperiled Planet*, which was published in 2016.

While teaching at City College, I studied for my Master's degree in civil engineering. I was enjoying my teaching and interactions with students so much that I decided to make college teaching my career. However, I didn't want to seek a Ph.D., because it would involve doing research in a relatively narrow area. Back then, many engineering colleges were accepting professional engineering licenses in lieu of a Ph.D., so I decided to pursue that path instead. This involved getting some experience working in the industry and passing several tests. My teaching experience and strong academic background made passing the tests a relatively easy matter, but I had to leave teaching for a while in order to get the required professional experience.

Before entering the work field, I decided to take care of my military obligations. At that time, the United States was in a major technological race against the then Soviet Union. In 1958, the Soviets had surprised the world by launching Sputnik I, the world's first artificial satellite. This was a wake-up call to the US government, a warning that we were falling behind in technology. As a result, engineers were classified by the military into a special category called "Critical Skills." The government's philosophy at the time was that everyone should get some basic training in order to be ready if the United States was attacked, but that people with special skills should not be taken away for long periods from the more important work of improving the nation's technological abilities.

Therefore, I only had to be in the US Army for three months. Those few months in the army were the only substantial time in my adult life when I was not focused on studying for tests, preparing class lectures and other talks, researching and writing articles and books, and dealing with other professional concerns. It was a valuable time for organizing my thoughts about social issues.

After leaving the army, I worked at Ammon & Whitney, an engineering company in lower Manhattan that designed the Verrazano-Narrows Bridge connecting Staten Island and Brooklyn. I didn't work on that particular project, but I did work on many other civil engineering design projects. Although I enjoyed working with other engineers and applying what I had learned, my desire to return to college teaching remained strong.

As soon as I had sufficient practical experience, I arranged to take the necessary tests for my professional engineering license. Fortunately, because of my academic and teaching background, I easily passed.

My next step was to seek a position teaching civil engineering at a college. I thought that my academic achievements, my teaching experience, my professional experience, and my professional engineer's license would make this easy, but that was not the case. The only civil engineering department willing to hire me was at Rutgers University, and then only if I also enrolled as a Ph.D. candidate there. Seeing no other possibility that would enable me to resume teaching, I agreed. So, I moved to New Brunswick, New Jersey, with my wife and first child, Susan Esther.

I enjoyed my new teaching activities, and once again did well in my engineering studies. However, I had difficulty choosing a topic for my Ph.D. thesis. This was a source of great frustration to me. I loved teaching and desperately wanted to continue it, but I absolutely hated the idea of spending endless hours researching a relatively minor topic that few people outside a specialized field would ever be interested in. I would much prefer to spend the time teaching and promoting positive causes. I became so frustrated over this that I even thought of dropping out of the Ph.D. program altogether. When people warned me that this would end my chances of maintaining a college teaching position, I replied that I would just teach at a two-year college.

Had I dropped out of the Ph.D. program, it would have greatly hindered my teaching career, because even community colleges began to require Ph.D. degrees for full-time teachers. Fortunately, I finally found a topic, "Analysis of Circular Plates on Elastic Foundations Under Radially Symmetrical Loadings," that enabled me to use my mathematical and other skills. I also received National Science Foundation grants for two consecutive summers, which provided me with the time to work on the project. In 1967 I received my Ph.D. in "Applied Mechanics." This enabled me to continue my teaching career until my retirement from the College of Staten Island as a full professor in 1999.

As I was completing my Ph.D. requirements, I was informed that Rutgers had a "no inbreeding" policy. This meant that they did not continue employing people who had taught at Rutgers while getting their Ph.D. degrees there. The Rutgers philosophy was that, by hiring people from a wide variety of other schools, they would get the greatest possible cross-fertilization of ideas. An academically laudable position, but one that left me without a job.

So once again, I sent out resumes, and this time I received an invitation to teach at Pratt Institute in Brooklyn. They offered me a position as an assistant professor with the possibility of a rapid promotion to associate professor, and I accepted. Pratt did not have a civil engineering department, so I worked in the mechanical engineering department, because many of the courses that I had taught were equally applicable to both civil and mechanical engineering.

In 1968, my wife and I moved to Staten Island to be closer to Pratt Institute. By then we had three children: Susan Esther, David Elliot, and Deborah Ann. In 1970, I learned that there was an opening at what was then called Staten Island Community College (SICC). That was only about five minutes by car from my house, which would make it easier to help out with the kids. The position had a better salary and benefits as well, so I decided to apply. I was accepted, but only as a substitute in the civil technology department for a professor who had left for a year to help set up Hostos Community College in the Bronx.

I was told that the professor for whom I was substituting probably wouldn't return. However, he did decide to return, and that put me in a very difficult position. I had given up a tenured post at Pratt Institute to be a substitute at SICC. Now it looked as if I would have to leave. My efforts at finding another position were not panning out, and I was becoming increasingly desperate.

Fortunately, the City University started its "Open Admissions" policy at that time, providing remediation to students who did not meet entrance requirements in

Mathematics and English. Because of that program, I was able to join the SICC mathematics department, teaching remedial math. It wasn't the ideal job, but it helped feed my family.

Needless to say, this was a very difficult time in my life. But, as the Chinese philosopher Lin Yutang said in his book *The Importance of Living,* one does not know what is "good luck" or "bad luck" until the end of a sequence of events, because what appears to be a negative event often leads to a positive result and vice versa. In the Jewish tradition, there is a similar teaching: Joseph, who is sold into slavery by his brothers, ends up becoming an important official in Egypt and saves thousands of people from famine, including those very same brothers who had betrayed him in the first place.

And so, it turned out for me, that my "bad luck" became my good fortune. During the difficult period when I was trying to find a new teaching position, I went to the director of an experimental department at SICC known as "The Place," which offered a number of interdisciplinary courses. I asked about the possibility of teaching in their department. They had no opening at the time, but later, after I was teaching in the mathematics department, they asked me to teach a course, "The Impact of Science on Human Values and Problems."

At first, I hesitated. This topic was completely different from anything I had previously taught or even considered in much detail. At the same time, it offered the possibility of applying my interest in social issues. I decided to accept the offer. That was a major turning point in my life, because teaching that course started me on the path of environmental activism that I still pursue today.

Through the use of essays, short stories, and plays, I explored with the students the implications of the rapid explosion of scientific and technological advances on society and its problems.

This was right after the first Earth Day in April 1970, when there was widespread interest in environmental threats, so we devoted a lot of discussion time to ecological issues. As I became increasingly concerned about the environment, the original course was replaced by a new one called "Environmental Issues on Staten Island."

I was a relatively new resident of Staten Island, so I had to rely on local resources to help me teach the course. I pored over old newspapers and reports, interviewed Staten Island environmentalists, invited guest speakers, and showed films and videos. I led field trips to places like Fresh Kills landfill (then the world's largest garbage dump). We also visited sewage treatment plants, natural areas, and different types of housing developments. Instead of a final examination, the students were required to write a report and give an oral presentation about some current environmental issue impacting Staten Island.

Because this course was so different from anything I had previously taught, I devoted a great deal of my time, energy, and thinking to developing it. In the process, I became increasingly active in responding to environmental issues, often writing letters to the editor for publication in the *Staten Island Advance* about local, national, and global environmental and other societal concerns. I also spoke on these topics to various groups at the college and in the community.

After a number of years teaching "Environmental Issues on Staten Island," budgetary considerations led to an end of "The Place." As a result, I was no longer able to offer the course. At first, this was a big blow. But I soon recognized that this "disaster" had, in fact, freed up a lot of time and energy that I could now devote to other activities. I was determined to continue educating people about environmental issues, and it dawned on me that perhaps I could teach a course relating mathematics to environmental and other global concerns.

At the time, I was teaching a basic math course for liberal arts majors. This was a course that students had to take in order to fulfill the requirements for their degrees. Most of the students were poorly prepared and poorly motivated. So, instead of the usual course that included a smorgasbord of unconnected topics, I decided to offer a course called "Mathematics and the Environment," in which basic mathematical concepts and problems would be used to explore current critical problems. We considered such issues as pollution, resource scarcities, hunger, energy, population growth, nutrition, and health, using basic calculations, ratios and proportions, circle diagrams, bar charts, line graphs, scatterplots, sequences, and elementary statistics and probability. In short, my course covered similar math concepts to those in the old course, but all the examples and exercises connected with environmental concerns.

The course was well received. I found plenty of valuable material in the daily newspapers and weekly magazines, which I used to create mathematical problems. The annual World Population Data Sheet of the Population Reference Bureau and that group's many demographic reports were also very valuable. The class considered issues like percentages of the world's population in the United States versus China, projected increases in world population, effects of infant mortality, and so on. Analyzing the computer-generated graphs in a book entitled *The Limits to Growth*, we saw that the world would face severe future problems if global population and industrial production continued to increase exponentially. Once again, instead of a final exam, I required written and oral reports on environmentally related topics, using the mathematics that students had learned in the course.

Designing this course resulted in my reading, thinking, and teaching about a wide variety of environmental crises. As I worked with the statistics related to these issues, I became increasingly aware of environmental threats and the urgent need to respond to them. During my first sabbatical, in the 1978 79 academic year, I wrote a course text called *Mathematics and Global Survival*. This book was updated and revised every few years to reflect changing conditions, and became the foundation for my later book, *Judaism and Global Survival*.

* * * * *

Throughout my academic career, my involvement in Judaism was also growing. After moving to Staten Island in 1968, my family immediately joined the local Young Israel of Staten Island, a Modern Orthodox synagogue. I have met wonderful, generous, sincere, deeply committed people in this congregation. I have found many members to be extremely charitable, kind, and deeply involved in learning and davening.

Given these involvements and my personal friendships, as well as an awareness of own limitations and weaknesses, it is not easy to be critical of my own community. But I think some constructive criticism might be valuable. Through the application of Jewish teachings on social activism, we can join in the process of moving our endangered planet to a more just, peaceful, and environmentally sustainable path. It is no longer enough to ask, "Is it good for the Jews?" We must now also ask, "Is it good for the planet?"

I am deeply disturbed by the seeming lack of concern for universal issues among many of my religious Jewish brethren (as well as most other people). Within their own communities, they are very caring and generous, but they often seem oblivious to issues that affect the rest of humanity. It sometimes seems that one can be more readily accepted in certain circles if one has intolerant, reactionary ideas, than if one has a commitment to Jewish universal values.

For this reason, I often need to go outside my immediate synagogue group in order to find support for my Jewish activism. Through my articles, talks, books, and letters to editors, I am able to express my societal concerns, but I often feel alienated from my local community in the process. How grateful I am to be living in the age of email, the Internet, and Zoom.

The electronic age has enabled me to be in regular contact with many like-minded people around the world, express my ideas to a wider audience, and to reach beyond the limitations of my own community.

In the early 1970s, partly in an attempt to increase my synagogue's involvement in social justice issues, I became coeditor of the synagogue's newsletter and frequently contributed articles. I was (and still am) searching for ways to demonstrate Judaism's meaning and relevance to the world. I sensed a great gap between the glorious Jewish teachings that I was learning about and the realities that I was seeing in my synagogue and Jewish community.

Jews have been chosen to be God's servants, a light unto the nations and a holy people, descendants of the prophets, the original champions of social justice. Why, then, was there so much complacency in the face of so many current critical problems? Why so few dreams of a better world through the application of Jewish teachings?

I saw great potential for applying the values I was reading about in Jewish texts to the real world around us. I wanted to help revitalize my religion, to harness it to help save our imperiled planet. My reaction to the Judaism of the time is summed up in the following paragraph from one of my articles for the synagogue newsletter:

> It is generally not religious values that dominate in churches and synagogues today, but rather materialistic, middle-class values. The problem is that far too few people (sometimes including myself) take God and religious teachings seriously enough. If we did, would we fail to protest against the destruction of the precious planet that God has given us as our home? Would we be so apathetic while an estimated nine million people die of hunger and its effects annually (when God has provided sufficient food for every person on earth), and additional millions suffer from poverty and a lack of shelter, clean water, and other necessities while hundreds of billions of dollars are spent creating newer and better ways to wage war? If a person took God and religious values seriously, he or she would be among the greatest critics of present society, where religious values are generally given lip service, at best. She or he would be among the greatest champions of peace and justice.

Unfortunately, these editorials were like crying into the wilderness. Nobody appeared to be listening. I felt as if I were tilting at windmills, engaging in a quixotic quest for "The Impossible Dream." This book is my latest attempt to turn these dreams into practical realities.

* * * * *

The "Mathematics and the Environment" course had another profound effect on my life—it set me on the road toward vegetarianism and later veganism.

Up until 1978, I was a typical American "meat and potatoes" eater. My mother would be sure to prepare my favorite dish, pot roast, whenever I came to visit with my wife and children. It was a family tradition that I would be served a turkey "drumstick" every Thanksgiving. And yet, I not only became a vegetarian, and later a vegan, but also now devote a major part of my time to writing, speaking, and teaching about the benefits of these diets and lifestyles.

What caused this major change?

While reviewing material on world hunger for my "Mathematics and the Environment" course in the 1970s, I became increasingly aware of the tremendous waste of grain that results from the production of beef. About 70 percent of the grain produced in the United States, and about 40 percent of the grain produced worldwide, is fed to animals destined for slaughter, while millions of people—many of them children—die of hunger and its effects annually.

Despite my own eating habits, I often led class discussions on the possibility of reducing meat consumption as a way of helping hungry people. After several semesters of this, I listened to my own advice and gave up eating red meat, while continuing to eat chicken and fish.

I then began to read about the many health benefits of vegetarianism and about the horrible living conditions of animals raised on factory farms. As a result, I was increasingly attracted to the vegetarian way of life. I was very fortunate to attend a course on "Judaism and Vegetarianism" at Lincoln Square Synagogue (LSS) in Manhattan taught by Jonathan Wolf, founder and first president of Jewish Vegetarians of North America. I learned many things and gained much insight from him. We became good friends, and Jonathan has provided valuable advice and editing skills for my Judaic writings.

On January 1, 1978, I decided to join the International Jewish Vegetarian Society. The membership form offered two choices: 1) practicing vegetarian (one who refrains from eating any flesh); or 2) non-vegetarian (one who is in sympathy with the movement, but not yet a vegetarian). I decided to become a full-practicing vegetarian. I checked that box on the form, and ever since that moment I have avoided eating any meat, fowl, or fish.

In 2000, I became a vegan, abstaining from using any animal products as much as possible, except those employed for religious purposes to make such ritual objects as Torah scrolls, *mezzuzot*, and tefillin.

Following that decision in 1978, I learned a great deal more about vegetarianism's connections to health, nutrition, ecology, and animal welfare. I also began wondering about the deeper connections between my vegetarianism and Judaism. I learned that the first biblical dietary regimen (Genesis 1:29) was strictly vegetarian, and that the future age of world peace and harmony, the Messianic period, will also be a vegan time.

I soon became convinced that there are important Jewish mandates to preserve our health, be kind to animals, protect the environment, conserve natural resources, share with hungry people, and seek and pursue peace—all of which point to vegetarianism, and even more so veganism, as the ideal diet for Jews. To get this message out to a wider audience, I wrote a book, *Judaism and Vegetarianism*, which was first published in 1982, with revised and expanded editions published in 1988 and 2001.

The more I have learned about the wastefulness of meat production, the negative health effects of animal-based diets, and the cruelties of factory farms—and their inconsistencies with Jewish values—the more I have come to see a switch toward vegetarianism (and later veganism) as not only a personal choice, but a societal and a Jewish imperative. Reducing meat consumption is an essential component in the solution of many national and global problems, as well as an important symbolic religious move toward the peaceable kingdom envisioned by the prophets. As discussed in Chapter 8, the most effective way to address climate threats is through a major shift toward vegan diets.

In recent years, I have been devoting considerable time and energy toward making others aware of the importance of applying Jewish values in efforts toward healing our imperiled planet.

I wrote a book, *Vegan Revolution: Saving Our World, Revitalizing Judaism*, that was published in 2020. In an effort to encourage many dialogues that will help promote a better world, I have been emailing a complimentary digital copy of the book to as many people as possible.

I wrote an e-book, *Restoring and Transforming the Ancient Jewish New Year for Animals: An Idea Whose Time Has Come*, that was published in August 2022. I am using it as part of a major campaign, along with other Jewish activists, to help restore the ancient holiday and to transform it into a day devoted to increasing awareness of Judaism's compassionate teachings about animals and how far current realities for animals are from these teachings. To further that objective, I have emailed the e-book to many rabbis and other Jews, urging them to consider setting up events related to the restored holiday and also to share the e-book widely. I have also organized and led several related Zoom events, with leading activists taking part.

I helped produce and appeared in the documentary *A Sacred Duty: Applying Jewish Values to Help Heal the World*, which premiered in Jerusalem in November 2007. Because the issues are so important and the threats are so great, I helped distribute over 40,000 complimentary copies of the DVD and made it freely available on YouTube. The video was produced as a labor of love and dedication, with no professional fee being received, by multi award–winning producer, director, writer, and cinematographer Lionel Friedberg, along with his wife Diana, a professional film editor. The documentary has been acclaimed by Jews, Christians, and others and has had a significant impact.

In addition, as part of my activism, I have:

* Appeared on over 100 radio and cable television programs;
* published many letters and several op-ed articles in a variety of publications;
* spoken frequently at conferences and meetings;

* given dozens of talks on vegetarianism, veganism, animal rights, environmental sustainability, and related issues;
* started a podcast, with which I plan to interview many vegan, animal rights, and environmental activists;
* contributed many blogs in both *Jewcology* and the *Times of Israel*;
* written two previous editions of *Judaism and Global Survival*, which were published in 1984 and 2002;
* set up a website on which I have over 250 articles and 25 podcasts at JewishVeg.org/Schwartz. They include articles relating Shabbat and all the Jewish holidays to vegetarianism and veganism;
* served as president emeritus and as a board member of Jewish Veg, formerly known as Jewish Vegetarians of North America (JVNA). Previously, I was president from 2002 to 2012, during which time I produced and sent out almost weekly email newsletters to keep Jewish vegetarians informed;
* served as president of the Society of Ethical and Religious Vegetarians (SERV), an inter-religious group dedicated to spreading vegetarian messages in many religious communities;
* served for several years as director of Veg Climate Alliance, a group dedicated to spreading awareness that a major shift to plant-based diets is essential to avert a climate catastrophe.

I have been fortunate in getting some recognition for my activities. In 1987, I was selected as "Jewish Vegetarian of the

Year" by JVNA, and in 2005, I was inducted into the "Hall of Fame" of the North American Vegetarian Society (NAVS).

* * * * *

In 2016, my wife and I moved to Israel, where I have remained active in promoting veganism and related causes through letters to editors, articles, talks, and personal conversations.

I have also averaged at least one published letter a month in the *Jerusalem Post*, and in May 2022 had letters published in seven consecutive issues of the publication. I have also had several articles published in that paper, including the following: "Climate Change: An Existential Threat to Israel, the U.S., and the World;" "Why Belgium's Ban on Kosher Slaughter Is Wrong;" and "Can a Climate Catastrophe Be Averted?"

My co-authored article, "Climate Change: An Existential Threat to Humanity and How We Can Survive," was a cover story in the *Jerusalem Report*, as were my article about Rabbi David Rosen, former chief rabbi of Ireland, and my article, "Why Jews Should Be Vegans." That publication also had a feature article about me entitled, "The Israeli Environmental Activist Seeking to Save Our World."

I have spoken often at the Protea Hills retirement village, where I and my wife now live, in the Shoresh area of Israel on topics in my Judaica books. Also, using Zoom, I led *Tu BiShvat* Seders in Israel and in the U.S. in 2021 and 2022, and moderated a 'teach-in" organized on Earth Day, April 22, 2021, involving twenty-one distinguished speakers, including six rabbis.

Having joyfully celebrated the weddings of four grandchildren and the births of six great-grandchildren since moving to Israel, I have a special interest in creating a decent, habitable world for future generations. I hope you will join me in this essential, holy task. I welcome comments, suggestions, questions, and constructive criticism. You may contact me at VeggieRich@gmail.com.

* * * * *

As I reflect on all of the above, I am so thankful that I have been blessed by God to have been able to make at least a small difference in trying to help create a better world. Of course, there is much more that needs to be done, and I hope to be able to devote much of the time that I will be granted by God to continuing the struggle. I hope that this volume will help inspire many others, especially young people, to work in the struggle to shift our very imperiled planet onto a healthier, more just, peaceful, more humane, and environmentally sustainable path.

APPENDIX C: GLOBAL SURVIVAL-RELATED ORGANIZATIONS

Listed below are just a few of the many Jewish and non-Jewish organizations working in a wide variety of areas to improve the world, to organize members of their communities to contribute and help, and to involve people in changing society. All of these websites have links to numerous other groups; you can also contact other organizations near you to find opportunities to join in and help make a difference.

A. Jewish Global Survival-Related Organizations and Their Websites

- American Jewish World Service: ajws.org.
- Animals Now, formerly Anonymous for Animal Rights: animals-now.org/en/.
- Arava Institute for Environmental Studies: arava.org.
- Aytzim: Ecological Judaism: aytzim.org.
- Coalition for the Advancement of Jewish Education (CAJE): myjewishlearning.com.
- Canfei Nesharim (Wings of Eagles): canfeinesharim.org.
- Coalition on the Environment and Jewish Life (COEJL): coejl.org.

- Concern for Helping Animals in Israel (CHAI): chai-online.org.
- EcoPeace Middle East, formerly Friends of the Earth Middle East (FoEME): foeme.org.
- Green Course (Megamah Yeruka): green.org.il.
- Hazon: hazon.org.
- Heschel Center for Environmental Learning and Leadership: www.heschelcenter.org.
- International Jewish Vegetarian Society: jvs.org.uk.
- Israeli Jewish Vegetarian Society (Ginger): ginger.org.il.
- Israel Union for Environmental Defense (IUED): iued.org.il.
- Jewish Veg, formerly known as Jewish Vegetarians of North America (JVNA): jewishveg.org.
- Let the Animals Live: secrettelaviv.com/best/services/let-the-animals-live.
- Mazon: A Jewish Response to Hunger: mazon.org.
- National Council of Jewish Women (NCJW): ncjw.org.
- Religious Action Center of Reform Judaism (RAC): rac.org.
- Richard Schwartz's collection of articles: jewishveg.org/schwartz.
- Shamayim V'Aretz, Jewish Animal Advocacy: shamayimvaretz.org.
- Shalom Center: theshalomcenter.org.
- Society for the Protection of Nature in Israel (SPNI): www.spni.org.
- Teva Learning Center: tevalearningcenter.org.
- Vegetarian Mitzvah: brook.com/jveg.
- Vegan Friendly: vegan-friendly.co.il.
- Vegan Nation: vegannation.io.

B. Non-Jewish Global Survival-Related Organizations and Their Websites

- Farm Animal Rights Movement (FARM): farmusa.org.
- Food First: foodfirst.org.
- GreenFaith: greenfaith.org.
- International Vegetarian Union: ivu.org.
- Mercy for Animals: mfa.org.
- National Library of Medicine (NLM): nlm.nih.gov.
- Natural Resources Defense Council: nrdc.org.
- Physicians Committee for Responsible Medicine (PCRM): pcrm.org.
- Population Reference Bureau: prb.org.
- Sierra Club: sierraclub.org.
- Union of Concerned Scientists (UCS): ucsusa.org.
- US Environmental Protection Agency (EPA): epa.gov.
- Vegetarian Resource Group: vrg.org.
- VegSource: vegsource.com.
- Worldwatch Institute: worldwatch.org.

BIBLIOGRAPHY

Books by Jews Relating Judaism to Current Issues

Amsel, Nachum. *The Jewish Encyclopedia of Moral and Ethical Issues*. Northvale, NJ: Jason Aronson, 1996.

Ben-Ami, Jeremy. *A New Voice for Israel: Fighting for the Survival of the Jewish Nation*. New York: Macmillan, 2011.

Benstein, Jeremy. *The Way into Judaism and the Environment*. Woodstock, VT: Jewish Lights Publishing, 2006.

Bernstein, Ellen, editor. *Ecology and the Jewish Spirit: Where Nature and the Spirit Meet*. Woodstock, VT: Jewish Lights Publishing, 1998.

Bernstein, Ellen and Dan Fink. *Let the Earth Teach You Torah: A Guide to Teaching Ecological Wisdom*. Wyncote, PA: Shomrei Adamah, 1992.

Broyde, Michael and John Witte (eds.). *Human Rights in Judaism: Cultural, Religious, and Political Perspectives*. Northvale, NJ: Jason Aronson, 1998.

Bush, Lawrence, and Jeffrey Dekro. *Jews, Money, and Social Responsibility: Developing a "Torah of Money" for Contemporary Life*. Philadelphia: The Shefa Fund, 1993.

Cardozo, Rabbi Nathan Lopes. *Jewish Law and Rebellion: A Plea for Religious Authenticity and Halachic Courage*. Jerusalem/New York: Urim Publications, 2018.

Carmell, Aryeh. *Masterplan: Judaism: Its Program, Meanings, Goals*. Jerusalem: Feldheim, 1991.

Dorff, Elliot. N., *The Way into Tikkun Olam*. Woodstock, VT: Jewish Lights Publishing, 2005.

Eisnitz, Gail A. *Slaughterhouse: The Shocking Story of Greed, Neglect, and Inhumane Treatment Inside the US Meat Industry.* Amherst, NY: Prometheus Books, 1997.

Fisher, Adam D. *To Deal Thy Bread to the Hungry.* New York: Union of American Hebrew Congregations, 1975.

Foer, Jonathan Safran. *Eating Animals.* New York: Little, Brown and Company, 2009.

Fuhrman, Joel, MD. *Fasting and Eating for Health: A Medical Doctor's Program for Conquering Disease.* New York: St. Martin's Press, 1995.

Greenberg, Rabbi Irving. *The Jewish Way: Living the Holidays.* New York: Summit Books, 1988.

Greger, Michael, MD. *How Not to Die: Discover the Foods Scientifically Proven to Prevent and Reverse Disease.* New York: Macmillan, 2015.

Gross, Aaron S. *The Question of the Animal and Religion: Theoretical Stakes, Practical Implications.* New York: Columbia University Press, 2015.

Heschel, Abraham J., *The Insecurity of Freedom: Essays on Human Freedom.* New York: Farrar, Straus and Giroux, 1967.

—— *The Prophets.* Jewish Philadelphia: Publication Society, 1962 (two volumes).

Hirsch, Richard G. *The Way of the Upright: A Jewish View of Economic Justice.* New York: Union of American Hebrew Congregations, 1973.

—— *Thy Most Precious Gift, Peace in Jewish Tradition.* New York: Union of American Hebrew Congregations, 1974.

Hirsch, Samson Raphael. *Horeb,* translated by Dayan I. New York/London/Jerusalem: Grunfeld, Soncino Press, 1962.

—— *The Nineteen Letters.* Jerusalem/New York: Feldheim, 1969.

Jacobs, Jill, *There Shall Be No Needy: Pursuing Social Justice Through Jewish Law & Tradition.* Woodstock, VT: Jewish Lights, 2010.

—— *Where Justice Dwells: A Hands-On Guide to Doing Social Justice in Your Jewish Community.* Woodstock, VT: Jewish Lights, 2011.

Kalechofsky, Roberta, editor. *Judaism and Animals Rights: Classical and Contemporary Responses.* Marblehead, MA: Micah Publications, 1992.

—— *Vegetarianism and Judaism: A Guide for Everyone.* Marblehead, MA: Micah Publications, 1992.

——. Vegetarian Judaism. Marblehead, MA: Micah Publications, 1998.

——, editor. *Rabbis and Vegetarianism: An Evolving Tradition.* Marblehead, MA: Micah Publications, 1995.

Kushner, Tony and Alisa Solomon, editors. *Wrestling with Zionism.* New York: Grove Press, 2005.

Lamm, Norman, editor. *The Good Society.* New York: Viking Press, 1974.

Landau Yechezkel. *Violence and the Value of Life in Jewish Tradition.* Jerusalem : Oz V'Shalom, 1984.

Labenz, Jacob Ari, and Rabbi Shmuly Yanklowitz, editors. *Jewish Veganism and Vegetarianism.* Albany: SUNY Press, 2019.

Lerner, Michael. *Jewish Renewal: A Path to Healing and Transformation.* New York: G. P. Putnam's Sons, 1994.

—— Embracing *Israel/Palestine: A Strategy to Heal and Transform the Middle East.* San Francisco: Tikkun Books, 2012.

Levine, Aaron. *Free Enterprise and Jewish Law: Aspects of Jewish Business Ethics.* New York: Ktav, 1980.

Merzer, Glen. *Food Is Climate: A Response to Al Gore, Bill Gates, Paul Hawken, & The Traditional Narrative on Climate Change.* Atlanta, GA: Vivid Thoughts Press, 2021.

Neril, Yonatan, and Evonne Marzouk, editors. *Uplifting People and Planet: Eighteen Essential Teachings on the Environment.* Elizabeth, NJ: Canfei Nesharim, Jewcology, and Jewish Eco Seminars, 2013.

Nerl, Yonatan and Leo Dee, editors. *Eco Bible: Volume 1: An Ecological Commentary on Genesis and Exodus*. Jerusalem: Interfaith Center for Sustainable Development, 2020.

—— *Eco Bible: Volume 2: An Ecological Commentary on Leviticus, Numbers, and Deuteronomy*. Jerusalem: Interfaith Center for Sustainable Development, 2022.

Ornish Dean, MD. *Dr. Dean Ornish's Program for Reversing Heart Disease*. New York: Ballantine, 1990.

Polner, Murray, and Stefan Merken, editors. *Peace, Justice and Jews: Reclaiming Our Tradition*. New York: Bunim & Bannigan, 2007.

Polner Murray, and Goodman, Naomi, editors, *The Challenge of Shalom: The Jewish Tradition of Peace and Justice*. Philadelphia: New Society Publishers, 1994.

Regenstein, Lewis. *Replenish the Earth: The Teachings of the World's Religions on Protecting Animals and the Environment*. New York: Crossroads, 1991.

Rifkin, Jeremy. *Beyond Beef: The Rise and Fall of the Cattle Culture*. New York: Dutton, 1992.

Robbins, John. *Diet for a New America: How Your Food Choices Affect Your Health, Happiness and the Future of Life on Earth, 25th Anniversary Edition*. Novato, CA: New World Library, 2012.

—— *The Food Revolution: How Your Diet Can Help Save Your Life and the World*. Berkeley, CA: Conari Press, 2001.

Rose, Aubrey (editor). *Judaism and Ecology*. New York/ London: Cassell, 1992.

Sacks, Chief Rabbi Jonathan. *The Dignity of Difference: How to Avoid the Clash of Civilizations*. London/New York: Continuum, 2003.

Schlottmann, Christopher, and Jeff Sebo. *Food, Animals, and the Environment: An Ethical Approach*. New York: Earthscan/ Routledge, 2019.

Schochet, Rabbi Elijah J. *Animal Life in Jewish Tradition*. New York: K'tav, 1984.

Schwartz, Richard H. *Judaism and Vegetarianism*. New York: Lantern, 2001.

—— *Vegan Revolution: Saving Our World, Revitalizing Judaism*. New York, Lantern, 2020.

Schwartz, Richard H., with Rabbi Yonassan Gershom and Rabbi Shmuly Yanklowitz. *Who Stole My Religion: Revitalizing Judaism and Applying Jewish Values to Help Heal Our Imperiled Planet*. Jerusalem/New York: Urim Publications, 2016.

Sears, David. *Compassion for Humanity in the Jewish Tradition*. Northvale, NJ: Jason Aronson, 1998.

—— *The Vision of Eden: Animal Welfare and Vegetarianism in Jewish Law and Mysticism*. Jerusalem/New York: Meorei Ohr, 2015.

Seidenberg, David. *Kabbalah and Ecology: God's Image in the More-Than-Human World*. New York/Cambridge, UK: Cambridge University Press, 2015.

Shapiro, Paul. *Clean Meat: How Growing Meat Without Animals Will Revolutionize, Dinner and the World*. New York: Simon & Schuster, 2018.

Shatz, H., Chaim I. Waxman, and Nathan J. Diament, editors. *Tikkun Olam: Social Responsibility in Jewish Thought and Law*. Northvale, NJ: Jason Aronson, 1997.

Singer, Peter. *Animal Liberation*. New York: New York Review of Books Publishers, 1990.

Slifkin, Natan, *Man and Beast: Our Relationship with Animalism in Jewish Law and Thought*. New York: Yashar Books, 2006.

—— *Perek Shirah: Nature's Song*. Zoo Torah, second edition, 2011.

Strassfeld, Sharon and Michael. *The Third Jewish Catalog–Creating Community*. Philadelphia: Jewish Publication Society, 1980.

Tal, Alon. *Pollution in a Promised Land: An Environmental History of Israel*. Berkeley: University of California Press, 2002.

—— *The Land Is Full: Addressing Overpopulation in Israel,* New Haven and London: Yale University Press, 2016.

Tamari. Meir. *With All Your Possessions: Jewish Ethics and Economic Life.* Northvale, NJ: Jason Aronson, 1998.

Vorspan, Albert and David Saperstein. *Jewish Dimensions of Social Justice: Tough Moral Choices of Our Time.* New York: Union of American Hebrew Congregations Press, 1998.

Vorspan, Albert. *Great Jewish Debates and Dilemmas: Jewish Perspectives on Moral Issues in Conflict in the Eighties.* New York: Union of American Hebrew Congregations, 1980.

Waskow, Arthur I. *Godwrestling –Round 2: Ancient Wisdom, Future Paths.* Woodstock, VT: Jewish Lights, 1996.

Waskow, Arthur I., editor. *Torah of the Earth: Exploring 4,000Years of Ecology in Jewish Thought.* Woodstock, VT: Jewish Lights, 2000 (two volumes).

Yanklowitz, Shmuly. *Jewish Ethics & Social Justice: A Guide for the 21st Century.* Pompano Beach, FL: Derusha Publishing, 2011.

Yanklowitz, Shmuly. *The Jewish Vegan.* Santa Fe Springs, CA: The Shamayim v'Aretz Institute, 2015.

——, editor. *Kashrut and Jewish Food Ethics.* Boston, MA: Academic Studies Press, 2019.

Books by Non-Jews About Current Issues

Bingham, the Rev. Canon Sally G. *Love God, Heal Earth: 21 Leading Religious Voices Speak Out on Our Sacred Duty to Protect the Environment.* Pittsburgh: Saint Lynn's Press, 2009.

Brown, Lester R. *Plan B 4.0: Mobilizing to Save Civilization.* New York/London: W.W. Norton and Company, 2009.

—— *World On the Edge: How to Prevent Environmental and Economic Collapse.* New York/London: W. W. Norton and Company, 2011.

Campbell, T. Colin, with Thomas M. Campbell II. *The China Study: The Most Comprehensive Health Study Ever Conducted and the Startling Implications for Diet, Weight Loss and Longterm Health.* Dallas: Benbella Books, 2004.

Coats, David C. *Old McDonald's Factory Farm.* New York: Continuum, 1989.

Gore, Albert, *An Inconvenient Truth: The Planetary Emergence of Global Warming and What We Can Do About It*. Emmaus, PA: Rodale Press, 2006.

—— *Our Choice: A Plan to Solve the Climate Crisis*. Emmaus, PA: Rodale Press, 2009.

Harrison, Ruth. *Animal Machines*. London: Vincent Street, 1964.

Hoggan, James. *Climate Cover-Up: The Crusade to Deny Global Warming*. Vancouver/Toronto/ Berkeley: Greystone Books, 2009.

Lappe, Frances Moore. *Diet For a Small Planet*. New York: Ballantine, 1991.

Kong, Joanne, editor. *Vegan Voices: Essays by Inspiring Changemakers*. New York: Lantern, 2021.

Kradjian, Robert M., MD. *Save Yourself from Breast Cancer: Life Choices That Can Help You Reduce the Odds*. New York: Berkeley Publishing Group, 1994.

Lequire, Stan L. (editor). *The Best Preaching on Earth: Sermons on Caring for Creation*. Valley Forge, PA: Judson Press, 1996

Lymbery, Philip. *Farmageddon: The True Cost of Cheap Meat*. London: Bloomsbury, 2014.

Mason, Jim, and Peter Singer. *Animal Factories*. New York: Harmony Books, 1990.

McDougall, John A., MD. *McDougall's Medicine: A Challenging Second Opinion*. Piscataway, NJ: New Century Publishers, 1985.

McDougall, John A., MD., and Mary A. McDougall. *The McDougall Plan*. Piscataway, NJ: New Century Publishers, 1983.

Messina, Mark, and Virginia Messina. *The Dietitians' Guide to Vegetarian Diets: Issues and Applications*. Wilmington, DE: Aspen Publishers, 1996.

Moran, Victoria. *Compassion: The Ultimate Ethic*. Wellingborough, U.K.: Thorsons, 1985.

Perussello, Camila. *Food for Thought: Planetary Healing Begins on Our Plate*. New York: Lantern, 2022.

Rao, Sailesh, editor. *Agriculture Is Immoral: An Anthology.* Phoenix, AZ: Earth Healers, 2022.

Rowe, Martin. *The Way of Compassion: Survival Strategies for a World in Crisis.* New York: Stealth Technologies. 1999.

Schlottmann, Christopher, and Jeff Sebo. *Food, Animals, and the Environment: An Ethical Approach.* New York: Earthscan/ Routledge, 2019.

Tuttle, Will. *The World Peace Diet: Eating for Spiritual Health and Social Harmony.* New York: Lantern, 2005.

Walters, Kerry S., and Lisa Portress, editors. *From Pythagoras to Peter Singer.* New York: State University of New York Press: 1999.

Weis, Tony. *The Ecological Hoofprint: The Global Burden of Industrial Livestock.* London: Zed Books, 2013.

ENDNOTES

Preface

1. Heschel, Abraham Joshua. *The Earth Is the Lord's & The Sabbath*. New York: Harper Torchbooks, 1966, 107.
2. King, Jr., Martin Luther. "Remaining Awake Through a Great Revolution." An address at the Episcopal National Cathedral, Washington, D.C., March 31, 1968.
3. United Nations Meetings Coverage and Press Releases. "Secretary-General Calls Latest IPCC Climate Report 'Code Red for Humanity,' Stressing 'Irrefutable' Evidence of Human Influence." August 9, 2021.
4. United Nations Department of Economic and Social Affairs. "World Population Projected to Reach 9.8 Billion in 2050, and 11.2 billion in 2100." June 21, 2017.
5. Ritchie, Hannah, Pablo Rosado, and Max Roser. "Meat and Dairy Prouction." Our World in Data, November 2019.

Chapter 1: Involvement and Protest

1. Loew, R. Judah. *Netivot Olam, Shaar Hatochaha*, end of Chapter 2. The result of failing to speak out against injustice is well expressed by the following statement by the German theologian Martin Niemoller: "In Germany, the Nazis first came for the Jews, and I didn't speak up because I was not a Jew. Then they came for the communists, and I didn't speak up because I was not a communist. Then they came for the trade unionists, and

I didn't speak up because I wasn't a trade unionist. Then they came for the gypsies, and I didn't speak up because I was not a gypsy. Then they came for the Catholics, and I didn't speak up because I was not a Catholic. Then they came for me . . . and by that time, there was no one to speak up for me." Quoted from Jack Doueck, *The Chesed Boomerang: How Acts of Kindness Enrich Our Lives*, Deal, New Jersey: Yagdiyl Torah Publications, 1999, 83.

2. *Orchot Tzaddikim* 24. Jerusalem: Eshkol, 1967, 160. See also Rabbeinu Yonah, *Sharei Teshuvah, Shaar Sh'lishi*, no. 5, 187, 195.

3. American Jewish Congress. *Congress Bi-Weekly* 38, no. 1 (May 11, 1964): 6.

4. Heschel, Abraham Joshua. *The Insecurity of Freedom*. New York: Farrar, Straus and Giroux, 1967, 92.

5. Hammerman, Joshua. "Fight or Flight: The Rabbi, the Journalist and the Protester in Sodom." *The Times of Israel*, March 19, 2022.

6. American Jewish Congress. *Judaism* 19 (1970): 38–58.

7. Heschel, Abraham Joshua. *The Insecurity of Freedom*, 9–13, 92–93.

8. Lamm, Norman. *The Royal Reach*. New York: Feldheim Publishers, 1970, 131.

9. Shatz, David, Chaim I. Waxman, and Nathan J. Diament, eds. *Tikkun Olam: Social Responsibility in Jewish Thought and Law*. Northvale, New Jersey: Jason Aronson, 1997, 3.

10. Ibid, 4. See also Joseph B. Soloveitchik, "Confrontation," *Tradition: A Journal of Orthodox Jewish Thought* 6, no. 2 (1964): 5–29.

11. Sacks, Johnathan. *The Persistence of Faith*. London: Jews College, 1990, 27.

12. Social Action Commission. "Why We Went." In Rabbi Henry Cohen, *Justice, Justice: A Jewish View of the Black Revolution*, New York: Union of American Hebrew Congregations, 1968, 18.

13. Many Jewish groups that are actively working on environmental and social justice issues are discussed in Appendix C. This section focuses on components of the Jewish community that are not sufficiently involved.

14. Heschel, *The Prophets*, 10–11.

15. Heschel, *The Insecurity of Freedom*, 3, 4.

16. In Samuel Chiel, *Spectators or Participants*, New York: Jonathan David, 1969, 57.

17. In Albert Vorspan and Eugene Lipman, *Justice and Judaism: The Work of Social Action*, New York: Union of American Hebrew Congregations, 1969, 231.

Chapter 2: Human Rights and Obligations

1. In Rabbi J. H. Hertz, *The Pentateuch and Haftorahs*, London: Soncino Press, 1958, 17.

2. Maimonides, Moses. *The Guide for the Perplexed.* Mineola, New York: Dover Publications, 2000, Chapter 54.

3. Heschel, Abraham Joshua. "The Last Days of Maimonides." In Abraham Joshua Heschel, *The Insecurity of Freedom*, New York: Farrar, Straus and Giroux, 1967, 291.

4. Hertz, *The Pentateuch and Haftorahs*, 563.

5. Buber, Martin. *Tales of the Hasidim.* New York: Schocken Books, 1947, 227.

6. In Hertz, *The Pentateuch and Haftorahs*, 563.

7. Eliyahu of Vilna, Rabbi Pinchas. *Sefer HaBrit*, 2:13. In Dovid Sears, *Compassion for Humanity in the Jewish Tradition*, Northvale, New Jersey: Jason Aronson, 1998, 6.

8. Ibid, 13:31. In Sears, *Compassion for Humanity in the Jewish Tradition*, 8.

9. Ibid, 13:5. In Sears, *Compassion for Humanity in the Jewish Tradition*, 7.

10. In Samuel Dresner, *Prayer, Humility, and Compassion*, Philadelphia: The Jewish Publication Society, 1957, 196.

11. In Hertz, *The Pentateuch and Haftorahs,* 504. In Jewish numerology, the number thirty-six is associated with righteousness, and the Talmud states that there are thirty-six tzaddikim (righteous individuals) in the world at any time (*Sukkot* 45b).
12. Ibid.
13. Ibid.
14. There were several privileges that the "stranger" did not share. The cancellation of debts every Sabbatical year applied only to natives. While the Israelite was prohibited from charging a fellow Israelite interest on loans, this was not applicable when the loan was to a non-Israelite. Also, a foreigner, if captured, did not enjoy the benefits of the laws requiring the periodic freeing of all enslaved people.
15. Cohen, Rabbi Henry. *Justice, Justice: A Jewish View of the Black Revolution.* New York: Union of American Hebrew Congregations, 1968, 51–52.
16. Many other statements by Jews of the Middle Ages indicated concern for the treatment of non-Jews by Jews. Levi b. Isaac ha-Hasid, a French Jew of the tenth century, stated: "Treat with equal honesty the Christian as your brother in faith. If a Christian make a mistake to his loss, call his attention to it. If a Jew be a tax gatherer, he should demand no more from a Christian than from a Jew. A Jew shall not be untruthful in business with Jew or gentile." Rabbi Yehudah ben Samuel of Regensburg wrote in his *Sefer Hasidim*: "Mislead no one through thy actions designedly, be he Jew or non-Jew. . . . Injustice must not be done to anyone whether he belongs to our religion or another." In his *Sefer Mitzvot Gadol*, Moses ben Coucy wrote in 1245: "Those who lie to non-Jews and steal from them belong to the category of blasphemers, for it is due to their guilt that many say the Jews have no binding law." These quotations are found in "Jew and Non-Jew," no. 3,

Popular Studies in Judaism, Cincinnati: Union of American Hebrew Congregations.

17. *Tradition: A Journal of Orthodox Jewish Thought*, no. 2 (Summer 1966): 8.

18. Soloveichik, Rabbi Ahron. *Logic of the Heart, Logic of the Mind: Civil Rights and the Dignity of Man.* Jerusalem: Genesis Press, 1991. In Sears, *Compassion for Humanity in the Jewish Tradition*, 53.

19. Soloveichik, *Logic of the Heart, Logic of the Mind.* In Sears, *Compassion for Humanity in the Jewish Tradition*, 19.

20. Ibid.

21. Heschel, *The Insecurity of Freedom*, 86.

22. Ibid, 87.

23. Ibid, 93.

24. Ibid, 95.

Chapter 3: Social Justice

1. In Rabbi J. H. Hertz, *The Pentateuch and Haftorahs*, London: Soncino Press, 1958, 820. Rabbi Hertz also offers a Chassidic rebbe's interpretation of this Biblical verse: "Do not use unjust means to secure the victory of justice" (820).

2. Rackman, Rabbi Emanuel. "Torah Concept of Empathic Justice Can Bring Peace." *The Jewish Week* (April 3, 1977): 19.

3. Horowitz, Rabbi Levi Yitzchak. "And You Shall Tell Your Son." *Young Israel Viewpoint* (Spring 1997). In David Sears, *Compassion for Humanity in the Jewish Tradition*. Northvale, New Jersey: Jason Aronson, 1998, 22.

4. Maimonides, Moses. "Gifts to the Poor." *Mishneh Torah: Sefer Zeraim*, 10:7.

5. Ibid.

6. Maimonides, Moses. *Mishneh Torah: Hilchot Avadim*, 9:8.

7. Schachter, Fishel, and Chana Nestlebaum. *Chofetz Chaim: Loving Kindness*. Rahway, New Jersey: Mesorah Publications, 2006.

8. Hirsch, Samson Raphael. *Horeb*. Translated by Dayan Dr. I Grunfeld. London: Soncino Press, 1962, vol. 1, Section 125, 54–55.

9. Ibid, Section 126.

10. Dresner, Samuel. *Prayer, Humility, Compassion*. Philadelphia: Jewish Publication Society, 1953, 183.

11. For a detailed study of the Jewish tradition on compassion for animals, see Noah J. Cohen, *Tsa'ar Ba'alei Chayim: The Prevention of Cruelty to Animals, Its Basis, Development, and Legislation in Hebrew Literature*. New York: Feldheim, 1976.

12. Cordover, Rabbi Moshe. *Tomer Devorah*. In Sears, *Compassion for Humanity in the Jewish Tradition*, 3.

Chapter 4: Environment

1. Hirsch, Samson Raphael. *Horeb*. Translated by Dayan Dr. I. Grunfeld. London: Soncino Press, 1962, vol. 1, 398.

2. Story told by Rabbi Shlomo Riskin in *Biblical Ecology: A Jewish View*, directed by Mitchell Chalek and Jonathan Rosen.

3. Kook, Rav. *A Vision of Vegetarianism and Peace*, Section 2. Also see Joe Green, *"Chalutzim* of the Messiah: The Religious Vegetarian Concept as Expounded by Rabbi Kook," lecture given in Johannesburg, South Africa, 2.

4. Ibid.

5. Maimonides, Moses. "Laws of Kings and Wars." *Mishneh Torah: Hilchos Melachim*, 6:8, 10.

6. *Sefer Ha-Hinukh*, 529.

7. Hirsch, *Horeb*, Sections 397–398.

8. Ibid, Section 400.

9. In David Miller, *The Secret of Happiness*, New York: Rabbi David Miller Foundation, 1937, 9.

10. Flucke, Paul. "For the Sin of Terricide." In *New Prayers for the High Holy Days*, ed. Rabbi Jack Riemer, New York: Media Judaica, 1970, 44.
11. Union of Concerned Scientists. "World Scientists' Warning to Humanity," 1992.
12. Ripple, William J., Christopher Wolf, Thomas M. Newsome, et al. "World Scientists' Warning of a Climate Emergency." *BioScience* 70, no. 1 (January 2020): 8–12.
13. Nunez, Christina. "Why Deforestation Matters—and What We Can Do to Stop It." *National Geographic*, December 7, 2022.
14. Mackenzie, Jilliane, and Jeff Turrentine. "Air Pollution: Everything You Need to Know." Natural Resources Defense Council, June 22, 2021.
15. Farge, Emma. "Pollution Causing More Deaths Than COVID, Action Needed, Says U.N. Expert." *Reuters*, February 15, 2022.
16. Hirsch, Samson Raphael. "The Sabbath." In *Judaism Eternal*, ed. Dayan Dr. I. Grunfeld, London: Soncino Press, 1956, 22, 23.

Chapter 5: Climate Change

1. For a comprehensive overview of the threats, see Oliver Milman, Andrew Witherspoon, Rita Liu, et al., "The Climate Disaster Is Here: Earth Is Slready Becoming Unlivable. Will Governments Act to Stop This Disaster Before It Is too Late?" *The Guardian*, October 14, 2021. My coauthored article with Prof. Dan Brook, "Climate Change: An Existential Threat to Humanity —and How We Can Survive" is in the September 30, 2020 *Jerusalem Report*.
2. Cockburn, Harry. "World Heading for Catastrophe Without Bolder Climate Plans, UN Warns." *The Independent*, October 26, 2021.
3. The Climate Reality Project. "How Feedback Loops Are Making the Climate Crisis Worse," January 7, 2020.

4. NASA. "Scientific Consensus: Earth's Climate Is Warming," https://climate.nasa.gov/scientific-consensus/. For a grim overview of the realities, see David Wallace-Wells, *The Uninhabitable Earth*, New York: Crown, 2019; and Dale Jamieson, *Reason in a Dark Time: Why the Struggle Against Climate Change Failed–and What It Means for Our Future*, Oxford, U.K.: Oxford University Press, 2014.

5. UN Sustainable Development Goals. "UN Climate Change Conference Paris 2015," https://www.un.org/sustainabledevelopment/cop21/. Also see *BBC News*, "COP26: What Was Agreed at the Glasgow Climate Conference?," November 15, 2021.

6. IPCC. "Summary for Policymakers of IPCC Special Report on Global Warming of 1.5°C Approved by Governments," October 8, 2018.

7. Ripple, William J., Christopher Wolf, Thomas M. Newsome, et al. "World Scientists' Warning of a Climate Emergency." *BioScience* 70, no. 1 (January 2020): 8–12.

8. Slezak, Michael. "Climate Emergency Declared by 11,000 Scientists Worldwide Who Warn of 'Catastrophic Threat' to Humanity." *ABC News Australia*, November 5, 2019.

9. Carrington, Damian. "Climate Crisis: 11,000 Scientists Warn of 'Untold Suffering'." *The Guardian*, November 5, 2019.

10. Ibid.

11. Sengupta, Somini. "'Bleak' U.N. Report on a Planet in Peril Looms Over New Climate Talks." *The New York Times*, November 26, 2019. Teirstein, Zoya. "Paris Agreement Targets Need to Be 5 Times Stronger to Actually Work." *Grist*, Novemner 26, 2019.

12. Harvey, Fiona, and Jennifer Rankin. "Paris Climate Deal: World Not on Track to Meet Goal Amid Continuous Emissions." *The Guardian*, December 3, 2019.

13. Chestney, Nina, and Andrea Januta. "U.N. Climate Change Report Sounds 'Code Red for Humanity'." *Reuters*, August 9, 2021.

14. Fountain, Henry. "Carbon Dioxide Levels Are Highest in Human History." *The New York Times*, June 3, 2022.

15. Johnson, Andrew. "Retired Generals, Admirals Warn Climate Change Is a 'National Security Concern'." *National Review*, May 14, 2014.

16. Borger, Julian. "Dafur Conflict Heralds Era of Wars Triggered by Climate Change, UN Report Warns." *The Guardian*, June 23, 2007.

17. Fischetti, Mark. "Climate Change Hastened Syria's Civil War." *Scientific American*, March 2, 2015.

18. Schilling, Janpeter, Elke Hertig, Yves Tramblay, et al. "Climate Change Vulnerability, Water Resources and Social Implications in North Africa." *Regional Environmental Change* 20, no. 15 (2020).

19. Townsend, Mark, and Paul Harris. "Now the Pentagon Tells Bush: Climate Change Will Destroy Us." *The Guardian*, February 21, 2004.

20. Brook, Dan, and Richard H. Schwartz. "In Depth: Are You Taking Global Warming Personally?" World.edu, October 27, 2010.

21. Nichols, Michelle. "Ban Calls Climate Change as Dangerous as War." *Reuters*, March 1, 2007.

22. Kaplan, Sarah, and John Muyskens. "The Past Seven Years Have Been the Hottest in Recorded History, New Data Shows." *The Washington Post*, January 13, 2022.

23. Fountain, Henry. "2020 Ties 2016 as Hottest Yet, European Analysis Shows." *The New York Times*, January 8, 2021.

24. Rice, Doyle. "2020 Expected to Be Earth's Warmest Year on Record, Scientists Say." *USA Today*, April 16, 2020.

25. Shumaker, Lisa, and Andrea Januta. "Killer Heatwaves and Floods: Climate Change Worsened 2021 Weather

Extremes." *Reuters*, December 13, 2021. Siese, April. "Climate Change Is Making It Harder to Avoid Extreme Weather Events." *Daily Kos*, June 21, 2022.

26. Fountain, Henry. "The Hurricanes, and Climate Change Questions, Keep Coming. Yes, They's Linked." *The New York Times*, October 10, 2018.

27. Fountain, Henry. "Climate Change Is Accelerating, Bringing World 'Dangerously Close' to Irreversible Change." *The New York Times*, November 10, 2021.

28. Rivers, Brendan. "NOAA: 'Sunny Day Flooding' Becoming More Common Across Fla. as Sea Levels Rise." *WJCT News*, July 15, 2021.

29. Carrington, Damian. "Polar Ice Caps Melting Six Times Faster Than in 1990s." *The Guardian*, March 11, 2020. Braine, Theresa. "Greenland Ice Sheet Melting Exponentially Faster Than 1990s, Study Shows." *The Jerusalem Post*, December 14, 2019.

30. Pappas, Stephanie. "How Fast Are Glaciers Melting? Just Listen to Them." *Scientific American*, May 29, 2018.

31. Ibid.

32. Science Alert. "Greenland Was 40 Degrees Hotter Than Normal This Week, and Things Are Getting Intense," June 16, 2019.

33. Gaulkin, Thomas, Raymond Pierrehumbert. "Hooray, the Arctic Is Melting! Say WHAT?" *Bulleting of the Atomic Scientists*, June 25, 2019.

34. Onishi, Norimitsu, and Jeffrey Moyo. "Cyclone Idai Destroys 'Ninety Percent' of a City of Half a Million in Southern Africa." *The New York Times*, March 18, 2019.

35. Smith, Mitch, Jack Healy, and Timothy Williams. "'It's Probably Over for Us': Record Flooding Pummels Midwest When Farmers Can Least Afford It." *The New York Times*, March 18, 2019.

36. Neslen, Arthur. "Insurance Could Become Unaffordable, Due to Climate Change." *Bulletin of the Atomic Scientists*, March 22, 2019.

37. Ibid.

38. Zhong, Raymond. "Climate Scientists Warn of a 'Global Wildlife Crisis'." *The New York Times*, February 23, 2022.

39. Plumer, Brad, and Raymond Zhong. "Climate Change Is Harming the Planet Faster Than We Can Adapt, U.N. Warns." *The New York Times*, February 28, 2022.

40. Ibid.

41. Zhong, Raymond. "5 Takeaways From the U.N. Report on Climate Hazards." *The New York Times*, February 28, 2022.

42. Harvey, Fiona. "'Tipping Points' Could Exacerbate Climate Crisis, Scientists Fear." *The Guardian*, October 9, 2018. Also see Yasemin Saplakoglu, "The Planet Is Dangerously Close to the Tipping Point for a 'Hothouse Earth'," *Live Science*, August 6, 2018; and The Climate Reality Project, "How Feedback Loops Are Making the Climate Crisis Worse," January 7, 2020.

43. Rose, Chris. "California Governor Brown Warns of Increasing Drought, Wildfire Costs, Decries Climate Denial." DeSmog, May 21, 2014.

44. Lenton, Timothy M., Johan Rockström, Owen Gaffney, et al. "Climate Tipping Points—Too Risky to Bet Against." *Nature*, April 9, 2020.

45. Berwyn, Bob. "Climate Tipping Points Are Closer Than We Think, Scientists Warn." *Inside Climate News*, November 27, 2019.

46. Ibid.

47. Ibid. Also see University of Exeter, "Nine Climate Tipping Points Now 'Active,' Warn Scientists," *Science Daily*, November 27, 2019.

48. Ibid.

49. Ibid.

50. Watts, Jonathan. "Global Atmospheric CO₂ Levels Hit Record High." *The Guardian*, October 30, 2017.

51. Gammon, Katharine. "Global Carbon Dioxide Levels Continued to Rise Despite Pandemic." *The Guardian*, June 8, 2021.

52. Fountain, "Carbon Dioxide Levels."

53. Nebehay, Stephanie. "Climate Change Hits Health, Yet Funds Lacking: WHO." *Reuters*, December 3, 2019.

54. Ibid.

55. Ibid.

56. Ibid.

57. Henderson, Rebecca M., Sophus A. Reinert, Polina Dekhtyar, et al. "Climate Change in 2017: Implications for Business." Harvard Business School, June 27, 2017.

58. Hoggan, James, and Richard Littlemore. *Climate Cover-Up: The Crusade to Deny Global Warming.* Vancouver, BC: Greystone Books, 2009.

59. Mann, Michael, Stefan Rahmstorf, Gavin Schmidt, et al. "Senator Inhofe on Climate Change." RealClimate, January 10, 2005.

60. Worland, Justin. "Donald Trump Called Climate Change a Hoax. Now He's Awkwardly Boasting About Fighting It." *Time*, July 8, 2019.

61. Union of Concerned Scientists. "Debunking Misinformation About Stolen Climate Emails in the 'Climategate' Manufactured Controversy," August 25, 2011.

62. Waskow, Rabbi Arthur. "Rabbinic Letter on Climate—Torah, Pope, & Crisis Inspire 425 + Rabbis to Call for Vigorous Climate Action." The Shalom Center, October 29, 2015.

Chapter 6: Environmental Issues in Israel

1. Fine, Arlene. "Environment Ranks Low on Israel's Radar Screen." *Cleveland Jewish News*, October 4, 2011.

2. Ibid.

3. Schuster, Ruth. "Mideast Climate Change: Hotter, Drier and More Dangerous." *Haaretz*, February 11, 2015.

4. Gutman, Lior. "Israel Will See Less Rain, Higher Temperatures by 2050." *CTech*, December 3, 2019.

5. Bernstein, Rachel. "How Our Home Is Slowly Becoming Uninhabitable." *The Jerusalem Post*, September 16, 2021. Vohra, Anchal. "The Middle East Is Becoming Literally Uninhabitable." *Foreign Policy*, August 24, 2021.

6. TOI Staff. "Torrential Rains in Northern Israel Break 51-Year Record." *The Times of Israel*, January 9, 2020.

7. Haas, Saar, and Yaron Druckman. "Israel Warming Up Almost Twice as Fast as Rest of World, Data Shows." *Ynetnews*, November 1, 2021.

8. *Haaretz*. "Heat Wave Scorches Israel—but the Real Sizzle Is Yet to Come," August 5, 2021. Surkes, Sue. "Relentlessly Hotter: Sizzling Heat Increasingly the Norm in Israel, Data Shows." *The Times of Israel*, August 3, 2021.

9. Ibid.

10. Yaron, Lee. "Heat Waves Killed Hundreds of Israelis in a Decade, Government Study Finds." *Haaretz*, May 31, 2022.

11. Hasson, Nir. "The Age of Mega-Fires: Jerusalem Blaze Is a Wake-Up Call for Israel." *Haaretz*, August 16, 2021.

12. Yaron, Lee. "'Climate Crisis Will Lead to Increase in Unstoppable Massive Wildfires in Israel'." *Haaretz*, July 25, 2022.

13. Harel, Amos. "'Israel Will Have to Fortify Its Borders': Israeli Military Finally Sees Climate Change as Strategic Threat." *Haaretz*, November 26, 2021.

14. Efron, Shira, et al. "The Implications of Climate Change for Military Intelligence." The Institute for National Security Studies, November 22, 2021.

15. Ibid.

16. Tal, Alon. *Pollution in a Promised Land: An Environmental History of Israel*. Berkley: University of California Press, 2002.

17. Much of the material below about various Israeli environmental problems is from Aytzim: Ecological Judaism, unless otherwise indicated.

18. Rosenberg, David. "A Danger to Millions: The Middle Eastern Threat No One's Talking About." *Haaretz*, May 29, 2022.

19. Tal, Alon. "Israel Can Do Better: A 70-Year Report Card of Environmental Underachievement." *The Tel Aviv Review of Books*, 2019.

20. Sommer, Allison Kaplan. "Meet the U.S.-Born, Ex-Paratrooper About to Shake Up Israel's Environmental Policy." *Haaretz*, June 17, 2021.

21. Israeli Government Press Release. "PM Bennett Declares the Tackling of Climate Change as a New National Security Interest of Israel," October 24, 2021.

22. Knesset News. "Minister of Environmental Protection: 'Climate Crisis Requires Us All to Take Action'," January 17, 2022.

23. Yaron, Lee, and Shira Kadari-Ovadia. "Israeli Schools to Make Classes on Climate Crisis Mandatory for All Ages." *Haaretz*, May 30, 2022.

Chapter 7: Hunger

1. Tanenbaum, Rabbi Marc H. "Remarks Following 'Report on Rome—The Challenge of Food and Population'," 1974. In The Jacob Rader Marcus Center of the American Jewish Archives, *MS-603: Rabbi Marc H. Tanenbaum Collection, 1945–1992*. Series D: International Relations Activities, 1961–1992.

2. Rifkin, Jeremy. *Beyond Beef: The Rise and Fall of the Cattle Culture*. New York: Dutton, 1992, 177.

3. *The Philadelphia Inquirer*, October 13, 1974, 9B.

4. Brown, Lester R. *In the Human Interest: A Strategy to Stabilize World Population*. New York: W.W. Norton & Company, 1974, 21.

5. *UN News*. "Act Now to Avert COVID-19 Global Food Emergency: Guterres," June 9, 2020.

6. Ibid.

7. Paper on world hunger by Mazon, ad hoc Jewish Committee on Hunger, 1975.

8. Class attended by the author before Passover at the Young Israel of Staten Island.

9. Dinshah, Jay. "The Vegetarian Way." Proceeding of the 24th World Vegetarian Conference, Madras, India, 1977, 34.

10. "The Energy–Food Crisis: A Challenge to Peace—A Call to Faith." Statement from the Inter-religious Peace Colloquium, held in Bellagio, Italy, May 1975.

11. Balch, Oliver. "The Relevance of Gandhi in the Capitalism Debate." *The Guardian*, January 28, 2013.

Chapter 8: Should Jews Be Vegans?

1. Steinfeld, Henning, Pierre Gerber, Tom Wassenaar, et al. *Livestock's Long Shadow: Environmental Issues and Options*. Rome: FAO, 2006. FAO's original estimation that global livestock production was responsible for 18 percent of global GHGs was lowered to 14.5 percent in 2013.

2. Goodland, Robert, and Jeff Anhang. "Livestock and Climate Change." *World Watch Magazine* (November 2009).

3. Rao, Sailesh. "Animal Agriculture Is the Leading Cause of Climate Change. A Position Paper." *Journal of Ecological Society* 32–33, no. 1 (April 1, 2021): 155.

4. Carrington, Damian. "Plant-Based Meat by Far the Best Climate Investment, Report Finds." *The Guardian*, July 7, 2022.

5. Ibid.

6. Pennisi, Elizabeth. "Earth Home to 3 Trillion Trees, Half as Many as When Human Civilization Arose." *Science*, September 2, 2015.

7. For an overview of animal agriculture's effect on the environment and climate change, see Christopher Schlottmann and Jeff Sebo, *Food, Animals, and the Environment: An Ethical Approach*, New York: Routledge, 2018. Another overview can be found in Tony Weis, *The Ecological Hoofprint: The Global Burden of Industrial* Livestock, London: Zed Books, 2013.

8. Much information about the negative environmental effects of animal-based diets can be found in John Robbins, *Diet for a New America*, Novato, CA: HJ Kramer/ New World Library, 2012; Frances Moore Lappé, *Diet for a Small Planet*, New York: Ballantine Books, 1991; and Jonathan Safran Foer, *Eating Animals*, New York: Black Bay Books, 2010. Additional valuable information on this issue is in the FAO report, *Livestock's Long Shadow*; and in Bibi van der Zee, "What Is the True Cost of Eating Meat?," *The Guardian*, May 7, 2018.

9. Sauven, John. "Why Meat Eaters Should Think Much More About Soil." *The Guardian*, May 16, 2017.

10. World Resources Institute. "Eutrophication and Hypoxia," n.d. See also Tom Philpott, "The Gulf of Mexico Is About to Experience a 'Dead Zone' the Size of Connecticut," *Mother Jones*, June 17, 2016.

11. Cooke, Christina. "North Carolina's Factory Farms Produce 15,000 Olympic Pools Worth of Waste Each Year." *Civil Eats*, June 28, 2016.

12. Butler, Rhett. "Controlling the Ranching Boom that Threatens the Amazon." Yale Environment 360, August 10, 2009; and Livestock Policy Brief 03, "Cattle Ranching and Deforestation," FAO.

13. Pearce, Fred. "Global Extinction Rates: Why Do Estimates Vary So Wildly?" Yale Environment 360, August 17, 2015.

14. IPBES. "Media Release: Nature's Dangerous Decline 'Unprecedented'; Species Extinction Rates 'Accelerating'," May 5, 2019.

15. Ibid.

16. Suza, Walter. "As Tropical Rainforests Disappear, So Do Potential Medicine Reservoirs." *Undark*, November 19, 2019.

17. Pearce, Fred. "Rivers in the Sky: How Deforestation Is Affecting Global Water Cycles." Yale Environment 360, July 24, 2018.

18. These examples are based on material from Toronto Vegetarian Association, "Meat and the Environment: Facts and Resources," February 2, 2007; and J. Frorip, E. Kokin, J. Praks, et al., "Energy Consumption in Animal Production—Case Farm Study," *Agronomy Research*, Biosystem Engineering Special Issue 1 (2012): 39–48.

19. Lappé, *Diet for a Small Planet*, 10.

20. Ibid., 74, 75.

21. National Geographic. "Freshwater Crisis," https://www.nationalgeographic.com/environment/article/freshwater-crisis.

22. Centers for Disease Control and Prevention. "Global WASH Fast Facts," May 31, 2022.

23. Gerbens-Leenes, P.W., M.M. Mekonnen, and A.Y. Hoekstra. "The Water Footprint of Poultry, Pork and Beef: A Comparative Study in Different Countries and Production Systems." *Water Resources and Industry* 1–2 (March–June 2013): 25–36.

24. Jacobson, Michael F. "More and Cleaner Water." In Michael F. Jacobson, *Six Arguments for a Greener Diet: How a Plant-Based Diet Could Save Your Health and the*

Environment, Washington, D.C.: Center for Science in the Public Interest, 2006.

25. Gerbens-Leenes, Mekonnen, and Hoekstra, "The Water Footprint of Poultry, Pork and Beef."

26. Loria, Joe. "Animal Agriculture Wastes One-Third of Drinkable Water (and 8 Other Facts for World Water Day)." Mercy for Animals, March 21, 2018.

27. Kristof, Nicholas. "Our Water-Guzzling Food Factory." *The New York Times*, May 30, 2015.

28. *Newsweek*. "The Browning of America," February 2, 1981. See also John Vidal, "Meat-Eaters Soak up the World's Water," *The Guardian*, August 23, 2004.

29. Johnson, Scott K. "About a Third of US Rivers Contaminated with Agricultural Runoff." *Ars Technica*, April 8, 2013.

30. Union of Concerned Scientists. "Grade A Choice? Solutions for Deforestation-Free Meat." Reports & Multimedia, June 10, 2012.

31. Rifkin, Jeremy. *Beyond Beef: The Rise and Fall of the Cattle Culture*. New York: Dutton, 1992, 1–2.

32. The facts in this section and many additional facts relating to diet and the utilization of resources can be found in Robbins, *Diet for a New America*; Rifkin, *Beyond Beef*; Foer, *Eating Animals*; and Keith Akers, *Vegetarian Sourcebook*, New York: Putnam, 1983. Also used are "Cowspiracy Facts," from *Cowspiracy*, directed by Kip Andersen and Keegan Kuhn, 2014, https://www.cowspiracy.com/facts.

33. Rifkin, Jeremy. "There's a Bone to Pick With Meat Eaters." *Los Angeles Times*, May 27, 2002; Robbins, *Diet for a New America*.

34. United States Department of Agriculture. "Farms and Farmland: Numbers, Acreage, Ownership, and Use." 2012 Census of Agriculture Highlights (September 2014).

35. U.S. Department of Agriculture. "Feed Grains Sector at a Glance." Economic Research Service, n.d.

36. Shepon, Alon, Gidon Eshel, Elad Noor, et al. "The Opportunity Cost of Animal Based Diets Exceeds All Food Losses." *Proceedings of the National Academy of Sciences* 115, no. 15 (April 2018): 3804–3809.

37. Cook, Rob. "World Beef Imports: Ranking of Countries." Beef2Live, March 12, 2013.

38. Central America Link. "Honduras Exports Beef to United States," March 7, 2017.

39. Feeding America. "Food Waste and Food Resources," https://www.feedingamerica.org/our-work/reduce-food-waste.

40. Ritchie, Hannah. "Food Waste Is Responsible for 6% of Global Greenhouse Gas Emissions." Our World in Data, March 18, 2020.

41. Huffstutter, P.J. "U.S. Dairy Farmers Dump Milk as Pandemic Upends Food Markets." *Reuters*, April 3, 2020.

42. Gerbens-Leenes, Mekonnen, and Hoekstra, "The Water Footprint of Poultry, Pork and Beef."

Chapter 9: Population

1. Arlosoroff, Meirav. "Israel's Population Is Growing at a Dizzying Rate. Is It Up for the Challenge?" *Haaretz*, January 4, 2021.

2. Mayer, Melissa. "What Are Environmental Problems Due to Population Growth?" *Sciencing*, June 11, 2018.

3. Population Reference Bureau. "2021 World Population Data Sheet Released," August 17, 2021.

4. Ibid.

5. Ghosh, Iman. "These Countries Will Have the Largest Populations—by the End of the Century." World Economic Forum, September 8, 2020.

6. Shapiro, David S. "Be Fruitful and Multiply." In Fred Rosner and J. David Bleich, eds., *Jewish Bioethics*, New York: Sanhedrin Press, 1979, 71–72.
7. Maimonides, Moses. *Sefer Hamitzvot*, 212.
8. Maimonides, Moses. *Mishnah Torah: Hilchot Ishut*, 15:16.
9. Arlosoroff, "Israel's Population Is Growing at a Dizzying Rate."
10. Döhler, Dominik. "Overpopulation in Israel: A Self-Made Crisis." Zavit, April 20, 2020.
11. Arlosoroff, "Israel's Population Is Growing at a Dizzying Rate."
12. Ibid.
13. Hoffman, Gil. "Israel Expected to Become Most Crowded Western Country by 2050." *The Jerusalem Post*, June 14, 2022.
14. Ibid.
15. Ibid.
16. Waxman, Chaim. "How Many Are We? Where Are We Going?" *Jewish Life* (Spring/Summer 1982): 44.
17. Rashi's commentary on Genesis 41:50, based on *Ta'anit* 11a.
18. Wikipedia. "Noah's Ark."
19. Rashi. "The Spiritual Outreach of Avraham and Sarah." Shema Yisrael.
20. This might be more appealing to Jews when it is considered that this can be read as Z-PIG, or "Zero Pig," since the dietary laws forbid the eating of pig flesh.
21. Population Reference Bureau. "2021 World Population Data Sheet Released."
22. Ibid.
23. A challenging analysis of the true causes of world hunger is in Frances Moore Lappé, Joseph Collins, Peter Rosset, et al., *World Hunger: Twelve Myths*, New York: Grove Press, 1998.

Chapter 10: International Issues

1. *Sanhedrin* 105a; also see *Yalkut*, II Kings, 296; Jerusalem Talmud *Pe'ah* 1:1; and David Sears, *Compassion for Humanity in the Jewish Tradition*, Northvale, New Jersey: Jason Aronson, 1998, 53–56.

2. Goodman, Philip, ed. *The Sukkot and Simchat Torah Anthology.* Philadelphia: The Jewish Publication Society, 1973, 114.

3. Buber, Martin. *Ten Rungs: Hasidic Sayings.* New York: Schocken Books, 1961, 81.

4. Nachman of Breslov, Rabbi. *Likkutei Moharan* I, 5:1, quoted in Sears, *Compassion for Humanity in the Jewish Tradition*, 93, 94.

5. Gordis, Robert. "The Vision of Micha." In R. Konvitz, ed., *Judaism and Human Rights*, New York: W. W. Norton & Company, 1972, 287.

6. Peer, Andrea. "Global Poverty: Facts, FAQs, and How to Help." World Vision, updated April 4, 2023.

7. Ibid.

8. The facts below are from Bernie Sanders, "The Rich–poor Gap in America Is Obscene. So Let's Fix It—Here's How." *The Guardian*, March 29, 2021.

9. Ibid.

10. Sidney E. Goldstein discusses this in *The Synagogue and Social Ethics,* New York: Block Pubs., 1955, 337.

11. Reinert, Erik S. "Why We Need a Global Marshall Plan." World Economic Forum, April 22, 2015.

12. Ibid.

13. Lerner, Rabbi Michael. "Our Global Marshall Plan." *Tikkun,* June 27, 2017.

Chapter 11: Peace

1. Eisendrath, Rabbi Maurice. "Sanctions in Judaism for Peace." In Homer A. Jack, ed., *World Religions and World Peace*, Boston: Beacon, 1968.

2. Quoted in "World Hunger," *WorldVision*, February 19, 1975, 5.

3. Fong, Susan. *Staten Island Advance*, July 1, 1980, 1.

4. *Avot de Rabbi Nathan*, Chapter 23.

5. Hertz, Rabbi J. H. *The Pentateuch and Haftorahs*. London: Soncino Press, 1957, 501, 502.

6. *Tanhuma Mishpatim* 1.

7. Quoted in Rabbi Samuel Belkin, *In His Image*, New York: Abelard Schuman, 1960, 227.

8. Maimonides, Moses. *Mishnah Torah: Hilchot Melachim*, 7:7.

9. Quoted in Richard G. Hirsch, *Thy Most Precious Gift, Peace in Jewish Tradition*, New York: Union of American Hebrew Congregations, 1974, 8.

10. Herold, J. C. *The Mind of Napoleon*. New York: Columbia University Press, 1955, 76.

11. *Chayei Moharan* 546. In Dovid Sears, *Compassion for Humanity in the* Jewish *Tradition*, Northvale, New Jersey: Jason Aronson, 1998, 34.

12. See "Judaism and Peacemaking," *Fellowship* (January– February 1976): 14, 15.

13. Maimonides, *Mishnah Torah: Hilchot Melachim*, 3:9.

14. Synagogue Council of America. "Action Memo," January 1970, 1.

15. Shawn Perry, ed. "Words of Conscience, Religious Statements on Conscientious Objection." National Inter-religious Service Board for Conscientious Objectors, Washington, D.C. Also see Allen Solomonow, ed., *Roots of Jewish Nonviolence*, Nyack, NY: Jewish Peace Fellowship, 1981.

16. Ibid.

17. Ibid.

Chapter 12: Seeking Peace for Israel

1. Sacks, Jonathan. *The Dignity of Difference: How to Avoid the Clash of Civilizations*. New York: Continuum, 2003, 189–190.

2. *Maariv*, Rosh Hashanah, 1975, quoted in David Bedein, "Genesis of an Israeli Religious Left," *New Outlook* (January 1976): 39.
3. Netivot V'Shalom poster.
4. Ronen, Gil. "'Hundreds of Civilian Deaths in Next War,' Says IDF." *Arutz Sheva*, January 12, 2011.
5. Lappin, Yaakov. "Israel Prepares Civilians for Threat of 230,000 Enemy Rockets." *Commentary*, September 15, 2016.
6. Keinon, Herb. "Abraham Accords Are Helping Israel Transform the Middle East." *The Jerusalem Post*, November 25, 2021.
7. Ravid, Barak. "European Parliament Passes Motion in Favor of Palestine Recognition." *Haaretz*, December 17, 2014.
8. TOI Staff. "UN Condemned Israel 17 Times in 2020, Versus 6 Times for Rest of World Combined." *Times of Israel*, December 23, 2022.
9. Eilam, Shahar, and Tom Eshed. "Increased Antisemitism in the United States Following Operation Guardian of the Walls: Permanent or Short-Lived?" *INSS Publications*, November 10, 2021.
10. Caine, Paul. "Report Finds Antisemitism on the Rise in America." *WTTW News*, November 25, 2021.
11. Ibid.
12. Magarik, Raphael. "Do Jewish Actions Ever Cause Anti-Semitism." *Forward*, September 24, 2014; Rosenberg, M.J. "Sorry, Jewish Organizations, the Cause of Spike in Antipathy Toward Jews is Israel's Behavior." *M.J. Rosenberg on Everything*, September 18, 2014.
13. Silkoff, Shira. "Israel's Health System Is Understaffed, Under Equipped—OECD Data." *The Jerusalem Post*, January 24, 2022.

14. Bassok, Moti. "Israel Shells out Almost a Fifth of National Budget on Defense, Figures Show." *Haaretz*, February 14, 2013.

15. United Nations Press Release. "Secretary General Calls Latest IPCC Climate Report 'Code Red for Humanity', Stressing 'Irrefutable' Evidence of Human Influence," August 9, 2021.

16. Yaron, Lee. "'Climate Crisis Will Lead to Increase in Unstoppable Massive Wildfires in Israel'." *Haaretz*, July 25, 2022.

17. Derfner, Larry. "To Be Israeli Today." *The Jerusalem Post*, January 13, 2010.

18. Israel's popularity climbs in annual BBC poll, but overall global impression is still negative.

19. *The Washington Post* blog. "America Is the Only Country with a Favorable View of Israel," July 25, 2014.

20. Magid, Jacob, and JTA. "ADL, Other Jewish Groups, Denounce 'Ongoing Terrorism' by Settler Extremists." *The Times of Israel*, January 25, 2022.

21. Ibid.

22. Myre, Greg. "Acting Israeli Leader Backs a Palestinian State." *The New York Times*, January 25, 2006.

23. Bickerton, Ian J. *A History of the Arab–Israeli Conflict*. New York: Pearson, 2009, 195.

24. BrainyQuote. "Yitzhak Rabin Quotes," https://www.brainyquote.com/authors/yitzhak-rabin-quotes#qiL3Xx40T3LkXws.

25. Information about the organization in this section is from the Commanders for Israel's Security website: http://en.cis.org.il/.

26. Ephron, Dan. "The Gatekeepers: Shin Bet Chiefs Air Peace Views in Documentary." *Newsweek*, February 5, 2013.

27. Israel National Security Project. "Two States for a Strong Israel."

28. Baskin, Gershon. "Encountering Peace: And We Will Dwell in Peace . . ." *The Jerusalem Post*, July 5, 2010.
29. al-Mughrabi, Nidal. "Hamas Would Honor Referendum on Peace with Israel." *Reuters*, December 1, 2010.

Chapter 13: Should Prayer Inspire Activism?

1. Heschel, Rabbi Abraham Joshua. Quoted in "On Prayer," in Susannah Heschel, ed., *Moral Grandeur and Spiritual Audacity*, New York: Farrar, Straus and Giroux, 1996, 257.
2. Nir, Ori. "U.S. Poll: Synagogue-Goers More Likely to Be Politically Conservative." *Haaretz*, February 7, 2005.
3. Sears, David. *The Vision of Eden: Animal Welfare and Vegetarianism in Jewish Law and Mysticism*. New York: Meorei Ohr, 2015.
4. Lerner, Rabbi Michael. "What Would A.J. Heschel Be Doing or Advocating Today?" *Tikkun*, January 8, 2013.
5. Heschel, Rabbi Abraham Joshua. *The Insecurity of Freedom*. New York: Farrar, Straus and Giroux, 1959, 87.
6. Waskow, Arthur. "My Legs Were Praying: Theology and Politics in Abraham Joshua Heschel." *Shalom Magazine*, October 10, 2012.
7. Ibid.

Chapter 14: Revitalizing Judaism

1. Heschel, Rabbi Abraham Joshua. *The Insecurity of Freedom*. New York: Farrar, Straus and Giroux, 1959, 218.
2. *The New York Times*. "For 'Peace of Mind'." February 23, 1986.
3. Heschel, Rabbi Abraham Joshua. *The Insecurity of Freedom*. New York: Farrar, Straus and Giroux, 1959, 1, 2.
4. Greenberg, Rabbi Irving. *The Jewish Way: Living the Holidays*. New York: Summit Books, 1988, 17.

Chapter 15: Summary and Conclusions

1. Heschel, Rabbi Abraham Joshua. *The Earth Is the Lord's &
   The Sabbath*. New York: Harper Row, 1950, 107.
2. Edmond Fleg (1874–1963) was a French essayist,
   playwright, and poet, whose main writings deal with
   Judaism and the Jewish people.

APPENDIX B: The Making of a Jewish Activist

1. Heschel, Abraham Joshua. *The Insecurity of Freedom*. New
   York: Farrar, Straus and Giroux, 1959.

ABOUT THE AUTHOR

RICHARD H. SCHWARTZ, PhD is the author of *Vegan Revolution: Saving Our World, Revitalizing Judaism; Judaism and Vegetarianism; Who Stole My Religion? Revitalizing Judaism and Applying Jewish Values to Help Heal Our Imperiled Planet; Mathematics and Global Survival;* and *Restoring and Transforming the Ancient Jewish New Year for Animals: An Idea Whose Time Has Come* and over 250 related articles at JewishVeg.org/schwartz. He is President Emeritus of Jewish Veg, associate producer of the video "A Sacred Duty: Applying Jewish Values to Help Heal the World," and professor emeritus at the College of Staten Island, New York. A father, grandfather, and now great-grandfather, he has lived with his wife in Israel since 2016.

ABOUT THE PUBLISHER

LANTERN PUBLISHING & MEDIA was founded in 2020 to follow and expand on the legacy of Lantern Books—a publishing company started in 1999 on the principles of living with a greater depth and commitment to the preservation of the natural world. Like its predecessor, Lantern Publishing & Media produces books on animal advocacy, veganism, religion, social justice, humane education, psychology, family therapy, and recovery. Lantern is dedicated to printing in the United States on recycled paper and saving resources in our day-to-day operations. Our titles are also available as ebooks and audiobooks.

To catch up on Lantern's publishing program, visit us at www.lanternpm.org.

facebook.com/lanternpm
twitter.com/lanternpm
instagram.com/lanternpm